ENDANGERED
PEOPLES
of North America

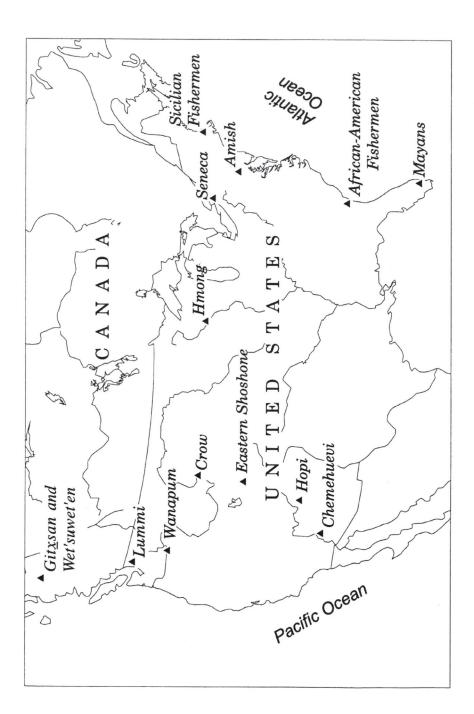

ENDANGERED PEOPLES
of North America

Struggles to Survive and Thrive

Edited by Tom Greaves

The Greenwood Press
"Endangered Peoples of the World" Series
Barbara Rose Johnston, Series Editor

GREENWOOD PRESS
Westport, Connecticut • London

Library of Congress Cataloging-in-Publication Data

Endangered peoples of North America : struggles to survive and thrive / edited by Tom Greaves.
    p. cm.—(The Greenwood Press "Endangered peoples of the world" series, ISSN 1525–1233)
    Includes bibliographical references and index.
    ISBN 0–313–30811–X (alk. paper)
    1. Indians of North America—Ethnic identity. 2. Indians of North America—Government relations. 3. Ethnicity—North America. 4. Minorities—North America. 5. North America—Social conditions. I. Greaves, Thomas C. II. Series.
E98.E85E53 2002
305.8'00973—dc21   2001023885

British Library Cataloguing in Publication Data is available.

Library of Congress Catalog Card Number: 2001023885
ISBN: 0–313–30811–X
ISSN: 1525–1233

First published in 2002

Greenwood Press, 88 Post Road West, Westport, CT 06881
An imprint of Greenwood Publishing Group, Inc.
www.greenwood.com

Printed in the United States of America

∞™

The paper used in this book complies with the
Permanent Paper Standard issued by the National
Information Standards Organization (Z39.48–1984).

10 9 8 7 6 5 4 3 2 1

Contents

Contents

Series Foreword

Barbara Rose Johnston

Two hundred thousand years ago our human ancestors gathered plants and hunted animals in the forests and savannas of Africa. By forty thousand years ago, *Homo sapiens sapiens* had developed ways to survive and thrive in every major ecosystem on this planet. Unlike other creatures, whose response to harsh or varied conditions prompted biological change, humans generally relied upon their ingenuity to survive. They fashioned clothing from skins and plant fiber rather than growing thick coats of protective hair. They created innovative ways to live and communicate and thus passed knowledge down to their children. This knowledge, by ten thousand years ago, included the means to cultivate and store food. The ability to provide for lean times allowed humans to settle in larger numbers in villages, towns, and cities where their ideas, values, ways of living, and language grew increasingly complicated and diverse.

This cultural diversity—the multitude of ways of living and communicating knowledge—gave humans an adaptive edge. Other creatures adjusted to change in their environment through biological adaptation (a process that requires thousands of life spans to generate and reproduce a mutation to the level of the population). Humans developed analytical tools to identify and assess change in their environment, to search out or devise new strategies, and to incorporate new strategies throughout their group. Sometimes these cultural adaptations worked; people transformed their way of life, and their population thrived. Other times, these changes produced further complications.

Intensive agricultural techniques, for example, often resulted in increased salts in the soil, decreased soil fertility, and declining crop yields. Food production declined, and people starved. Survivors often moved to new regions to begin again. Throughout human history, migration became the common strategy when innovations failed. Again, in these times, culture was essential to survival.

For the human species, culture is our primary adaptive mechanism. Cultural diversity presents us with opportunities to draw from and build upon a complicated array of views, ideas, and strategies. The Endangered Peoples of the World series celebrates the rich diversity of cultural groups living on our planet and explores how cultural diversity, like biological diversity, is threatened.

Five hundred years ago, as humans entered the age of colonial expansion, there were an estimated twelve to fourteen thousand cultural groups with distinct languages, values, and ways of life. Today, cultural diversity has been reduced by half (an estimated 6,000 to 7,000 groups). This marked decline is due in part to the fact that, historically, isolated peoples had minimal immunity to introduced diseases and little time to develop immunological defenses. Colonizers brought more than ideas, religion, and new economic ways of living. They brought a host of viruses and bacteria—measles, chicken pox, small pox, the common cold. These diseases swept through "new" worlds at epidemic levels and wiped out entire nations. Imperialist expansion and war further decimated original, or "indigenous," populations.

Today's cultural diversity is further threatened by the biodegenerative conditions of nature. Our biophysical world's deterioration is evidenced by growing deserts; decreasing forests; declining fisheries; poisoned food, water, and air; and climatic extremes and weather events such as floods, hurricanes, and droughts. These degenerative conditions challenge our survival skills, often rendering customary knowledge and traditions ineffective.

Cultural diversity is also threatened by unparalleled transformations in human relations. Isolation is no longer the norm. Small groups continually interact and are subsumed by larger cultural, political, and economic groups of national and global dimensions. The rapid pace of change in population, technology, and political economy leaves little time to develop sustainable responses and adjust to changing conditions.

Across the world cultural groups are struggling to maintain a sense of unique identity while interpreting and assimilating an overwhelming flow of new ideas, ways of living, economies, values, and languages. As suggested in some chapters in this series, cultural groups confront, embrace, adapt, and transform these external forces in ways that allow them to survive and thrive. However, in far too many cases, cultural groups lack the time and means to adjust and change. Rather, they struggle to retain the right to simply exist as other, more powerful peoples seize their land and resources and "cleanse" the countryside of their presence.

Efforts to gain control of land, labor, and resources of politically and/or geographically peripheral peoples are justified and legitimized by ethnocentric notions: the beliefs that the values, traditions, and behavior of your own cultural group are superior and that other groups are biologically, culturally, and socially inferior. These notions are produced and reproduced in conversation, curriculum, public speeches, articles, television coverage, and other communication forums. Ethnocentrism is reflected in a language of debasement that serves to dehumanize (the marginal peoples are considered sub-human: primitive, backward, ignorant people that "live like animals"). The pervasiveness of this discourse in the everyday language can eventually destroy the self-esteem and sense of worth of marginal groups and reduce their motivation to control their destiny.

Thus, vulnerability to threats from the biophysical and social realms is a factor of social relations. Human action and a history of social inequity leave some people more vulnerable than others. This vulnerability results in ethnocide (loss of a way of life), ecocide (destruction of the environment), and genocide (death of an entire group of people).

The Endangered Peoples of the World series samples cultural diversity in different regions of the world, examines the varied threats to cultural survival, and explores some of the ways people are adjusting and responding to threats of ethnocide, ecocide, and genocide. Each volume in the series covers the peoples, problems, and responses characteristic of a major region of the world: the Arctic, Europe, North America, Latin America, Africa and the Middle East, Central and South Asia, Southeast and East Asia, and Oceania. Each volume includes an introductory essay authored by the volume editor and fifteen or so chapters, each featuring a different cultural group whose customs, problems, and responses represent a sampling of conditions typical of the region. Chapter content is organized into five sections: Cultural Overview (people, setting, traditional subsistence strategies, social and political organization, religion and world view), Threats to Survival (demographic trends, current events and conditions, environmental crisis, sociocultural crisis), Response: Struggles to Survive Culturally (indicating the variety of efforts to respond to threats), Food for Thought (a brief summary of the issues raised by the case and some provocative questions that can be used to structure class discussion or organize a research paper), and a Resource Guide (major accessible published sources, films and videos, Internet and WWW sites, and organizations). Many chapters are authored or coauthored by members of the featured group, and all chapters include liberal use of a "local voice" to present the group's own views on its history, current problems, strategies, and thoughts of the future.

Collectively, the series contains some 120 case-specific examples of cultural groups struggling to survive and thrive in a culturally diverse world. Many of the chapters in this global sampling depict the experiences of indigenous peoples and ethnic minorities who, until recently, sustained their customary way of life in the isolated regions of the world. Threats to survival are often linked to external efforts to develop the natural resources of the previously isolated region. The development context is often one of co-optation of traditionally held lands and resources with little or no recognition of resident peoples' rights and little or no compensation for their subsequent environmental health problems. New ideas, values, technologies, economies, and languages accompany the development process and, over time, may even replace traditional ways of being.

Cultural survival, however, is not solely a concern of indigenous peoples. Indeed, in many parts of the world the term "indigenous" has little relevance, as all peoples are native to the region. Thus, in this series, we define cultural groups in the broadest of terms. We examine threats to survival and the variety of responses of ethnic minorities, as well as national cultures, whose traditions are challenged and undermined by global transformations.

The dominant theme that emerges from this sampling is that humans struggle with serious and life-threatening problems tied to larger global forces, and yet, despite huge differences in power levels between local communities and global institutions and structures, people are crafting and developing new ways of being. This series demonstrates that culture is not a static set of meanings, values, and behaviors; it is a flexible, resilient tool that has historically provided humans with the means to adapt, adjust, survive, and, at times, thrive. Thus, we see "endangered" peoples confronting and responding to threats in ways that reshape and transform their values, relationships, and behavior.

Emerging from this transformative process are new forms of cultural identity, new strategies for living, and new means and opportunities to communicate. These changes represent new threats to cultural identity and autonomy but also new challenges to the forces that dominate and endanger lives.

Introduction

Tom Greaves

This volume is about endangered peoples in North America. What do we mean by "endangered peoples"? "Peoples" signals that we are talking about people who think of themselves as members of groups and for whom their membership together is very important. "Endangered" means, in this case, that their future as a distinct people is in some way in doubt. In North America two types of peoples are often endangered: indigenous peoples (Indian tribes), and ethnic minorities. This book looks at both types of groups, beginning with Indians.

INDIGENOUS GROUPS

Are there any Indians left? Many Americans don't think so. To them Indians were the friendly people who helped the Pilgrims through a hard winter in the 1620s and sold Manhattan Island for almost nothing. Indians were the feathered hostiles who harassed the pioneers during the westward expansion of the 1800s. Many Americans who think Indians either died out or melded in conclude that their history came to an end a century ago.

Given the above assumption, it is not hard to understand why the average American today is startled, puzzled, maybe irritated when an Indian group intrudes on their lives. A garish casino opens up on an overlooked Indian reservation up the road. A big coastal oil spill occurs in Alaska and Indian representatives demand to be among the negotiating parties. A judge rules that certain Indian tribes have continuing treaty rights to fish or hunt without buying the state license other fishermen and hunters must have. An Indian delegation visits a state museum and demands that the museum return the human bones in its archaeological collection to the tribe that historically occupied that area. The museum complies. A land developer faces Indian protesters who argue that some of the land cannot be built upon because an Indian cemetery is located there, and it must not be disturbed.

A common reaction to these encounters is that these people cannot be "real" Indians. Even if they are Indians, they should be subject to the same laws other Americans have to obey. Further, they should not be able to block the lawful activities—like land development—of other Americans. Feelings of indignation, frustration, anger, injustice, and sometimes aggression well up. These situations are becoming more frequent and more intense, particularly as land development and other changes in the United States and Canada accelerate, bringing Indians and non-Indians more frequently face to face.

In point of fact, the descendants of many of the native societies who occupied North America before the Europeans arrived are very much still here. Today there are some 330 federally recognized tribes and bands in the "lower 48 states," nearly all of whom have reservations. In Alaska there are about 225 individually recognized, indigenous communities of Alaskan Natives. Canada has about 600 recognized Indian groups, which are called "bands." Today, as in the past, North American Indians *define* themselves as Indians of particular tribal groups and bands. Tribal councils administer their reservations and communities. Treaty rights remain in force, guaranteed by treaties signed when Euro-Americans wanted peace and land. Tribal cultural ways have everywhere changed greatly, but nearly all tribal peoples take pride in having protected and maintained a vital core of philosophical and religious ideas from their ancestors.

ETHNIC MINORITIES

Ethnic minorities are more familiar to the average American. Most Americans have direct experience with various ethnic groups in their midst. American cities have neighborhoods where Americans of, for example, Chinese, Mexican, Vietnamese, or Italian descent are concentrated and where their language, ethnic foods, architectural styles, music, religious practices, and social groups remain strong. Americans are accustomed to a good deal of cultural diversity around them, some of it from immigrant groups and some of it from regional variants that developed here, such as Appalachians, New Englanders, and Texans.

Like North American Indians, ethnic minorities, too, struggle to retain their distinctiveness. This book is about that struggle. Its chapters examine cases of both Indians and ethnic minorities. The reader is invited to compare one case with another, looking for commonalities and differences in their experiences, seeking to identify what works and what does not in their efforts to resist the forces that erode them.

Five ethnic groups are examined in this book, the Old Order Amish in Pennsylvania, African American fishermen along the coast of Georgia, Sicilian fishermen in Gloucester, Massachusetts, and two refugee groups, the Hmong in Wisconsin and Guatemalan Maya living in southern Florida. As with the book's eight chapters on indigenous groups, chapters 9 through 13 present us with powerful pressures threatening a lifeway and cultural heritage, and very different responses, ranging from sad resignation to exuberant ethnic pride.

BEING ENDANGERED

Human beings have a penchant for dividing themselves into separate groups, one from another. Other species, too, divide up into communities which stake out a territory and defend it from others. Humans, because they operate in a *cultural* universe, divide themselves not only by territory, but also by lifeway and custom. Oftentimes these groups live among one another in relative harmony and mutual interdependence, but at other times prejudice, exploitation, cruelty, and violence will set one group against another. Each group tenaciously guards its differences. A recurring fear is that its ancestry will be lost, its distinctive heritages will dissipate, and its children will forget from whom they came.

Staying different is hard work. Whenever human groups are in continuing contact with one another they have a tendency to grow more alike. This is caused by diffusion, when one group adopts something from the other's lifeway, and assimilation, when diffusion has gone so far that one group, or individuals from it, merge into the other. Diffusion and assimilation can be slowed, or even stopped, if one or both groups nurture prejudice, religious differences, and regulations that channel how one group can interact with the other. Diffusion and assimilation can also be countered by segregating where people live. The two groups may work and trade together, but they keep different home sites, home life, child rearing, religion, and marriage—the heart of cultural difference—safely separated. Nevertheless, the forces of diffusion and assimilation are always present, threatening those boundaries. If unopposed, the boundaries will eventually erode. In today's world, groups find themselves in increasing contact with each other, and thus the persistence and distinctiveness of every group becomes, to various degrees, endangered.

Your reaction to this may be, "What's wrong with everyone becoming one large society?" Engaging in a discussion on this question will bring out intriguing ideas and probably strong feelings. In this book, however, it is enough to observe that, for better or worse, we live in a world in which group identities are centrally important to people, and that is not going to change. To take one example, The bloody war between ethnic Albanians and ethnic Serbs in Kosovo, Yugoslavia, eventually achieved a resentful but fragile stalemate. The Kosovo conflict, a struggle between two peoples who emphatically oppose becoming more like each other, is far from unusual. The fierce determination to keep their lifeways separate and strong finds countless parallels all over the world, including North America. The world we humans live in continues to be one in which peoples value their ancestry and fight to defend their differing identities and histories.

On the North American continent the struggle to stay separate is highly unequal. In both the United States and Canada an enormous, mainstream culture dominates economic, political, and social life. The dominant culture is, of course, internally divided, as in French-speaking and English-speaking Canada, or Anglo Americans and Hispanic Americans. Imagine how much more disadvantaged a group feels when it numbers only a few hundred people who are surrounded by a dominant society of hundreds of millions. Imagine how a small group feels when television, music, clothing styles, advertising, career opportunities, and material luxuries trumpet the values and thoughts of the dominant society and for your children.

TOOLS OF SELF PRESERVATION

The chapters in this book are about small societies struggling to maintain their futures against the never relenting, insistent, intrusive, dominant society. While each group is conscious of the threat, the degree to which it has mounted an organized and effective defense varies. Some seem overwhelmed by what they see happening to themselves. Other groups, however, have been resolute and remarkably effective in defending their identities. And the effectiveness is spreading. Throughout North America there is a growing sense among most groups that they must act decisively if the societies conveyed by their ancestors are to exist for their children.

Awareness of the threat is the critical first ingredient in stemming the erosive action of diffusion and assimilation. The second ingredient is to begin to believe that these twin threats can be offset. The third ingredient of a successful defense is to learn from the experience of other groups what works and what does not. The stories of the groups that have had spectacular successes are now circulating widely. They are studied to determine how those successes were achieved. It is an exciting time for these endangered societies, and many have reason to believe that diffusion and assimilation, if not altogether stopped, at least can be controlled and managed.

The threats to these small-scale groups are many. There is threat in the vast imbalance of population size, economic resources, and political clout. These mostly small, poor, politically weak, societies are surrounded by a huge society which controls nearly all the common means of communication and the distribution of information (newspapers, magazines, radio, television, Internet). The surrounding society originates most of the new, powerful technologies, which produce much of the prevailing entertainment (movies, television, magazines, professional sports). The surrounding society manages the banks, insurance, transportation, most of the stores, the courts, the police, the regional and national government, foreign political and military affairs, education and the careers accessed through education, and jobs. No wonder we call it "the dominant society." The small society occupies an "enclave," a small place surrounded by the dominant other.

The external, dominant society also actually penetrates aggressively inside these communities. Local land is being bought up and developed; natural resources, such as coal, timber, and fisheries, are under commercializing pressure; tourism is increasing; water supplies may be in jeopardy; and local artistic and traditional symbols held dear by the small society appear, without consent, on commercial products. The languages of the dominant society (English and, in Quebec, French) hold sway. "Cool" products—designer jeans and shoes, popular music CDs, cigarettes, branded alcoholic beverages, gang symbols, drugs, and inhalants—entice the youth of these communities. These enclaved communities cannot simply ignore the "outside" because the outside is within their midst, demanding their attention. Against all of these forces, how can a small, enclaved lifeway persist?

Many of these communities are finding old and new strategies to use to preserve themselves. One old strategy is to withdraw and close themselves off from others. Indian reservations in many cases now prohibit strangers from entering most areas without permission. Another strategy is to take serious steps to preserve language, ceremonies, customs, and oral traditions and to make these more important in everyday life. Another is to attract more economic opportunities into the community, under greater degree of local control, in order to provide more job opportunities for the youth. Still another is to take greater control over schools in order to reinforce rather than undermine their lifeways. There also are some "new" tools to combat the forces eroding their lifeways.

One of the new tools is the Internet. Small enclaved groups can now communicate cheaply and quickly with others and develop united action. Many tribal groups, for instance, have websites (some are listed in this book's chapters) and e-mail "list serves" through which they develop a greater awareness of the threat, share information on any resources available for the fight, and spread the benefits of the experience of each. Fax machines and express delivery services are also important. These inventions are driving what is called "globalization," but, paradoxically, the very factors that are drawing the world into a single society are also enabling small societies to resist being homogenized into the whole.

Another tool is money. From a variety of sources—Indian casinos in the United States are the most visible—various Indian tribes and small communities are finding they have more money to spend. Land claims settlements, court-mandated damage awards, and successful business ventures also contribute. Money allows a group to defend its interests more successfully, to overcome the disadvantages of isolation and poverty when they must take the battle to the dominant society's turf, send out mailings, orchestrate press conferences, and hire expert advisors to map out strategy.

There are many more new defense tools in use, and the reader is invited to search them out in the chapters to follow. Here are three more to look for: the quality of leadership, powerful advocacy organizations (for instance, environmentalists and human rights groups) enlisted as allies, and the ability to influence public opinion in the dominant society by shaping what the news media report and by harnessing the power of film and video.

THE COUNTERREACTION

The increasing effectiveness of small, ethnic communities in North America has elicited counterreactions, some of them very powerful. For example, in the United States, Indian casinos have been legal since 1988. The casinos have become an important source of the money used to defend Indian rights. However, casinos have generated strong counterreactions, and the U.S. Congress may change existing legislation in ways that would limit the tribes' business success. Another, more general issue illustrates the counterreaction: throughout the centuries of contact with Euro-Americans, North American Indian tribes have demanded recognition of their sovereignty. Sovereignty is reflected in the group's ability to run its own affairs, to have its land and treaty rights honored, and to be dealt with on a government-to-government basis between their tribal governments and the U.S. and Canadian federal governments. As the dominant society increasingly intrudes, Indian demands that their sovereignty be honored have become more aggressively asserted. This engenders stiffened resentment and resistance among non-Indian citizens, and among many political leaders, who think Indian sovereignty threatens the political integrity of the American or Canadian state.

In Canada, Indian sovereignty has also generated resistance and resentment, but on a political level it seems better accepted than in the United States. The greater entrenchment of Indian sovereignty in Canada is well illustrated by the recent creation of the vast northern territory of Nunavut to accommodate Inuit (Eskimo) home rule desires, and by the reconceptualization of Indian groups as "first nations" and as significant players in Canadian politics and economics.

Ethnic minorities, too, encounter resistance to their efforts to preserve themselves. They struggle to preserve their collective integrity in the face of land development projects that invade their communities. They find their local stores and gathering places thrown aside by corporate chains. They find their traditional livelihoods displaced by incoming employers. They find outsiders grabbing their land, their fish, and their crafts and re-making the channels for selling what is produced. These struggles are well illustrated in the chapters that follow.

SCOPE

This section begins by clarifying the scope of the volume. First, although "North America" usually includes Mexico on the south and the Polar region on the north, there are no cases in this volume from Mexico or the Arctic. Those areas are dealt with in *Endangered Peoples of Latin America* and *Endangered Peoples of the Arctic*. Another factor: "endangered peoples" could include almost any type of human group in trouble. As a colleague, Dr. Joan Mencher, recently pointed out, one could argue that small-scale American farmers are an endangered people. True enough, but this book and the others in the series specifically focus on those endangered peoples whose differences are ethnic, not just occupational. Finally, the thirteen chapters in this book can only cover a small sampling of the great number and variety of ethnically defined endangered peoples in North America. Much effort has gone into getting as broad a diversity as possible; you should keep in mind that this book can only introduce you to a modest part of the enormous diversity of North American groups and their struggles. The stories and lessons of the many peoples not in these chapters await your exploration.

TERMINOLOGY

In this book, the tribal peoples are usually called "Indians," not "Native Americans." Among themselves, "Indian" is usually preferred, despite its 1492 origin in one of the most colossal geographic misconstruals in history. Similarly, "tribe" is used here because it is in widespread use among Indians, although in Canada, and increasingly in the United States, "tribe" is being replaced by "nation." Finally, in the United States "Americans" refers not only to those whose ancestors came from other continents, but also to those whose ancestors were here when they arrived. In the United States all are Americans, and in Canada all are Canadians.

THE IMPORTANCE OF YOU

As tribes and small ethnic groups struggle to hang on to their futures, public opinion among citizens of the dominant society is usually very important to the outcome. Consider the following cases:

1. A beer manufacturer brands his product with a heroic Indian name. The most promising avenue to halt such use is for the tribe to convince the broad buying public to boycott the product.

2. A traditional ethnic group sees its traditional fishing spots taken away by highly capitalized fishing corporations. One of the avenues of protest is to take the concern to consumers and mobilize an outcry to legislators to protect the traditional fishermen.

3. The National Park Service discovers that one of its properties has become a mecca for rock climbers, but the climbers are disturbing Indians who are conducting private religious ceremonies in what they regard as a very holy place. The Park Service is caught between the Indians who want privacy and the climbers who want to climb. A strong expression of public support for the Indians' privacy can make it easier for the Park Service to refuse access to the climbers.

4. A university wants to build a telescope on a mountain in the Southwest considered a very sacred site by an Indian tribe. The tribe believes the road, the construction, and the traffic will desecrate the spiritual sanctity of the site. After the university decides to proceed, the tribe's best hope may be to mobilize public opinion to pressure the university to halt or limit its project.

5. A small ethnic group, who have established themselves in a Midwestern community, wants to buy land, build churches, and enlarge their numbers by bringing relatives to the community. The town officials, fearing an "invasion" of these people, refuse building and zoning permits and in other ways block the group. To lower the resistance, the group must explain itself to the townspeople and seek supporters among its opinion leaders.

In each of these cases—all of them true—the knowledge, attitudes, and understanding of members of the dominant society can be crucial. If the public's knowledge is stronger than its fears, if there is understanding rather than ignorance, if there is courage to argue for justice rather than acquiescing to demagogues, the chances for justice and harmony improve.

What role do you have? If you are a member of the dominant society, you are one of those who make up the public opinion that either opposes a fair outcome, or insists on it. Find out what endangered peoples are all about. This book is an important place to begin.

ACKNOWLEDGMENTS

Producing a volume like this benefits from the support of many people. Limited space does not allow me to name most of them, but series editor Barbara Johnston's readily available counsel and assistance have been consistently supportive. I want also to acknowledge the wonderful assistance of three Bucknell students and one faculty colleague: Jill Owczarzak who lent fine manuscript skills to the work, Ryan Neenan and Professor Ben Marsh, who accomplished wonders with computerized maps, and Kristi Yingling, who contributed much to the index and proofing tasks. My thanks to all.

PART 1

INDIGENOUS SOCIETIES

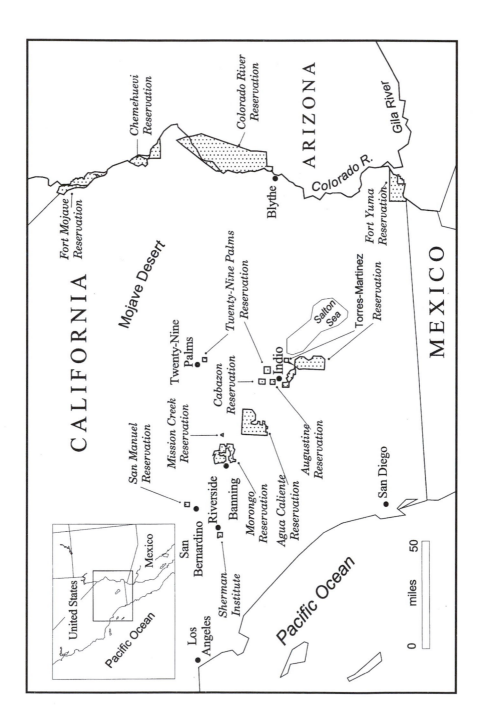

Chapter 1

The Chemehuevis in Nevada and California

Clifford E. Trafzer

Chemehuevi culture has always been and will forever remain a live and dynamic entity. In spite of years of threats to their existence, the people have adapted to changing circumstances within and outside their culture and have survived. Chemehuevis (pronounced ChemehWAYvees) remain a pragmatic people, but their culture has changed over time, particularly after contact with European-derived Americans. They have become an endangered people largely as a result of the pressures brought about by the invasion of Chemehuevi by the United States government and its citizens.

CULTURAL OVERVIEW

The People

Chemehuevis are Southern Paiute people who call themselves Nuwu or the People. They once occupied villages from Las Vegas, Nevada, south along the Colorado River to present-day Blythe, California. Chemehuevis also lived in villages in the Colorado and Mojave deserts of southeastern California. Anthropologist Alfred Kroeber estimated their precontact population at 1,000, although others believe they numbered 1,500 people.[1] Originally, Chemehuevis were hunters and gatherers, but those living along the Colorado River learned to farm from Mojaves. During the seventeenth century, Chemehuevis moved into the Mojave Desert, establishing villages near natural springs and mountain hunting areas. The desert Chemehuevis conducted limited farming near springs and in washes, including the Oasis of Mara that became known as Twenty-Nine Palms. This band once numbered forty-five to fifty people, but today, the band includes thirteen enrolled members. Approximately 1,500 Chemehuevis live along the Colorado River today on the Chemehuevi and Colorado River Indian Reservation, largely working for tribal, state, county, and federal agencies. Most members of the Twenty-Nine Palms Band work for the tribe. Although living in a modern world, Chemehuevis have not forgotten their creation stories, songs, and spiritual relationship with the earth, animals, and plants of their former homelands.

The Chemehuevis people's creation story is as follows: At the beginning of time, creative forces moved around and within the earth. Ocean Woman experienced a vision that the earth should be more than the rolling waves of an endless sea. So she used her body to create a solid earth of plains and plateaus, mountains and valleys. With her body she created the deserts, the natural home of Chemehuevis. But before the birth of Chemehuevis and other indigenous peoples of the Americas, creative characters like Ocean Woman, Coyote, Louse, and Wolf set the world into motion. At this time, the animal people interacted intimately with each other as well as with water, rocks, plants, mountains, and all natural features of earth. They formed a relationship with the sun, stars, moons, galaxies, and universes. They set into motion a cosmic drama in which the Chemehuevis were an integral part.

After Ocean Woman spread her body across the water, creating solid land, Coyote raced about through valleys, plateaus, swamps, forests, mountains, and canyons until he announced that the earth had been formed. But the creative process was not complete, as Wolf, Mountain Lion, Louse, and other animal people began their history with the natural features of the land. Fathers and mothers created sons and daughters, and the animal people intermarried with one another. One daughter was Poo'wavi (Louse). Poo'wavi was a beautiful girl, but powerful and dangerous. When Coyote initiated a courtship, she tried to drown him. Eventually, Poo'wavi and Coyote married and through their union produced many fertilized eggs which Coyote placed into a large woven basket crafted by Old Woman. Coyote carried the basket with its treasure on his journey to Nëvagante (Snow Having, probably Charleston Peak).[2]

Before he arrived at the sacred mountain, the basket became so heavy that Coyote opened the lid. He found that the larvae had become the first tribal people who then left the basket to begin a new life. Some remained in the desert, but most migrated to every corner of the earth. Nearly all of the people emerged in this way, created and sustained by the body of Ocean Woman. In the bottom of the basket were larvae that had been crushed by the weight of the other larvae. Coyote carried these on to Snow Having where he asked his brother Wolf what to do. Wolf took the crushed larvae, molded them with his hands, nurtured them into children, and breathed life into these people. From the creation of Coyote and Louse and the recreation of Wolf, Nüwü or Chemehuevi people were born.[3]

The Setting

Chemehuevis lived in a vast desert region, ranging from present-day Las Vegas, Nevada, south to Blythe, California. They established villages along the Colorado River, living in close proximity to Mojave Indians. In addition, some Chemehuevis lived in permanent and temporary village sites in the Mojave Desert which was the place of their origin.

The deserts of southern Nevada, eastern California, and western Arizona stretch out for miles, intercepted occasionally by valleys, arroyos, and mountains. It is a magical place for Chemehuevis, a place where the intense sun is born and dies each day, constantly altering the dramatic desert scene with shades and shadows, winds and calms, and colors that change hues throughout each day and each season.[4]

Contemporary Chemehuevis live in selected areas of their former domain and beyond. The people live primarily along the Colorado River near Parker, Arizona, and Havasu Landing, California. Members of the Twenty-Nine Palms Band live in the Coachella Valley, California, but some Chemehuevis choose to live on the Soboba and Cabazon reservations and near the city of Las Vegas.

Traditional Subsistence Strategies

The traditional homeland of Chemehuevis is dotted with mountains that deceptively appear arid and lifeless, but some of the larger mountain ranges contain evergreen trees, especially junipers and piñons. The mountains provide unique habitats for plants and animals as well as sanctuaries for birds, bats, and butterflies. The Mojave Desert contains hundreds of species of plants and animals, but Chemehuevis relied heavily on a small number for their survival. They gathered large quantities of the mesquite beans that came from groves of sweet mesquite. Women pounded mesquite beans into meal and mixed it with water to make bread or cakes.[5] Chemehuevi elder Gertrude Leivas remembers that people once made a drink from mesquite beans. When Gertrude was a child during the early twentieth century, her mother made a sweet, refreshing drink from mesquite beans that everyone enjoyed, particularly children who had no carbonated drinks or fruit juices. This drink was a special refreshment made in a traditional manner familiar to Native Americans living in the deserts of California, Arizona, and Nevada.[6] In addition, the people ate chia seeds, piñon nuts, tule roots, and screw beans. They ate small game including tortoises, quails, ducks, geese, rabbits, and lizards. The people were best known, however, for hunting desert mountain sheep and mule deer.[7]

Chemehuevis hunted throughout the vast Mojave Desert from present-day Las Vegas to Blythe and from the Hualapai Mountains of western Arizona into the San Bernardino Mountains in the region of Big Bear Lake,

California. Chemehuevis did not "own" their hunting areas in the modern sense of the word, but they believed they "owned" specific hunting areas through hereditary songs that tied humans to geographic areas where people had a physical, psychological, and spiritual relationship with the earth, plants, animals, and water resources. They also had a special relationship with the spirits inhabiting these lands.

The hunting complex of Chemehuevi people was spiritual in nature and closely tied hunters with prey. Chemehuevis sang sacred songs about mountain sheep and deer, and hunters "owned" songs about one or the other animal. Those families that owned mountain sheep songs called themselves mountain sheep people; those that owned deer songs called themselves deer people. The songs served several purposes. They reminded families of past generations of their people who hunted in the desert. The songs explained the relationship of hunters to the animals. The songs served as maps which laid out the features and geography of the hunting areas where the people took either mountain sheep or deer. If a man or woman owned a song, they owned the land addressed by the song. Proof of ownership was found in oral deeds known as deer songs and mountain sheep songs.[8] The songs reminded people of the gifts of life offered to them by the animals. In return for the sacrifice the animals made with their lives to the people, hunters followed prescribed rules of prayers, offerings, songs, and rituals before hunting. If they did not, harm could come to them. According to Chemehuevi elder Joe Benitez, one of his uncles once entered a hunting area without fulfilling all of his spiritual obligations and was approached by a spiritual being that frightened him away from the hunting ground.[9] Benitez did not know the exact nature of the spirit, but one anthropologist noted that Chemehuevis sometimes saw apparitions best described in English as "demons." The negative spirit may have been the phantom that appeared to the uncle of Joe Benitez.[10]

Chemehuevis were known as great hunters, and they developed a special hunting bow that powered arrows deep into the flesh of their favored game. In order to hunt, Chemehuevis developed great endurance, championing those among them who could run pell-mell in pursuit of game. In fact, running became a spiritual act for specific runners who could run in a special manner; that is, they could travel by teleportation or invisible flying via time and space. Although non-Indians have scoffed at the idea, Chemehuevi accounts exist in the works of John P. Harrington, George Laird, and Carobeth Laird that confirm the ability of Chemehuevi runners to travel great[11] distances in a period of time no other humans could possibly equal.

Social and Political Organization

Chemehuevis organized themselves in families or small groups of families. They enjoyed a great deal of autonomy, traveling and trading on foot over an extensive area. At times Chemehuevi hunters and their families traveled together for several months to take game.

Medicine men (shamans) held a unique place in Chemehuevi society. Usually these men were religious leaders who also served as local headmen. Although the two positions of leadership—one secular and one religious—could be separate, the shaman was often a village or band leader as well. Chemehuevis gravitated to the leadership of holy men who had power beyond that of others. The great-grandfather of Dean Mike and grandfather of Joe Benitez was William Mike, a famous shaman of the late nineteenth and early twentieth centuries. He was a man the people both revered and feared because of his power. All Chemehuevis could acquire power through dreams, visions, songs, and prayers, but shamans acquired unique and dangerous power that could be employed to do positive or negative acts. Medicine men could use their powers, for instance, to heal people, predict the weather, divine the location of game, and foresee wars. They could also muster their power to make other people ill or even kill them by shooting evil into the person or by placing the person in harm's way.[12]

Chemehuevi shamans were known for their ability to harness the power that was all about them. They spent a good deal of time by themselves in secluded spots, often in special caves in eastern California, western Arizona, and southern Nevada. One particular granite cave has been used by several generations of holy people, evidenced by the wear between the rocks at the entrance to the cave and the worn granite slab found immediately inside the cave. To enter the cave, the individual must stoop down and crawl into the space that opens into a larger, natural space, approximately five and one-half feet high. Pictographs painted in orange, yellow, and black decorate the walls. To the east, the cave opens up to a view of the desert and mountains, including the Chemehuevi range due east of Lake Havasu City, Arizona, and the Chemehuevi Reservation of California.[13] Chemehuevi shamans gained power in this sacred place and many others that held similar significance. Chemehuevis used such caves to conduct rituals and ceremonies. In this way, shamans had a reciprocal relationship to caves and other sacred areas. Usually they received power and employed it for the benefit of people within the rock walls of the earth.

Traditionally, each Chemehuevi band decided for itself where it would create a village site and how long the people would remain in a particular area. Some villages were permanently occupied; others were used seasonally as bands traveled about to hunt or gather. Throughout the vast Mojave Desert and beyond, Chemehuevis had specific village sites that were generally permanent and known to the people by name. When a local headman determined it was in the best interest of the group to move to a new hunting area, he informed the band of his decision and, by consensus, the people moved. If a family or portion of a family decided not to follow the plan, they were free to go their own way. In this sense, Chemehuevis enjoyed autonomy from group to group and within groups.

During the late nineteenth and early twentieth centuries, William Mike was the head of the largest group of Chemehuevis living in the Mojave Desert. Mike was a shaman and local headman who had a special power mountain (known today as Queen Mountain) he called his own. Mike's band was known by its location at an oasis at Twenty-Nine Palms, a place near the present-day headquarters of the Joshua Tree National Park. Although the Chemehuevis had known and used the Serrano Indian village site at Twenty-Nine Palms for generations, Chemehuevis are best known for inhabiting the village site after 1863 when Chemehuevis living along the Colorado River fought a major war with Mojaves. Mike's band of Chemehuevis settled among a Serrano Indian band at the Oasis of Mara— better known as Twenty-Nine Palms—where they lived in peace with one another in the middle of the desert far removed from Mojaves. Twenty-Nine Palms was distant from white settlements along the Colorado River, mining and transportation towns, and California settlements in present-day San Bernardino, Yucaipa, Palm Springs, and Banning. Chemehuevis under the leadership of William Mike determined to remain isolated from most Whites in order to maintain the band's sovereignty and independence. In this way, they retained their religious, political, and social structures largely without the interference of non-Indians until the mid-1890s. Although some white miners, merchants, and cattlemen passed by or lived nearby, the whites did not threaten William Mike or his band to any degree until the end of the nineteenth century when government policies dramatically altered their lives.

Religion and World View

Chemehuevis describe their religion as one that emerged at the time of creation when animal people, plants, and places interacted in a great drama that put the world into motion. Chemehuevis consider this time an actual part of their history, not simply a "myth" as often presented by scholars. The creative time of Chemehuevi history placed the people as part of creation, not superior to animals, plants, or places. The people also believed that creative time was important for all time, that the creative period always had (and has) influence in the lives of the people and their larger communities, past and present. Plants, animals, rivers, oases, mountains, and other natural occurrences were significant elements to the Chemehuevi, and today the stories of the relationship of the people to natural elements continue to be told. Many believe that the retelling of the ancient stories re-creates the first acts of creation and keeps them alive within contemporary people.[14] In similar fashion, the old songs of Chemehuevi people often tell of travels from one place to another or past hunts through particular areas. Songs and stories tell of specific animals and places where they lived, of the relationship of place, plants, and animals to humans, and of the journeys of

8

heroes and heroines which influenced the course of Chemehuevi history. Stories and songs continue to exert influence on the people today. Certain elements of traditional Chemehuevi religion, ritual, and ceremony are not openly shared with outsiders today, but Chemehuevi Salt Song singers do share some of their songs, at times interpreting them and singing them at such events as funerals and all-night sings with other Indians, particularly Paiute-speaking peoples.[15] In March 1999, Matthew Leivas, Vivian Jake, David Chavez, Larry Eddy, Betty Cornelius, Sylvia Polacca, and others formed the Salt Song Project to preserve and perpetuate these unique songs as well as oral knowledge relevant to their Salt Songs, stories, and other songs traditionally sung by Chemehuevis. The Chemehuevi Tribe and Twenty-Nine Palms Band of Chemehuevis, two distinct and sovereign people, have taken the lead in preserving Chemehuevi songs that are intimately connected to their religion.[16]

THREATS TO SURVIVAL

Today Chemehuevis believe that some aspects of their religion and culture are being threatened by real estate development, off-road vehicles, and modern entertainment that emphasizes a homogenous American culture rather than their own traditions, values, and beliefs. Although some Chemehuevis speak the old language, the number of native language speakers is declining. These conditions pose a threat to traditional Chemehuevi beliefs as do some locally active Christian sects (e.g., Presbyterians), which devalue native religions and traditional spiritual complexes.

Population

Chemehuevi people and their culture have been threatened for years, in part because they have always been a small population of people living at the southern end of the larger Paiute Indian culture area. Paiute-speaking people live in small groups throughout the Great Basin of the United States from present-day eastern Washington and Oregon and southern Idaho south through Nevada and Utah, into northern and western Arizona. Paiutes also shared with Shoshones the vast domain down the eastern slopes of the Sierra Nevada Mountains into the deserts of California. Chemehuevis represented the southernmost group of Paiute-speaking peoples, but their numbers have never been large. During the mid-nineteenth century, Chemehuevis were estimated to have numbered between 800 and 1,000 people, although the exact number is not known.[17] However, it is safe to state that the number of Chemehuevis has never been great, and that introduced diseases diminished the population during the second half of the nineteenth century. Spanish explorers crossed Chemehuevi lands a few times but never settled in Chemehuevi country. Spanish missions, presidios, and pueblos never existed on Chemehuevi lands, although the people may have contracted infectious disease spread from missions at San Gabriel, San Diego, San Luis Rey, San Pablo y San Pedro de Bicuñer, Concepcíon, or one of their *assistencias* (outposts).[18]

The American exploration of the Colorado River and Mojave Desert by Lieutenant Joseph Christmas Ives, Amiel Weeks Whipple, and Edward Fitzgerald Beal in the 1850s was a far greater threat to Chemehuevis than were the Spanish. American explorers and soldiers traveled through Chemehuevi lands and planned settlement of the region for military and commercial purposes. In the 1850s, the United States encouraged the Colorado Steam Navigation Company to operate steamboats up and down the Colorado River from the Gulf of Baja California to Black Canyon, the present site of Hoover Dam. Steamboats brought soldiers, miners, cattlemen, gamblers, merchants, whiskey traders, and prostitutes to Chemehuevi lands. Some of these foreigners resettled on Chemehuevi and Mojave lands; others ventured out into the Mojave Desert to prospect or travel through to the California coast. In 1861 soldiers of the United States Army built Fort Mojave, threatening the lifeway of Chemehuevi people. Although the Chemehuevi never fought a war against the United States, the U.S. Army's presence may have contributed to deteriorating relations between Chemehuevis and Mojaves, who far outnumbered the Chemehuevis.[19]

Between 1863 and 1867, Chemehuevis living in villages along the Colorado River fought a series of campaigns against Mojaves. The war caused the diaspora of Chemehuevi from the Colorado River into the deserts to the west. For generations, Chemehuevis had lived in villages in the Mojave Desert, hunting and gathering in the desert, but during and after the Mojave War, other groups moved permanently into the desert, as did the Twenty-Nine Palms Band of Chemehuevis. The latter are the ancestors of the contemporary Chemehuevis who live with Serrano Indians at Twenty-Nine Palms. They were the largest groups of Chemehuevis who lived in the desert, and they subsisted by hunting, gathering, and farming beans, squash, corn, melons, and other crops.[20]

During the late nineteenth century, the Twenty-Nine Palms Band and other Chemehuevis living in the Mojave Desert suffered horribly from disease. In the late nineteenth and early twentieth centuries, the people fell victim to tuberculosis, the scourge of all Americans but a disease that became extremely active among Native Americans between the 1890s and 1940s.[21] Chemehuevis suffered from other diseases and deaths from malnutrition brought on by a depleted food supply after the Indians began competing with non-Indians for game, land, and water. Whites hunted for food and sport, and they hunted with firearms, particularly long-range rifles, and sharply diminished the supply of game. In response, Chemehuevis living at Twenty-Nine Palms used their agricultural experience—which they had learned from Mojaves living along the Colorado River—and established farming while continuing to hunt and gather. They adapted to new circumstances, fencing their lands to prevent cattle, horses, mules, and burros from entering their gardens. Still, the food supply declined, especially after their forced removal from the oasis at Twenty-Nine Palms. Malnutrition of mothers and children contributed to lower birthrates and higher infant and childhood mortality, although there are no statistics to prove the point—only declining population figures. The number of desert Chemehuevis declined dramatically, but the Chemehuevi population living on the Colorado River stabilized and ultimately increased during the twentieth century.

Competition for Land and Water

Another major threat to Chemehuevi people living at Twenty-Nine Palms was competition for lands and water. The oasis at Twenty-Nine Palms stretches east to west, fed by an aquifer that reaches the surface and creates several pools of water. In the 1860s the Indians were the only inhabitants at Twenty-Nine Palms, but during the late nineteenth century, Whites settled on lands near the oasis, and commerce, cattle, and mining brought other non-Indians to and through the area. By the 1880s, the Chemehuevis lived on the west end of the oasis on lands currently owned by the Inn at Twenty-Nine Palms (a resort hotel located on the oasis about a half-mile from the north interpretive center of Joshua Tree National Park). The area included a host of palm trees native to California, a pond, and an abundance of natural grasses that was an inviting habitat for birds and game. Indians and non-Indians recognized this part of the oasis as native land, as did government agents, until the 1890s when, over the objection of lower-level government officials, the United States created a reservation of 160 acres for the Chemehuevis at Twenty-Nine Palms (not for Chemehuevis living along the Colorado River) that was some distance from the oasis and far from a water source.[22]

Through an executive order, the Chemehuevis lost nearly all their lands in Southern California, including hunting and gathering grounds that they had owned for generations. Furthermore, they lost all of their former lands, homes, gardens, and water supply at the oasis. Although the political maneuvering that created this situation is not known, it is likely that well-financed businessmen of the Southern Pacific Railroad recommended the removal of the Indians from the oasis. The state claimed the land in 1875 and sold it to the Southern Pacific Railroad. After the government established the reservation and tried to force the Indians to move to an arid spot at the base of the Queen Mountains, the Southern Pacific Railroad Company firmly claimed the oasis and controlled the precious water until it sold the land with the water to private owners.

The Twenty-Nine Palms Indian Reservation was an inhospitable piece of land located slightly south and west of the oasis on elevated ground which offered a splendid view of the palm trees among which they had lived since 1863. The Chemehuevis tried to dig a deep well on the land designated as their reservation but located no water there and refused to leave the oasis.[23] For years the United States had entertained a national policy of "civilizing" Indians by making them farmers. Chemehuevis were already farmers, but without water, they could not fulfill the assimilationist goals of the government. The reservation system proved detrimental to the Chemehuevis and resulted in malnutrition and diseases that affected their population. Census data for the Twenty-Nine Palms Band kept by the Bureau of Indian Affairs provide graphic evidence of a population in jeopardy and decline. In 1894 the Twenty-Nine Palms Reservation census suggests that four families lived at Twenty-Nine Palms with a total population of twelve people (this number may not have included all children or people who were in the desert and mountains hunting, gathering, or trading). The heads of these families included William and Maria Mike, Jim and Matilda Pine, and Jacinto and Carlota Do. Pancho Ramerez was not listed as having a wife, and a thirty-seven-year-old woman, Margarita Ramerez, did not have a husband. The twelve people listed in the census consisted of two in their sixties, one in her fifties, three in their forties, two in their thirties, one in her twenties, one teenager, and two children under ten and no infants. The 1897 census listed twenty-seven people. Most of these were older people ranging in age from forty to ninety years of age, and most of them appear on only one census at Twenty-Nine Palms. It is likely that these people were elderly refugees from other Chemehuevi villages in the Mojave Desert who migrated to Twenty-Nine Palms to spend the last days of their lives with fellow Chemehuevis. By 1922 the government listed only eight Chemehuevis on the Cabazon Reservation to which the United States had exiled them in 1910.[24]

Between 1895 and 1909, Chemehuevis lived on their waterless reservation at Twenty-Nine Palms. In 1909 Malki Agency Superintendent Clara True rode a wagon to Twenty-Nine Palms and offered to move the Indians to the Morongo or Agua Caliente reservations near her agency headquarters. When William Mike, Jim Pine, and Pancho Ramerez refused to leave Twenty-Nine Palms, True took the children with her so she could enroll them in school. After a brief council, most Chemehuevi elders—but not all—packed their belongings and moved to Banning, California, to be near their children and grandchildren. That same year, a Chemehuevi-Paiute young man named Willie Boy shot and killed William Mike. According to Chemehuevi elders, Willie had fallen in love with Mike's daughter Carlotta, and the couple had run away to be married. William Mike foiled the elopement. After a brief time spent apart, Willie and Carlotta planned another marriage. Contemporary Chemehuevis say that Mike disapproved of the marriage because Willie and Carlotta were too closely related to be married. Whatever the reason, Willie feared Mike, and when he approached the elder to ask for his permission to marry Carlotta, Willie carried a rifle. The two men argued, fought, and in the melee, Willie shot William Mike to death then fled Banning with Carlotta. A posse, including white lawmen and Cahuilla Indian trackers, followed the couple into the desert. According to one account, Willie murdered Carlotta and committed suicide.[25] Recent scholarship suggests that someone in the posse shot Carlotta by accident.[26] Contemporary California Indians say that the posse never captured Willie Boy. He escaped by running in the "old way" (teleportation) and lived out his days among Paiutes east of Bishop, California.[27]

Willie Boy's murder of William Mike encouraged the government to remove Chemehuevis from the Banning area. The government forced the Chemehuevis to resettle on the Cabazon Reservation, located on the eastern edge of the Coachella Valley. In 1910 the Bureau of Indian Affairs added a section of land to the Cabazon Reservation to be held jointly by Cahuillas already living at Cabazon and the Chemehuevis. According to Chemehuevi elder Joe Benitez, as soon as the Chemehuevis arrived, the Cahuillas informed them that they did not belong on the Cabazon Reservation.[28] Chemehuevis and Cahuillas were (and are) two separate peoples in terms of culture, language, and religion. The people at Cabazon had secured for themselves a small portion of their former domain and had no interest in sharing the reservation with Chemehuevis. Over the course of the twentieth century, most Chemehuevis left the Cabazon Reservation even though they were enrolled there. Susie Mike remained at Cabazon, where she raised her three-year-old son Joe, but members of the Mike family moved away, including Jessie Mike who relocated to Palm Springs where she worked for a living and raised her children, Dean, Darryl, and June.[29]

The survival of the members of the Twenty-Nine Palms Band of Chemehuevis during the twentieth century depended on the sheer will and perseverance of individuals. While the Mike family moved into Palm Springs, the Pine family (Serranos) moved to the Mission Creek Reservation before going to the Morongo Reservation. Serrano Indians, longtime friends of Chemehuevis, lived on these reservations and intermarried with Chemehuevis. During the course of the twentieth century, some Chemehuevi families—including those of Larry Eddy, Mat Leivas, David Chavez, Mary Lou Brown, Adrian Fisher, Patrick Lytle, and Alberta Van Fleet—moved to the Colorado River Indian Reservation in Arizona or lived on or near the present-day Chemehuevi Indian Reservation.[30] Chemehuevis could no longer live as they had in the past, as their economic culture of hunting, gathering, and farming gave way to wage earning. Some Chemehuevis continued to hunt, gather, and raise gardens, but this could not be their sole means of survival. By the 1950s, the traditional economy of Chemehuevis had been discontinued but not their reverence for the earth, plants, place, and animals. Those beliefs were a constant, a thread that tied the past to the present and was perpetuated and reinforced by singing the ancient songs.

RESPONSE: STRUGGLES TO SURVIVE CULTURALLY

Chemehuevi people and their culture have faced many threats over time. Invasion, war, removal, reservations, disease, and depression have all been a part of the Chemehuevi past. However, in spite of these difficulties, Chemehuevis survived, particularly those living along the Colorado River where their agriculture sustained them and where they could find wage labor by working on ranches, transportation systems, mines, cities, and government projects. Those Chemehuevis who lived in the Mojave Desert declined in numbers and never recovered. Today, only thirteen people are enrolled with the Twenty-Nine Palms Band, but approximately 1,500 live on the Chemehuevi Reservation, Twenty-Nine Palms Reservation (in Coachella, not Twenty-Nine Palms), Colorado River Indian Reservation, and Moapa Reservation.[31] In spite of their small numbers, Chemehuevi people have survived many cultural calamities, and they are the first to point out that they will survive and prosper in the future. Several factors that have entered into Chemehuevi survival are briefly described below.

Traditions

Perhaps most important to the people is their relationship with the past, a tradition that emphasizes the sacred connection between the people, deserts, mountains, mountain lions, wolves, bighorn sheep, deer, rattlesnakes, rabbits, hummingbirds, monarch butterflies, mesquites, piñons, junipers, ironwood, palo verde, chia, and other flora and fauna. In addition, place has been a significant element of survival for the Chemehuevi who revere the vast expanses of deserts, the many mountains that break the horizons of the Mojave Desert, and the rock formations that have meaning in the sacred knowledge of the people.

Protecting traditional food sources, including bighorn sheep and groves of mesquite trees, may help the people treat diabetes, a chronic problem from which the Chemehuevis have suffered since World War II. A return to traditional diets may be of communal and spiritual benefit to Chemehuevis who could also renew their relationship with plants, animals, and places significant to the people.

Ancient songs (Salt Songs) speak of the sacred relationship of humans to other components of nature. Chemehuevis still sing these songs and recreate their connection with their world through words, sounds, and motion. There is a new multitribal association to collect, record, and sing the songs, teaching the young.

Political Activism and Economic Development

Since World War II, Chemehuevis have become politically astute about the way in which federal, state, county, and local governments and non-native citizens deal with native people. They have organized tribal governments and have dealt with others in a sovereign, government-to-government relationship. This significant development among all Chemehuevis has been particularly important for the small group of the Twenty-Nine Palms Band of Chemehuevis who existed as a familial confederacy until the 1990s when the few remaining members formed a cohesive tribal government. It was then that they planned the development of Spotlight 29 Enterprises, located on trust lands adjacent to Interstate 10 in Coachella, California.[32] In 1975 an act of Congress created a separate reservation for the Twenty-Nine Palms Band, and in 1994 they opened a casino. Initially, Spotlight 29 was not a success but with patience and the able leadership of Chairman Dean Mike, the business council, and the staff, the casino became a success.

Revenues from gaming and entertainment have contributed to the economic improvement of the people. Revenue raised from gaming has also financed improved housing, utilities, and education for the people, and it has provided a future for children who will be the leaders of the tribe. Revenues from Spotlight 29 Enterprises has also financed a tribal cultural heritage project led by Dean Mike, Jennifer Mike, Theresa Mike, Joe Benitez, Luke Madrigal, and Anthony Madrigal.

Cultural and Community Projects

The cultural heritage project of the Twenty-Nine Palms Band encompasses several initiatives. The Cultural Committee of the Twenty-Nine Palms Band of Chemehuevi has worked closely with the chairman and the business council to conduct monthly cultural nights featuring traditional singers, native linguists, dancers, lecturers, and historians. The committee has also conducted oral histories with Chemehuevi elders, making audio tapes and video tapes of the interviews. These have been used to create a tribal history, *Chemehuevi People of the Coachella Valley*.[33] In 1997 the Twenty-Nine Palms Band founded the Native American Land Conservancy (NALC) a not-for-profit association, which brought together Indians and non-Indians interested in preserving natural sanctuaries on lands important to Native Americans. NALC's focus has been to protect plant and animal habitats from development, off-road vehicles, and the destructive activities of pot hunters, grave robbers, and individuals who deface pictographs. NALC protects Native American cultural resources and works closely with the University of California and other educational institutions to conduct historical, archaeological, and biological studies of protected lands. NALC

The Cultural Committee of the Twenty-Nine Palms Band of Chemehuevis. From left to right: Anthony Madrigal (Cahuilla), Clifford Trafzer (Wyandot), Luke Madrigal (Cahuilla), Dean Mike (Chemehuevi), Theresa Mike (Lummi), Bernie Thomas (Lummi), and Joe Benitez (Chemehuevi).

preserves landscapes for learning and healing for future generations. Through NALC, the Twenty-Nine Palms Band has worked closely with other Chemehuevis, Cahuillas, and Serranos to protect the earth.[34] The Twenty-Nine Palms Band also plans to establish a museum that will graphically portray the tribe's history and its relationship to the elements of nature and other humans important in the Chemehuevi story.[35]

Chemehuevis have begun to recover and preserve their material culture through the Native American Graves Protection and Repatriation Act (an act of the U.S. Congress that allows Indian tribes to recover remains and sacred objects from museums, universities, and institutions that receive federal funding), and they will use these elements of cultural patrimony to perpetuate their connection with the past. They will also focus on preserving other sacred sites, including caves and villages.

The Twenty-Nine Palms Band of Mission Indians is a sovereign native nation that prides itself on its accomplishments in many areas of life. Each member of the Twenty-Nine Palms group of Chemehuevis, as well as each member of the Chemehuevi Tribe, is committed to the positive growth and development of their people. They draw on native traditions to plan for the future, and no area of tribal business is more important to the business council than the well-being of their people as a community. Old and young identify strongly with their traditional past, not to replicate every aspect of past culture but to draw on elements of traditional culture to strengthen themselves in mind, body, and soul as individuals and as a community. Chemehuevis will continue to strengthen their tribal identity because of their commitment to cultural, historical, and language preservation. The people have exhibited a strong responsibility to work with one another for the benefit of the entire community.

FOOD FOR THOUGHT

Chemehuevis living on and off reservations today rely heavily on familial connections, and they use elements of their traditional culture to enable them to adapt to modern society. Like many other American Indians in North America, Chemehuevis pool their resources and ideas, sharing both to benefit their entire community. They use modern technologies to advance their communities and families, exchanging information through computers, telephones, faxes, printed matter, and transportation systems. They use these same technologies to revitalize and maintain their culture to preserve their traditions, rituals, history, language, and landscapes.

Questions

1. What factors account for the fact that the Chemehuevis did not disappear after the white people came?
2. How can Chemehuevis use elements of their past and present to perpetuate a modern Chemehuevi culture in the future?
3. Why is preserving the native language so important to the Chemehuevi and most other American Indian groups? In the long term, what would be the best strategies for preserving Chemehuevi as a living language?
4. How do state-run educational systems threaten or enhance Chemehuevi culture? Can Chemehuevis find value in individual initiatives and accomplishments as well as in kin-related communal activities?
5. Can the Chemehuevi maintain their spiritual ties to their lands while living apart from the majority of their traditional homelands?

NOTES

The author wishes to thank Lee Ann Smith-Trafzer for helping to prepare this chapter and the members of the Twenty-Nine Palms Band of Mission Indians for sharing oral histories, particularly Dean Mike. Joe Benitez of the Cabazon Reservation and Gertrude Leivas and Matthew Leivas of the Chemehuevi Reservation informed this chapter with their knowledge. Theresa Mike offered her intelligent and constructive thoughts about native history and helped me see the larger picture.

1. Alfred Kroeber, *Handbook of the Indians of California* (Berkeley: California Book, 1953).

2. Carobeth Laird, *The Chemehuevis* (Banning, Calif.: Malki Museum Press,

1976), 148–49; Carobeth Laird, *Mirror and Pattern: George Laird's World of Mythology* (Banning, Calif.: Malki Museum Press, 1984), 32.

3. Laird, *The Chemehuevis*, 149–51.

4. John P. Harrington, "The Chemehuevi: Their Name, Character, and Habitat," papers of John P. Harrington, Smithsonian Institution, Microfilm Collection 1907–1957, Rivera Library, University of California, Riverside, Reel 147, Part 3, p. 4. Hereafter cited as Harrington Papers.

5. The best volume on native use of plants in the Mojave and Colorado deserts is Lowell John Bean and Katherine Siva Saubel, *Temalpakh: Cahuilla Indian Knowledge and Usage of Plants* (Banning, Calif.: Malki Museum Press, 1972).

6. Oral interview by Clifford E. Trafzer, Theresa Mike, Matthew Leivas, Anthony Madrigal, and Bernie Thomas, May 1, 1999.

7. Richard Charles Jenkins, "A Study of Aboriginal Land Use: Southern Paiute Subsistence in the Eastern Mojave Desert" (master's thesis, University of California, Riverside, 1982): 14–28.

8. Laird, *The Chemehuevis*, 7–9.

9. Clifford E. Trafzer, Luke Madrigal, and Anthony Madrigal, *Chemehuevi People of the Coachella Valley* (Coachella, Calif.: Chemehuevi Press, 1997); 21; Oral interview by Clifford E. Trafzer, Luke Madrigal, and Anthony Madrigal with Joe Benitez, September 10 and 17, 1997, author's files. Hereafter cited as Benitez interviews.

10. Harrington, Harrington Papers, 12.

11. Laird, *The Chemehuevis*, 48; Benitez interviews.

12. Benitez interviews; Carobeth Laird, "Chemehuevi Religious Beliefs and Practices," *Journal of California Anthropology* 1 (Spring 1974): 19–25; Laird, *The Chemehuevis*, 148–52.

13. "Site Survey of Old Woman Mountain," Gerald Smith Collection, Smiley Library, Redlands, California. No date.

14. Oral interview by Clifford E. Trafzer, Luke Madrigal, and Anthony Madrigal with Dean Mike, September 3, 1997, author's collection. Hereafter cited as Dean Mike interview.

15. Trafzer, Madrigal, and Madrigal, *Chemehuevi People*, 16–27.

16. In the spring of 2000, Matthew Leivas headed the Salt Song Project, a preservation effort to perpetuate sacred Chemehuevi songs. The project now has the support of the Native American Land Conservancy.

17. Alfred Kroeber, *Handbook of the Indians of California* (Berkeley: California Book, 1953), 593–95; Edward D. Castillo, "American Indians in San Bernardino County: A Status Report," Community Services Department, July 1983, in Tribal Library, Twenty-Nine Palms Band, Coachella, California.

18. Trafzer, Madrigal, and Madrigal, *Chemehuevi People*, 40–44, 69–76.

19. Ibid., 56–62.

20. A.L. Kroeber and C.B. Kroeber, *A Mojave War Reminiscence, 1854–1880* (Berkeley: University of California Press, 1973), vii, 5, 27–32, 39–46, 83–87.

21. Harrington, Harrington Papers, 12.

22. Oral interview by Clifford E. Trafzer with Paul Smith and Jane Smith, September 7, 2000.

23. Ibid.; Trafzer, Madrigal, and Madrigal, *Chemehuevi People*, 81–85.

24. Census of the Twenty-Nine Palms Band, 1894 and 1922. National Archive, Pacific-Southwest Region, Laguna Niquel, Record Group 75.

25. Harry Lawton, *Willie Boy: A Desert Manhunt* (Balboa Island, Calif.: Paisano Press, 1960).

26. James A. Sandos and Larry E. Burgess, *The Hunt for Willie Boy: Indian Hating and Popular Culture* (Norman: University of Oklahoma Press, 1997).

27. Oral interview by Clifford E. Trafzer with Katherine Saubel, September 15, 2000. Saubel explained that her father was a close friend of the Cahuilla trackers who confided that they had never captured Willie Boy.

28. Public Law 94–271, "An Act to Provide for the Division of Assets between the Twenty-Nine Palms Band and the Cabazon Band of Mission Indians, California." 94th Congress, H.R. 1465, April 21, 1976, Washington, D.C.: U.S. House of Representatives.

29. Dean Mike and Benitez interviews.

30. Telephone interview by Clifford E. Trafzer with Matthew Leivas, August 1, 2000.

31. Oral interview by Clifford E. Trafzer with Theresa Mike, June 14, 2000, author's collection.

32. Tribal Enrollment as of 2001, Twenty-Nine Palms Band, Tribal Offices, Coachella, California.

33. Trafzer, Madrigal, and Madrigal, *Chemehuevi People* was the tribe's first book, but another volume, *A Chemehuevi Song*, was published in 2001.

34. The Native American Land Conservancy. Brochure published on the Cabazon Reservation on behalf of the conservancy, 1998.

35. Minutes of the Business Council, Twenty-Nine Palms Band of Mission Indians, November 1, 2000; Trafzer, Madrigal, and Madrigal, *Chemehuevi People*, 1–8, 114–17, 133–34.

RESOURCE GUIDE

Published Literature

Bean, Lowell John, and Katherine Siva Saubel. *Temalpakh: Cahuilla Indian Knowledge and Usage of Plants*. Banning, Calif.: Malki Museum Press, 1972.

Bee, Robert L. *Crosscurrents Along the Colorado: The Impact of Government Policy on the Quechan Indians*. Tucson: University of Arizona Press, 1981.

Culp, Georgia Laird. "The Chemehuevis." *Desert*, March 1975, 18–21, 38.

Harrington, John P. National Anthropological Archives 1907–1957, Smithsonian Institution, Washington, D.C., commonly called the Harrington Papers, microfilm copy, Rivera Library, University of California, Riverside. Included in this large collection is "The Chemehuevi: Their Name, Character, and Habitat" as well as notes and oral histories.

Ives, Joseph Christmas. "Report upon the Colorado River of the West," executive document prepared for the U.S. Senate, 36th Cong., 1st sess., Washington, D.C.: U.S. Government Printing Office, 1861.

Kroeber, Alfred L. *Handbook of the Indians of California*. Berkeley: California Book Co., 1953, 593–95.

Kroeber, A.L., and C.B. Kroeber. *A Mohave War Reminiscence, 1854–1880*. Berkeley: University of California Press, 1973.

Laird, Carobeth. "Chemehuevi Religious Beliefs and Practices." *Journal of California Anthropology* 1 (Spring 1974): 19–25. Reprint of a portion of the article is found in AVAS Newsletter (March 1982).

———. *The Chemehuevis*. Banning, Calif.: Malki Museum Press, 1976.

———. "Behavioral Patterns in Chemehuevi Myths." In *Flowers of the Wind: Papers on Ritual, Myth, and Symbolism in California and the Southwest*, edited by Thomas C. Blackburn. Socorro, N.M.: Ballena Press, 1977.

———. *Mirror and Pattern: George Laird's World of Mythology*. Banning, Calif.: Malki Museum Press, 1984.

Lawton, Harry. *Willie Boy: A Desert Manhunt*. Balboa Island, Calif.: Paisano Press, 1960

Miller, Ronald Dean, and Peggy Jeanne Miller. *The Chemehuevi Indians of Southern California*. Banning, Calif.: Malki Museum Press, 1967.

Sandos, James A., and Larry E. Burgess. *The Hunt for Willie Boy: Indian Hating and Popular Culture*. Norman: University of Oklahoma Press, 1997.

Trafzer, Clifford E. 1997. "Invisible Enemies: Ranching, Farming, and Quechan Indian Deaths at the Fort Yuma Agency, California, 1915–1925." *American Indian Culture and Research Journal* 21 (1997): 83–117.

Trafzer, Clifford E., Luke Madrigal, and Anthony Madrigal. *Chemehuevi People of the Coachella Valley*. Coachella, Calif.: Chemehuevi Press, 1997.

WWW Site

www.spotlight29Casino.com

Organization

Chemehueve Tribe
P.O. Box 1976
Havasu Lake, CA 92363

Chapter 2

The Crow/Apsaalooke in Montana

John A. Grim and
Magdalene Medicine Horse-Moccasin Top

There is no question but that both kin and clan affinities are extensive
and inclusive, and the result is mutual and wide affection throughout
the whole [Crow] tribe. Tribal unity and harmony is thus maintained
. . . the influence of the Whites has not yet affected this kinship system.
School children who had been away would return and try to disasso-
ciate themselves from tribal customs and traditions, but invariably
would be reclaimed through the kinship route. It is so affectionate, so
real and embracing that before they know, it has melted their individ-
ualistic tendencies into the Indian nature which is sympathetic, understanding and philanthropic.

Joseph Medicine Crow[1]

CULTURAL OVERVIEW

The People

The Apsaalooke/Crow have a reservation in the state of Montana and
speak the Sioux language. There are 9,985 Crow tribal members; 4,100
are younger than eighteen years of age. In the pre-Columbian period the
Crow were one settled agricultural people with the Hidatsa in the northern
drift plains of the Missouri River. The ancestors of the Crow, led by their
visionary ancestor, No-Vitals, parted from the Hidatsa probably in the fif-
teenth century. After a lengthy migration No-Vitals' group became the formative core of the Apsaalooke (pronounced Ap-sä-low-käy). In the early
seventeenth century they settled on the northern Missouri River drift plains
neighboring the Wolf, Big Horn, and Pryor mountains of the North Amer-

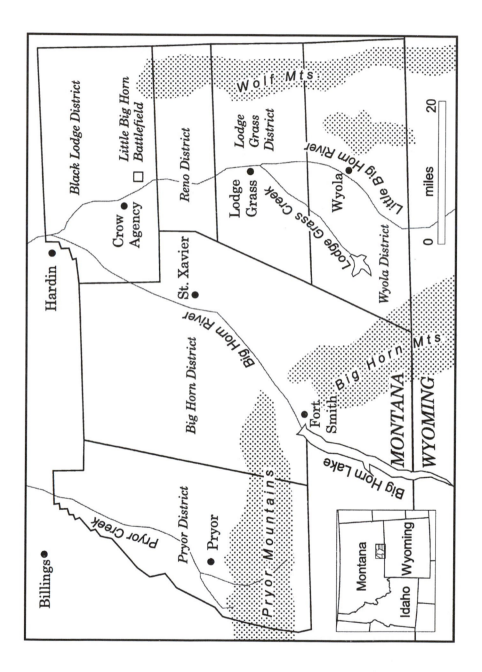

ican continent. This people's name for themselves, Apsaalooke, means "large beaked bird" and refers to a creature in their oral tradition. Various spellings have been used for this tribal name, including Apsaalooke, Absaalooka, Absaroka, Absaroke, Apsaalookee, and Absaroko. How, then, did these people come to be called the "Crow" by English speakers? Crow tribal historian Joseph Medicine Crow explained,

In the Hidatsa language, Apsaalookee means "Children of the Large-beaked Bird" (*absa* meaning "large-beaked bird" and *rokee* meaning "children" or "offspring"). Other Indian tribes called these people the "Sharp People," implying that they were as crafty and alert as the bird, absa (probably the raven), for which they were named. In referring to them in the hand-sign language, they would simulate the flapping of bird wings in flight. White men interpreted this sign to mean the bird crow and thus called the tribe the "Crow Indians."[2]

While "Crow" is the more familiar term in English, both terms, Crow and Apsaalooke, are used in this chapter. Use of both terms may reflect the reemergence in the late twentieth century of the Crow's right to govern themselves, on the one hand, and the impossibility, in Apsaalooke understanding, of any one person fully explaining Crow ways, on the other.

The Setting

The geographical boundaries of Crow country are currently set by their reservation in south central Montana. Of the reservation's two and one quarter million acres, approximately 55 percent is owned by the Apsaalooke, the remainder is held by non-Crow. The value Crow place on independent thought is well known on the high plains of North America: it is the right of individuals to speak for themselves and on behalf of their family lineages. Seasonal spring gatherings of the traditional Apsaalooke promoted tribal unity and shared narratives as did the late summer buffalo hunts which sustained the tribe across the winter months. The Crow's oral history describes four bands: the Mountain Crow, River Crow, Kicked in the Bellies, and one group, the Beaver Dries Its Fur (Bilapiiuutche), which has been lost. These fours bands of old have been replaced by the contemporary division of the Crow Reservation into six districts: Black Lodge, Reno, Lodge Grass, Wyola, Big Horn, and Pryor.

Traditional Subsistence Strategies

Buffalo figured prominently in Crow traditional subsistence strategies. Stories of the separation of the Crow from the Hidatsa peoples in what is now North Dakota tell of a quarrel between two chiefs over parts of a buffalo.[3] There is evidence in oral narratives and archaeological finds that, before the horse was used in hunting, buffalo were either trapped in box canyons or stampeded over cliffs.[4] The proto-Crow were also village cultivators especially of corn, beans, and squash. The different groups that came together to form the Crow people certainly retained memories of those early farming practices as well as the gathering of wild roots, berries, and plants. No doubt they carried them into their early tribal formative period and adapted farming, hunting, and gathering practices to the region of the Missouri River drift plains.

No doubt trade also played some role in the early separation of the Crow from the Hidatsa and led to their migration in the mid to late seventeenth century into the Yellowstone River region. Early accounts of the Crow by the La Verendrye trapping party in 1738 and the trading post experiences of François Larocque with the Crow in 1805–1807 all mention that these people were at the center of a robust trade bringing together nomadic tribes to the south with more northerly peoples already trading with Hudson Bay posts. In the 1820s the Crow experienced more conflict with other tribes moving southwestward such as the Cheyennes and Arapahos and finally the powerful Teton Lakota. These migrations placed increasing pressure on plant-gathering locations and the buffalo hunting grounds, especially after the southern and northern buffalo herds were cut by the transcontinental railroads of the westward-moving United States.

In the Indian Wars of the 1860s and 1870s, the Crow allied themselves with the United States and began in earnest the integration of Western goods into their economy. With the end of buffalo hunting in the late 1880s, the Crow increasingly adopted Western farming methods, subsisted on reservation rations, and developed ranching on allotment lands. During this disheartening period, the women's gathering of plant materials endured, but their sense of domestic ownership of the nomadic household and the male warrior and hunter ethos began to change fundamentally. The Crow entered into a culture-building period in which they adapted various American subsistence practices to their core culture in order to preserve other essential parts of their way of life.

Today, the Crow people still engage in ranching and farming, but tribe members are also making their careers in education, computer science, law, and the whole range of employment available to the Internet generation. Hunting of elk, mule deer, white tail deer, and bear still occurs, and the mountains continue to provide the Crow with the foods, medicines, and contemplative places that are significant components of traditional Crow life.

Social and Political Organization

To understand Crow social and political life properly, one must explore their universe of kinship, mythology, and religious values. The world of the Crow contrasts sharply with that of Western people.

Apsaalooke people still treasure their clan system, *ashammaleaxia*, in which every individual is embedded in an intricate web of kinship. Crow anthropology of the sacred, associated here with the term *baxpe* (sacred power) is subtly woven into the Crow kinship system. At Little Big Horn College, the Crow tribal college on the reservation, contemporary cultural studies courses explore this kinship system, considered a model form among the indigenous peoples of North America.

In Apsaalooke mythic understanding, from the period after creation the spirit beings called "Two Men" established the clan system. Through the clans flowed the evocation, transfer, and return of sacred, political, and material power through the paternal and maternal lines. An individual takes his clan identification from his mother's people. Maternal clan members traditionally give assistance during need and, in the buffalo-hunting days, joined revenge raids. Clan members address one another as brother and sister and, as an ideal that is now weakened, marry outside their own clan. One's maternal relatives respond to physical and emotional needs by giving material assistance and emotional support as well as by mourning at death. An individual is also a "child" of his or her father's clan. The child's paternal relatives transfer spiritual power that brings good health, wealth, and social status. Paternal relatives promote a child's status by announcing achievements and dream-blessings and also by testing the individual in the role of the person's "teasing clan." Maternal relatives feast and celebrate their paternal relatives for their gifts of efficacious power given through prayers and public narrations of praise.

In the buffalo-hunting days, the eleven clans of the Crow were arranged in five larger groupings, called phratries, for cooperative work efforts. The first phratry joined the Greasy Mouth (Uutuwasshe) and Sore Lips (Ashiiooshe) clans. The second brought the Whistling Waters (Bilikooshe) together with the Bad War Deeds (Ashkapkawiia). A third consisted of the Ties in a Bundle (Xukaalaxche), the Filth Eaters (Ashpeennusshe), and Brings Home the Game Without Shooting (Uussaawaachiia). A fourth united the Treacherous Lodge (Ashbatsua) and the Blood Indian Lodge (Ashkaamne). The fifth phratry was composed of Big Lodges (Ashitchite) and the Newly Made Lodges (Ashhilaalioo).

Remnants of the phratry system still persist, and six of the still functioning eight clans have paired relations in distinct regions of the Crow Reservation in Montana. The eight clans that continue into the present are Newly Made Lodges, Big Lodges, Greasy Mouth, Sore Lips, Bad War Deeds, Whistling Waters, Ties in a Bundle, and Blood Indian Lodge/Piegan. The relations between allied clans are activated in Crow ceremonial life when, for example, financial and material support is provided at "giveaways." So, too, labor and trees are contributed through the clan system for the building of Ashkisshe (Sun Dance) lodges.

On June 24, 1948, the tribe adopted a written constitution. Under this constitution the tribe has a general council form of government in which every enrolled adult has a vote. A quorum must be present before a vote is legal. Under the constitution the general council elects a chairman, vice chairman, secretary, and vice secretary. The treasurer is the agent of the Bureau of Indian Affairs of the federal government.

The adoption of the 1948 constitution marked the end of the ancient system of chiefs. The last Crow chief, Plenty Coups, died in 1932. That chief was the representative of the Crow Nation. When he died, his war-bonnet and staff, along with a flag, were placed on the Tomb of the Unknown Soldier in Washington, D.C. Although there were various candidates from whom to choose a successor to Plenty Coups, the tribe decided not to follow the old system, with its association between the office of chief and leader in war. Nevertheless, the ideals of the warrior have persisted among the Crow.

Military service has long been considered an honorable path among the Crow. Although Indian men were not required by U.S. law to serve as soldiers, Crow Indians have served bravely in the U.S. armed forces. This assistance to the United States began even before the treaty of 1868. The Crow served in many military engagements: the Indian Wars of the 1860s and 1870s, the Spanish-American War, World War I, World War II, the Korean Conflict, the Vietnam War, the Granada Action, and the Persian Gulf military action known as Desert Storm. When the United States again goes to war, Crow warriors will be among the fighting men.

Religion and World View

The Apsaalooke often say, "It's up to you!" This simple phrase suggests the decidedly personal exchange believed to occur between *baxpe*.[5] The spiritual beings who confer these efficacious blessings are associated with the Crow world view. A creator, Acbadadea, is believed to have set the world in motion. He is known by such names as First Maker, Starter or Maker of All Things, the One Above, the Old White Man Above, the Above Person with Yellow Eyes, He That Hears Always, and He That Sees All Things. Every Crow person who experiences the sacred has "to bring it [*baxpe*] out" in their own way. In expressing this gratuitous and sacred gift, the traditional Crow of the buffalo-hunting days acquired both personal status and spiritual identity as well as positions of leadership in warrior societies. Crow perspectives on the sacred changed both in the period before contact with Europeans and during interactions with mainstream America. Yet, a vibrant cultural sense of the sacred continues.

Among the Apsaalooke a human seeks with sincerity and purpose (*diakaashe*) his or her own experiences of sacred power (*baxpe*). It is in this sense that the Crow speak of "one's own religion," *alachiwakiia*. In the buffalo-hunting days, as well as among traditionally minded Crow today, devotion to one's Medicine Father (*Iilapxe*), or spirit being, who gives a

26

Violet Birdinground, a.k.a. Medicine Horse, "Catches the Sorrel Horse: (Newly Made Lodge Clan), and Adam Birdinground, "Buffalo That Sings" (Piegan Clan). Shown in Native American Church, or Peyoteway, dress these elders were also practitioners of traditional Crow religion, and members of the Crow Baptist Church of Wyola, MT. Photo: John A. Grim, Religion Department, Bucknell University.

blessing, is primary. That relationship, however, does not preclude belonging to other ritual organizations or participating in other ritual activities. He or she may be assisted by an older shaman (*akbaalia*, "one who brings things about") through fasting ordeals (*baawalishtakooshtechiiluua*, "fasting in hopes of acquiring a dream") and with the interpretation of extraordinary dreams and visions. While the sacred opens the possibility of any individual's acting as a healer or diviner for herself or her family, an *akbaalia* is believed to be able to evoke power consistently and to heal the sick upon request.

Through the conjunction of these time-honored patterns of older mentor, personal effort, and spirit blessing, a traditional Apsaalooke seeks a lifetime spiritual helper from the supernatural clans. Those spiritual beings who manifest *baxpe* power within the Apsaalooke world are called "Those Who Have No Bodies" or "Other Side Camp." This term stands in contrast to an informal Crow referent for themselves as *Biiluuke* or "Our Side." The animal and spiritual beings-in-the-land, who have no need for fire and the cultural comforts it supplies, are called the "Without Fires." The *baxpe* beings respond to the sincere efforts of fasting humans of Our Side. The spiritual beings may also give sacred inspiration to an adopted human sacred inspiration through dreams or visions instructing him or her to gather a sacred medicine bundle (*xapaalia*).

The specific religious exchange between an individual and his or her Medicine Father, which might result in a medicine bundle, takes place in the context of the larger Apsaalooke world view. The Apsaalooke see their region and everything in it as, at once, both ordinary and highly spiritual. These relationships are framed for Apsaalooke individuals by such religious experiences as sacred dreams, vision fasts, and ritual participation. This world view is further explained by the Crow's oral traditions, ancient narratives about the mysterious world of powerful beings. The Apsaalooke's mythic narratives describe trickster beings like Old Man Coyote, heroes like Lodge Boy, Thrown Away, and Old Woman's Grandchild (*Karicbapituac*, or *Ihkaleaxe*, Morning Star), as well as dangerous beings like Red Woman.

Medicine bundles (*xapaalia*), which typically result from encounters with spiritual beings, are groupings of material objects that have been revealed to an individual. Technically, these groupings can be called composite liturgies—the synthesis of various material items with chants, ritual manipulations, and mental attitudes—all of which constitute the medicine bundle. The actual objects gathered, such as individual feathers and whole wings of selected birds, colored clays, animal skins and horns, fossil-bearing rocks, dream objects crafted from wood or leather, and multiple wrapping cloths, do not in themselves constitute a medicine bundle. What defines the medicine bundle are the chants; the way of handling them; the rules about seasonal openings, attending guests, and storage of the bundle; and offerings to the bundle spirits. Bundles are typically stored by owners in personal, private locations in their homes or nearby buildings. It is important that, as persons, these medicine bundles have access to circulating air and occasional exposure to sunlight.

Another ancient Crow religious practice, which has these same dimensions, is the sweat lodge. The purifying sweat bath, or sweat lodge (*awushua*) enables intimate contact with the spiritual world. The ritual is conducted in a specially prepared lodge built of saplings bent over and tied so as to form a dome with a radius of from five to eight feet. The privilege of building a sweat lodge is carefully monitored among the Crow as is the right to pour water during the ritual. Among the Apsaalooke the sweat bath is an accepted means for individuals to gain access to the sacred because it is presumed that the individual seeking the sacred object is also motivated by *diakaashe*, or sincerity of effort. The sweat lodge is the most appropriate place for evoking sincerity of purpose. Thus, the sweat-lodge ceremony is often a daily occurrence as well as a ritual performed prior to all ceremonial activity.

The Apsaalooke also have a special ceremony which, they believe, tells the story of their ancient journey when they first became a distinct people. This is the Tobacco Society (*Baasshussheelaakbisuua*, or "tobacco dance adoption"). The Crow say that the stars, especially Morning Star, gave their founding ancestor, No-Vitals, a vision of a unique, four-petaled tobacco plant. It was revealed to No-Vitals that this tobacco plant grew in the Big Horn Mountains. Eventually the Crow developed elaborate dances, songs, and complex ceremonies woven around the narratives of this gift of the stars. No other Native North American peoples have a ceremony in which the planting and harvesting of this special tobacco tells the story of their history.

In the case of the Crow and their Tobacco Society . . . investigating ritual is investigating history; their "historical consciousness" results from a dialectic with their religious consciousness: their rituals are validated by their history, their history is legitimized by their rituals. As tobacco seeds are carried to the sacred lodge during the adoption ritual, so were the original tobacco seeds born by the legendary No-Vitals to the Big Horn Mountains.[6]

This is a good example of the ways in which myths and rituals are often used by native peoples to reinforce and reenact their tribal histories.

THREATS TO SURVIVAL

Historical Overview

The pre-reservation homeland of the Apsaalooke, a large area within what is now the states of Montana and Wyoming, was described at a council meeting in 1873 by Sits-in-the-Middle-of-the-Land (or Blackfoot) who used the metaphor of four tepee poles: "When we set up our lodge poles, one reaches to the Yellowstone; the other on the White River [Milk River]; another one goes to Wind River; the other lodges on the Bridger Mountains. This is our land."[7] The image of the tepee is not simply an indication of boundary. Rather, this symbolic image distinguishes each tepee pole as a mythic marker describing the Crow's relation to the land. The tepee is a spiritual habitat that symbolically embraces her occupants as a mother. Thus, the tepee, as a sacred metaphor for Apsaalooke land, carries an image of a nourishing and nurturing country. Moreover, the habitat metaphor resonates with the Crow matrilineal clan system in which succor and aid are sought from one's maternal relatives.

The major threat to the Crow is loss of land, either by sale or through legislation that might terminate the special status of tribal lands. Loss of land by the Apsaalooke over the past 100 years is a complex historical issue interwoven with the civilizing and Christianizing drives of dominant America. The Crow believe that their elders predicted the arrival of whites and that they welcomed the whites as allies against their enemies on the plains. The Lakota, Cheyenne, Blackfoot, Piegan, Shoshone, and other tribal groups contested the claim of the Apsaalooke to hunting and grazing lands. By the 1830s, the movements of tribespeople onto the northern plains, especially the Lakota and the Blackfoot, threatened to overwhelm the Crow. In this military setting, the Apsaalooke allied themselves with the westward-moving Americans in an effort to preserve their way of life. Toward that end, the Crow were willing to part with some of their land. Thus, the Apsaalooke, in addition to serving as scouts for numerous U.S. military expeditions against their mutual enemies, agreed to demands for land by American settlers, miners, ranchers, and politicians by selling 30 million acres in 1880 after the Indian Wars of the 1860s and 1870s.

During the 1880s Catholic missionaries and other Christian religious groups established themselves on the Crow Reservation in accordance with President Ulysses S. Grant's Peace Policy, which turned over the governance of Indian agencies to missionaries from various Christian denominations. Catholic and Baptist missionaries established day-boarding schools for Crow children, and by 1887 they were prohibiting these children from speaking Apsaalooke while the schools were in session. Today, only 50 percent speak the native Apsaalooke language.[8]

In 1882 the Apsaalooke were coerced to sell another 1.5 million acres. Buffalo had become scarce, forcing the Crow in 1883 to follow the suggestion of their agent to move from the mountains onto the plains around Crow Agency and accept food rations. There they encountered prohibitions against Crow religious practices and intertribal raiding in the warrior tradition. Both contributed to a spiritual malaise among the Apsaalooke. In 1887 a group of young warriors under Wraps-Up-His-Tail, a twenty-four-year-old visionary who subsequently received the name Sword Bearer, led a successful revenge raid against the Piegan/Blackfeet. Following this raid, Sword Bearer attempted to foment a rebellion against the U.S. agent at Crow Agency. During these events, Sword Bearer, a Crow woman, and one soldier were killed; after it ended, eight Apsaalooke were imprisoned. While the rebellion did not develop into a major military incident, this episode reflects the individual and group crises through which the Crow passed at this time. More important, this rebellion signaled the resistance to assaults against Crow traditions by Indian agents, the army, missionaries, and other representatives of dominant America. The Sword Bearer event marks the loss of two major paths for expressing pride and purpose among Crow warriors: military societies and intertribal warfare. Moreover, in this period, political pressures were being brought to bear that destroyed the fundamental linkage between the Crow people and their communally held land.

In the Allotment Act of 1887 (often called the Dawes Act) provisions were made for the Crow Reservation, as well as all other Indian lands set aside under specific treaties, to be divided into parcels and allotted to native individuals. Unallotted land left over after the allotment reverted to the U.S. government for resale to Whites. The Dawes Act was only one of a long series of initiatives taken by the federal government to acquire the assets of the tribes for dominant American interest groups. The Crow fought this legislation until the passage of the Crow Act in 1920 which divided the reservation into individually owned tracts and marked the transition of the Crow to settled communities.

The Crow, like other indigenous peoples in the United States, were subject to unilateral congressional reinterpretation of treaties. Moreover, the implementation of imposed treaty stipulations was undertaken by bureaucratic federal government agencies such as the Indian Office and later the Bureau of Indian Affairs (BIA). Accompanying governmental pressures to dismember the tribe's land holdings were racial tensions with local settler communities which intensified after the turn of the century as white populations increased. The practice of government-directed leasing of Crow land to local white farmers and ranchers reinforced these anxieties. As a result, the Crow lost control over their economic future. Crow farmers and ranchers were encouraged to enter into larger markets by the Indian Office where they were overwhelmed by their white competitors who had access to financial capital. Forced on the Crow in the name of "progress," these ideological, economic, religious, and political pressures further fragmented Crow understanding of communally held land that was central to their lifeway. The Apsaalooke fought this and other legislation, but meanwhile the military, technological, and ideological strength of the United States had subverted the integral religious life of their former Crow allies. Apsaalooke population fell below 2,000 at the turn of the twentieth century and only recently has recovered to pre-contact numbers of more than 9,000.[9]

Language issues are also part of the pattern of control and exploitation. Many Crow feel that, while they speak English, they do not understand the underlying purposes and deception masked by technical, political, and legal language. Governmental treaties, made by individual negotiators working with the Crow, were often changed by distant congressional legislation. The orally exchanged word, which is remembered and repeated in Crow narrative traditions, was cast aside by the written word. Contemporary Apsaalooke feel that the written word has no mercy and no memory: no mercy for the people from whom the land was unjustly taken, and no memory of the deception, fraud, and broken promises used to deprive the Crow people of their homelands. The Crow know that, even though they were allies of America, they have become its victims. They sense that government agents sought to sweep the Crow off the land forever and that any means could be used to accomplish that removal.

To this day, then, Crow believe that the U.S. government intentionally misuses language to avoid their financial obligations to native peoples. Such terms as "wards of the state" and "domestic and dependent nations" have been imposed on the Crow, as well as other American Indian peoples, to rob them of their integrity as a nation and to undermine their ability to imagine themselves as a people in their own language, their own stories, and their own lifeway. Ironically, even such conservation activities as setting aside park lands and protecting archaeological sites associated with living native peoples have been implemented with little or no consultation with resident Crow.

The opening of a Crow-run casino has raised the same concerns. The Crow feel capable of addressing this business in their own governmental context rather than being subject to both state limitations and BIA control. Yet, the Crow have a gaming casino that is limited by the same state regulations that apply in any gaming site throughout the state. The Crow object to this intrusion into their reservation sovereignty. Again, the use of "wardship" and other legal language enables the state of Montana and U.S. government agencies to subvert the capacity of the Crow people to make their own decisions. That there are ethical issues involved in gaming are evident to the Crow—their ancient narratives discuss these questions— but the Crow know they must make their own decisions about these issues to survive as a people.

Other crises today relate to housing, health care, and unemployment. The federal Department of Housing and Urban Development (HUD) program built 540 housing units on the reservation between 1969 and 1999. One public health hospital and three clinics serve both the Crow and the Northern Cheyenne peoples whose combined numbers total 15,985.[10]

Between 1991 and 1994, unemployment hovered around 75 percent.[11] There is an expectation that employment will increase in 2001 due to construction of commercial shops in Crow Agency as well as extensive construction of new buildings and renovation of existing buildings at Little Big Horn College.

RESPONSE: STRUGGLES TO SURVIVE CULTURALLY

The Crow have been profoundly transformed by their accommodation to the English language, consumer lifestyles, and the Christian values of dominant American society. Crow political leaders and the tribal government have navigated through such different policies as the allotment of remaining Crow lands, the Indian Reorganization Act in 1934, the termination policies of the 1950s, and the rebuilding of American Indian sovereignty since the 1960s. Land issues continue to be major concerns for both individual Crow, in terms of complicated ownership patterns resulting from land inheritance, and for the tribal government which seeks stronger support from the Bureau of Indian Affairs to terminate abusive leasing and ownership practices on the Crow Reservation.

Leadership

The traditional Crow chiefs, despite the erosion of their political power with the death of Plenty Coups in 1933, provided ongoing local stability and cohesion. This steadiness was especially significant when the Crow experienced the first intratribal tensions between the "long-hair" traditionals and the "progressive" factions whose shorter hairstyle was acquired when members were educated in white schools. The emergence of a business committee, after the turn of the century, and a tribal committee, in 1920, increasingly tied politics to community economic concerns. When Crow politician Robert Yellowtail became superintendent of the Crow in 1934, a new era was inaugurated in which attention to the rights of the Crow was often linked to larger American Indian issues. Although Yellowtail sought to convince the Crow to sign the Indian Reorganization Act of 1934, which established federally approved tribal governments, the Crow's rejection reflected their awareness of how little actual political control would be given to those tribal governments.

Religious Strongholds

Throughout the transformations of the last century, traditional Crow religion has been a central arena through which the Crow responded to changes they faced. Four particular religious practices exemplify how the Crow have resisted threats to community survival: the enduring Crow relationship with their land; the adoption of the Peyote Way (Native American Church); the ceremony of *Ashkisshe*, or the "Sun Dance"; and, finally, the adoption of Apsaalooke Pentecostal Christianity. All of these give us insight into the types of religious adaptations brought about by the oppressive conditions imposed upon Crow life in the mid-twentieth century.

First, and central to the understanding of Apsaalooke survival as a people, is their continuity with the land. The sacred relationship of the Crow with their mountainous homeland is not articulated vaguely but in robust statements of life lived within that world. "The sky is my Father and these Mountains are my Mother." This prayer is often heard at Crow ceremonies. In the Apsaalooke world view, the mountains are sources of fecundity and material blessings. This relationship between the Crow people and the mountains is especially evident in the New Year dance held on the last day of Crow Fair, the major late summer reunion centered around a powwow and rodeo. Originally an agricultural fair, Crow Fair has become a vibrant expression of Apsaalooke vitality and self-determination. The New Year dance with its four stops (symbolizing autumn, winter, spring, and summer) is led by a pipe carrier across whose path no human or animal should pass. This honored leader prays that everyone will be healthy for the year and will return again to Crow Fair. Crow participants dance behind him in traditional garb, and others arrange themselves along the dance route. During this dance all the participants gesture in unison toward the mountains as a sign of loving respect for their Mother, the mountains. The New Year dance at Crow Fair strikingly expresses an ancient world view and a ritual evocation of human-earth relations.

Second, Peyote Way came to the Crow from the Northern Cheyenne in 1890. While this ceremony was not original to the Crow, it did involve like-minded Crow men and women in a ritual evocation of sacred power, in property giveaways, and in traditional prayer forms. Peyote Way arrived at a time in Crow history when the people suffered from both dominant American pressures to abandon the Apsaalooke lifeway and internal controversies regarding the best course to follow. Both a Christian altar and the half-moon altar forms of Peyote Way were built on the Crow Reservation. However, the traditional half-moon form of this ceremony has since become dominant among the Crow. Participants sing highly structured peyote songs, which are often transmitted from other tribal groups, as they consume peyote, a vision-inducing plant substance. Prayers filled with emotion echo traditional concerns for sincerity (*diakaashe*). These alternate with singing in a specific sequence. Participants in the ritual reach a significant catharsis point when, at early dawn, the Water Woman brings water and prays for all the participants' needs. The deeply moving and personal narratives, the finely controlled fire, the skillful manipulation of the smoke flaps of the tepee, and the beaded patterns decorating the various fans all work in concert with the singing to create a profound religious moment for the Crow participant.

Third, the *Ashkisshe*, or Crow Sun Dances, are held in June and July in a specially prepared structure called the Big Lodge. The lodge has a central, forked cottonwood tree ringed by twelve smaller forked trees that are joined by rafter poles often made of lodgepole pine. The older, traditional Crow Sun Dance (*Baaiichkiisapiliolissua*, or "fringed ankle dance"), oriented toward the clan revenge ideal, was last sponsored in 1875. In 1941 the current Crow-Shoshone Sun Dance, or *Ashkisshilissuua* "temporary lodge dance" was brought back to the Crow by the Crow-Shoshone Sun Dance Chief, John Trujillo, at the invitation of William Big Day. The original impulse for many Crow to join in the 1941 *Ashkisshe* ceremony was spiritually to support sons and relatives who were fighting in World War II. The structure of the *Ashkisshe* was changed in the early 1950s when women entered the lodge and began to dance with the men. In this and other ways the scope of the *Ashkisshe* has significantly increased from 1941 when it was marginal to the more central "bundle way." Now, many Crow regard it as at the center of traditional Apsaalooke religion and their sense of self-integrity.

A fourth expression of Crow religious response to contemporary domination is the Crow Pentecostal Church. The evangelical Christian sect, identified with "holiness gifts" and "Pentecostal manifestations of the Holy Spirit," arrived on the Crow Reservation early in the twentieth century, stimulated by Four Square Gospel Mission evangelist Aimee Semple Mc-Pherson. In 1923 a Crow, Nellie Stewart, with five other Apsaalooke attended a revival held by McPherson in Miles City, Montana. The Holiness Pentecostal movement among the Crow came at a time of accelerated social, political, and economic change for these people. The Crow traditional lifeway, which had been tied to intertribal warfare, status based on military exploits, and community activity based on band needs, had come to an end, abruptly replaced by reservation districts, the end of the male military role, and settled agricultural life.

The settlement established around Crow Agency became, during the 1920s and 1930s, the site of intense debates among the Crow regarding acceptance of the Crow Allotment Act of 1920 and the Indian Reorganization Act of 1934. Both of these political acts struck Crow social and political life like a maelstrom, disrupting traditional lifeway patterns of subsistence, governance, and ritual expression. Horses were at the center of these changes. The Crow used horses in many ritual transactions, and when the U.S. government sought stock reductions, ostensibly to save pastureland, the Apsaalooke considered this policy a direct attack on their traditional lifeway. When their horses were taken from them, many adult Crow men completely lost hope in any restoration of a meaningful life.

The Holiness Pentecostal church partially alleviated some of these pressures by connecting older Apsaalooke views of the sacred with Christian rituals. For example, holiness gifts associated with speaking in tongues, interpreting tongues, and prophecy all paralleled Crow traditional narratives. In the traditional understanding, a person had to have had a vision to speak of sacred matters, to validate ownership of specific modes of spoken and sung prayer, and to deliver public rhetoric as a signal of leadership. The holiness gifts associated with power, such as personal faith, miracles, and healing, were adopted by Crow Pentecostals and filled the spaces previously filled by older belief systems, healers (*akbaalia*), and rituals. These gifts of power mimicked the older bundle way minus the physical objects gathered in a *xapaalia* bundle, the animal *baxpe* exchange, and the specific symbol system of the older Apsaalooke world view.

Gradually the Crow Holiness Pentecostal Church became a major religious group, with political power on the Crow Reservation when they voted as a bloc. Since the 1970s Apsaalooke Pentecostal sects have been a significant factor in every tribal election, providing tribal chairpersons in all but two elections since the 1980s. Ironically, the Crow Pentecostal churches became much more politically involved earlier on than their mainstream Christian counterparts in American fundamentalism. Moreover, the Pentecostal movement, which had drawn on Apsaalooke traditional beliefs and practices during its founding period, has been at times hostile to many traditional Crow practices, including the prayers of clan aunts and uncles after special events, kinship transactions (especially giveaways), and rituals such as the sweat lodge, Tobacco Society, *xapaalia* bundles, Peyote Way, and *Ashkisshe*.

Education

Education is another positive development. Bilingual and bicultural programs are active in both public and parochial schools on the reservation. Thirty-five years ago Head Start programs actively subverted Crow cultural life by teaching English and cultural forms from dominant America. Now Crow cultural education is being reintroduced even into Head Start educational programs.

The major center on the reservation for language instruction, job training, and cultural education is Little Big Horn College in Crow Agency. As of 1999 the college, which is run by Crow educators, has granted 188 associate of arts degrees. Crow students have gone on to earn 208 bachelor's degrees, 53 master's degrees, and 6 doctoral degrees.[12] Currently Little Big Horn College has begun a five-year construction plan that will result in a new library, classroom facilities, a gymnasium with pool, and a cultural center.

Federally funded teacher training programs over the past thirty years have resulted in native educators in both primary and secondary schools on the Crow Reservation. With the growth of Little Big Horn College there is a hope that native educators will fill new positions. There is also an expectation that Little Big Horn College will become a four-year institution granting bachelor's degrees.

FOOD FOR THOUGHT

Political leadership and traditional Crow religion provide the main intellectual and emotional arenas in which the integrity and vitality of the people are preserved. The Crow language, too, is instrumental in expressing the sacred, not only in words but in song, dance, visionary ways of knowing, and local community cohesiveness. A contemporary resurgence in the number of Crow individuals practicing traditional Apsaalooke rituals, such as the sweat lodge and Sun Dance, suggests that these older practices can coexist with newer religious frameworks such as Peyote Way, the Baptist Church, Roman Catholicism, and Christian Holiness Pentecostalism. The vitality of Crow religious dialogue and ceremony on the reservation suggests that *baxpe*, the sacred, is still a medium for conversation and communication among the people.

When the Crow think about their futures, they think about their children. The Crow people love their children deeply and instill in them a love of their reservation homeland. Most Crow do not choose to leave the reservation permanently and often return after pursuing a career away from their homeland. Indeed, some Crow parents do not allow their children to leave the reservation at all. This place is considered by many Crow to be a sanctuary from an outside world, a world they perceive as cruel. The hardships and homelessness of dominant American society are not sanctioned by Crow lifeway. They wish not to join it. A driving ideal for the Crow is to educate themselves and, in turn, to educate the people on the reservation. For a child to wish for education is considered a good dream, but to live apart from parents and grandparents subverts traditional Crow life. Even though housing is not plentiful on the Crow Reservation, Apsaalooke know that parents' and grandparents' homes are always open to all. There are no orphans among the Crow; they take care of their own. When one enters the Crow Reservation, he or she is among a people who care for guests as they care for their own.

Questions

1. Why do Crow/Apsaalooke peoples request that they be referred to by their own name for themselves, rather than names given to them by outsiders?

2. What roles has the Crow clan system had in their formation and ongoing identity as a people?

3. Why do the Crow have a continuous commitment to the military? How has this dimension of Crow life changed over the past century?

4. Why has religion been so important to the Aspaalooke peoples during the transitions to the nineteenth and twentieth centuries?

5. What forces for change from dominant America have actually been institutionalized on the Crow Reservation? Have they been beneficial or harmful?

6. How have the religious practices discussed in this chapter both bridged into dominant American culture and still affirmed traditional Crow cultures?

NOTES

1. Joseph Medicine Crow, *From the Heart of the Crow Country: The Crow Indians' Own Stories* (New York: Orion/Crown Publishers, 1992), 5.

2. Ibid., 2.

3. Cf. Edward S. Curtis, *The North American Indian: The Apsoroke, or Crow* (1909; reprint, New York: Johnson Reprint Corporation, 1970), vol. 4, 3–126; Edwin T. Denig, "Of the Crow Nation," John C. Ewers, ed., Bureau of American Ethnology Bulletin 151 (Washington, D.C.: Smithsonian Institution, 1953), 3–74.

4. Carling Malout, and Stuart Conner, eds., Symposium on Buffalo Jumps. Missoula: *Montana Archaeological Society, Memoire* no. 1, 1962.

5. Some writers express this term as *baaxpe, baxbe*, or *makpay*.

6. Peter Nabokov, "Cultivating Themselves: The Inter-play of Crow Indian Religion and History" (Ph.D. Diss., University of California, Berkeley, 1988), 395.

7. Medicine Crow, *From the Heart of the Crow Country*, 37.

8. Lanny Real Bird, "Ash-ammaa-éhkuua," a Report from the Director of the Learning Lodge Institute to the W.W. Kellogg Foundation, vol. 1, no. 1 (Winter, 2001).

9. Frederick E. Hoxie, *Parading Through History: The Making of the Crow Nation in America, 1805–1935* (New York: Cambridge University Press, 1995), 172.

10. Tribal Employment Rights Offices for the Crow and Northern Cheyenne Peoples, 2000.

11. Indian Health Service Annual Report for 2000 (Washington, DC: US Government Printing Office, 2000).

12. Data from Little Big Horn College, 2001.

RESOURCE GUIDE

Published Literature

Bernardis, Timothy. *Baleeisbaalishiwee: Crow Social Studies Teacher's Guide.* Crow Agency, Mont.: Bilingual Materials Development Center, 1986.

Frey, Rodney. *The World of the Crow Indians: As Driftwood Lodges.* Norman: University of Oklahoma Press, 1987.

Hoxie, Frederick E. *Parading Through History: The Making of the Crow Nation in America, 1805–1935.* New York: Cambridge University Press, 1995.

Linderman, Frank. *Plenty-Coups: Chief of the Crows.* Lincoln: University of Nebraska Press, 1962.

———. *Pretty-shield: Medicine Woman of the Crows.* 1935. Reprint, Lincoln: University of Nebraska Press, 1974.

Lowie, Robert H. *The Crow Indians.* 1935. Reprint, Lincoln: University of Nebraska Press, 1983.

McCleary, Timothy. *The Stars We Know: Crow Indian Astronomy and Lifeways.* Prospect Heights, Ill.: Waveland Press, 1997.

Medicine Crow, Joseph. *From the Heart of the Crow Country: The Crow Indians' Own Stories.* New York: Orion/Crown Publishers, 1992.

Nabokov, Peter, ed. *Two-Leggings: The Making of a Crow Warrior.* New York: Thomas Y. Crowell, 1967.

Voget, Fred W. *The Shoshoni-Crow Sun Dance.* Norman: University of Oklahoma Press, 1984.

Yellowtail, Thomas. *Yellowtail Crow Medicine Man and the Sun Dance Chief: An Autobiography, As Told to Michael Oren Fitzgerald.* Norman: University of Oklahoma Press, 1991.

Films and Videos

Contrary Warriors: A Film of the Crow Tribe. Rattlesnake Productions, distributed by Direct Cinema Limited, P.O. Box 69799. Los Angeles, California 90069. 1986.

Crow/Shoshoni Sundance. With Lloyd Old Coyote, Thunderous Productions, distributed by Unitel Videos, New York. 1991.

Spirit of the Dawn: Dramatic Changes in Native American Education. Heidi Schmidt, distributed by New Day Films, Ho-Ho-Kus, New Jersey. 1994.

Warrior Chiefs in a New Age. Dean Bear Claw, distributed by Montana Public Television, Bozeman, Montana 59717. 1991.

WWW Site

Little Big Horn College
http://www.lbhc.cc.mt.us

Organization

Little Big Horn College
c/o Magdalene Mocassin Top, Archivist
Library/Archives
P.O. Box 370
Forrestry Lane
Crow Agency, MT 59022

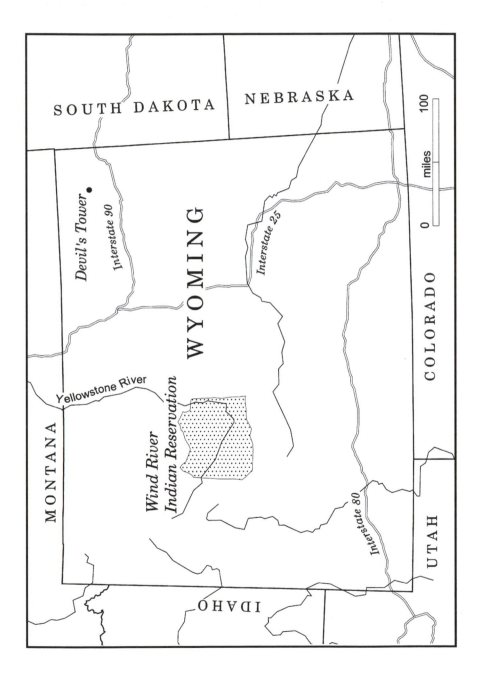

Chapter 3

The Eastern Shoshone in Wyoming

Ernest Olson and Brooke Olson

CULTURAL OVERVIEW

The People

The Eastern Shoshone (also spelled Shoshoni) of present-day Wyoming are a resilient and enduring people whose history in the Great Basin of the American West can be traced back at least 10,000 years. The Eastern Shoshone call themselves *Soesoenree*, or "people of the grass." The cultural traditions of the Eastern Shoshone are rooted in a foraging lifestyle that required great skill to ensure survival in the challenging environment of the Great Basin. The ingenuity of the Eastern Shoshone is evident in their cultural borrowings from Plains Indian cultures as they expanded their territory onto the Plains. Most notably, they adopted buffalo hunting, the tepee, and the horse. The continued adaptation and survival of the Eastern Shoshone can be witnessed in their struggles to maintain a sense of Shoshone culture and identity in the midst of continued threats and challenges from Anglo-American culture. The endurance of the Eastern Shoshone is exemplified in their strong leadership traditions. From the great leader Washakie, who was instrumental in securing a land base for his people in the mid-1800s, to the renowned contributions of Sacagawea in assisting the Lewis and Clark expedition in 1805, the Shoshones continue to exhibit a strong sense of leadership as they face threats to their treaty rights, access to resources such as water, and continued social and cultural changes.

The Eastern Shoshone, one group of the Great Basin Shoshones who pushed east and north out of the Great Basin of Utah, claimed western Wyoming as their home sometime before A.D. 1500. From that time on, they adapted to life on the Northern Plains among such neighboring groups as the Crow and Northern Cheyenne of southern Montana, the Lakota of South Dakota, and the Arapaho. These neighboring groups were traditionally enemies of the Eastern Shoshone and competed for the buffalo of the Northern Plains. With the arrival of white settlers, the competition for territory by these native groups was transformed through treaties to the present situation in which each group's territory has shrunk to the boundaries of its respective reservation land. In 1868 the Eastern Shoshone, through a treaty agreement with the U.S. government, became established on the Wind River Reservation of central Wyoming. After this date, the Eastern Shoshone shared the Wind River Reservation with the Arapaho on the only Indian reservation in the state of Wyoming. The Eastern Shoshone currently work with other Indian nations of the region in attempts to solve problems of employment, water rights, oil and mineral resources, education, and access to sacred sites.

The Setting

Until the beginning of the reservation period, the territory of the Eastern Shoshone included the Green River area of southwestern Wyoming, but they also ranged widely over the mountains and plains of Wyoming, Idaho, and Montana. Part of their traditional territory included what is now known as Yellowstone National Park. While many American Indian groups have traveled through Yellowstone, the Shoshones were among the few who called it home. This movement over a large land area has since been restricted to the Wind River Reservation, a territory that includes much natural beauty in its forests, mountains, rivers, and sagebrush areas. The 3,500 square miles of reservation, named after the Wind River Canyon, is located southeast of Yellowstone Park and adjacent to the Creek Mountains, the Wind River Mountains, and the Bridger and Shoshone National Forests. Sacred and culturally important areas for the Eastern Shoshone include Dinwoody Canyon and Bull Lake.

Traditional Subsistence Strategies

The Eastern Shoshone, unlike other related Shoshone groups in Utah and Idaho, followed a way of life similar to their Plains neighbors; the Crow, Arapaho, Cheyenne, and Lakota. This adaptation included nomadic movement, buffalo hunting on the Plains, and warfare and trade with neighboring tribes. The Eastern Shoshone came to resemble Plains tribes in terms of clothing, living in tepees, and dependence on the buffalo, but they still relied on a wide range of plant and animal foods.[1] Fish, particularly cutthroat trout and Rocky Mountain whitefish, were an important and relatively plentiful resource. As a supplement to the buffalo meat, deer, elk, and pronghorn antelope were important game resources. Plant resources, particularly various berries and roots, were gathered to round out the diet according to the seasonal availability of each plant, and late summer and fall were particularly important for gathering and harvesting ripened berries and mature roots. Berries were often used in the preparation of pemmican, a storable food resource made from a pounded mixture of berries, fat, and buffalo or elk meat. In addition to their use as food, many plants were used for medicinal purposes. The Shoshones used a compress of wet and heated plantain leaves to treat wounds and rheumatism. Plantain (*Plantago major*), a common herb with broad, oval, and ribbed leaves, was referred to by Native Americans as "white man's foot" because it was fond of the disturbed soil left in the wake of white settlements.

The already successful Shoshone adjustment to life on the Plains was greatly aided by the arrival of the horse at about the beginning of the eighteenth century, after which time horses became central to the activities of hunting, migrations, raiding, and warfare. Indeed, the Eastern Shoshone gained a reputation for their expertise in horsemanship and moved more easily over a wide territory. The adoption of the horse made the buffalo hunt the center of subsistence activities. The buffalo supplied food, hide for shelter, trade, and containers for gathering. Nearly every part of the buffalo was utilized by the Shoshone. For example, the buffalo provided material for tepee coverings, clothing, and blankets for the cold winters.[2]

Social and Political Organization

Perhaps the most important organizing aspect of social and political life has always been gender; men take the major roles of leadership among the Eastern Shoshone. The chief, who attained his status through military or shamanistic renown, organized hunts and was key in decisions that affected the whole group. In addition to the chief, leadership among the Shoshones was organized through assistants or aides and through two complementary military societies, the Yellow Brows and the Logs.

Women had crucial roles in managing the daily work of the group. Women fashioned leather, processed food, gathered plants, constructed tepees, maintained the camp area, reared the children, cared for pack animals, and collected firewood. In addition, midwifery and shamanism were highly valued roles for older women. To complement this, men had primary roles in hunting buffalo, managing horses, shamanism, religious activities, and raiding. Labor started very early for all members of the group, particularly the young girls, who were expected to contribute substantially to the workload.

The Eastern Shoshone traditionally had what is known as a band organization, meaning that there were a number of groups, often linked through extended family ties, each headed by a chief. Bands would come together or separate depending on local conditions and the seasons. In the mid-1800s, there were about three to five bands with a population count, depending on the season, of between 1,500 and 3,000.[3] Within each band, there were some individuals who had special duties for military activity, policing, and healing. Band membership was important for living together, hunting buffalo, raiding other tribes, and resource sharing. The band organization stressed unselfish support of the group in following orders from wise leaders.

Expert leadership was crucial for survival, especially for warfare, hunting, negotiations with other tribal groups, and securing food and winter shelter. The need for effective and wise leadership was paramount in dealing with whites, including fur traders, the U.S. Army, and settlers. It was also key in the negotiation of treaty agreements. Chief Washakie, undoubtedly the most important leader of the Eastern Shoshones in the 1800s, can be given much credit for the Shoshones' survival during a time of severe conflicts between Native Americans and the U.S. government. His skill as a gifted leader is evident from his role in establishing the Wind River Reservation, thereby securing a land base for his people. Washakie was also adept at maintaining peaceful relations with whites; he aided settlers, provided scouts for the U.S. military, and kept peaceful relations with trapper, guide, and frontiersman Kit Carson and American Mormon leader Brigham Young. Fort Washakie, his burial place, was named in Washakie's honor in 1878.[4]

Religion and World View

Religion has always been an integral part of the culture of the Eastern Shoshone. A primary belief was that a personal connection to a supernatural power, a guardian spirit, was essential for a successful and complete life. Their religion also celebrated the sacredness of creation stories, sacred sites found at various points of the landscape, and a seasonal cycle of rituals. Within their religious narratives, the creatures and features of nature were highlighted, and particular animals, mountains, and plants were given a prominent place in religious teachings. For example, sacred stories tell of the creation of humans, the capturing of fire by animals such as Coyote, and the gift of the Sun Dance.[5]

The religion of the Eastern Shoshone is based in the landscape that surrounds them. Sacred sites often contain pictographs, or stone etchings, representing hundreds of years of Shoshone expression. Areas where these pictographs are found, called *poha kahni*, or houses of power, are highly valued as spiritual places by the Shoshone. Dinwoody Canyon, located on the Wind River Reservation, is a place of great spiritual and historical significance to the Eastern Shoshones, evidenced in the pictographs that are found there of such important beings as the Water Ghosts and Rock

Ghosts. Sacred sites are also located within Yellowstone National Park. The continuity of Shoshone culture depends on maintaining access and rights to such areas. This has not always been easy.

Traditional Shoshone religion could not easily be separated from the rest of daily life. This is illustrated in the importance of spirituality for restoring health. Both men and women had special roles as curers or shamans. Shamans (religious healers), known as *pohakanti* or those who have power, have based their power on maintaining relations with the supernatural, and to do this they may have employed vision quests, medicine bundles, visiting sacred sites, and dreams.[6] Shamans were instrumental in the organization of special religious ceremonies, including the Father Dance, the Ghost Dance, and the Sun Dance.

The Sun Dance was the most important and elaborate of rituals for American Indian groups on the Plains. For the Eastern Shoshone, the Sun Dance was central to the ceremonial life; it celebrated the prosperity of the tribe and encouraged group solidarity. The Sun Dance had its designated leaders who gave instructions for the building of the special Sun Dance lodge, for the handling of the sacred buffalo head which was placed on the center pole, and for the performance of the dances. The Sun Dance was spectacular for the colorful regalia, intense singing and dancing, and connection to spiritual power. For the person participating in the Sun Dance, it was a quest for a spiritual vision. The Sun Dance was an enormous undertaking; the main ceremony lasted four days and three nights with a great feast at its conclusion.[7]

THREATS TO SURVIVAL

Health and Disease

The traditional way of life for the Eastern Shoshone was dramatically altered by the invasion of the Europeans.[8] One of the severest threats to Eastern Shoshone survival for the last two hundred years has been disease, specifically, diseases introduced by white populations, which have brought enormous suffering and death to all American Indian groups. The diseases invaded and spread from group to group even before Whites set foot in their territory. Even before the arrival of the first fur trappers and traders on Shoshone terrain, disease was devastating the people and culture.

The smallpox epidemic of 1781 seems to have been particularly harsh; it wiped out many Shoshones in Montana, Wyoming, and Idaho. Additional waves of disease took their toll, depleting the population, and, incidentally, weakening their defenses against other American Indian groups, such as the Lakota, the Crow, and the Cheyenne, who were pushed westward by the flood of White settlers moving west. Exact numbers are hard to estimate for earlier periods, but a population of perhaps 3,000 in 1840

45

continued to be decimated until they numbered less than 1,000 by the beginning of the twentieth century.[9] Today, the Eastern Shoshone tribal enrollment includes about 3,160 members, 10 percent of whom do not live on the Wind River Reservation.[10]

Diseases such as smallpox and tuberculosis continued to be serious problems up through the first part of the 1900s. In the 1930s, with only a small hospital serving the population on the reservation, tuberculosis and trachoma affected many Shoshones. During this time many Shoshones did not live beyond their twenties. While never totally eradicated, tuberculosis has been controlled in more recent times, although current reports indicate it may be on the increase again in American Indian populations.[11] Today, the biggest threats to health facing the Eastern Shoshone are diabetes, alcohol abuse, high blood pressure, sexually transmitted diseases, teen pregnancy, and accidents; HIV and AIDS loom on the horizon.

Diabetes is the biggest health problem facing the Eastern Shoshones on the reservation. In fact, American Indians have the highest rates of diabetes in the world, followed by Native Pacific populations.[12] Nearly all the Pima Indians of Arizona cope with the disease by the time they are in their thirties and forties, much earlier than the age when other populations experience diabetes. The kind of diabetes threatening American Indians is called Type II, or late-onset diabetes, which is triggered by a complex combination of factors including genetic predisposition, obesity, diet, and lifestyle. Yet, diabetes was almost unknown in Native American populations at the beginning of the twentieth century. Its epidemic increase, especially since the 1940s and 1950s, is the result of a number of pressures toward assimilation of native groups. Government rations given to American Indians as part of treaty agreements brought lard, sugar, coffee, sweetened canned fruit, and other unhealthy foodstuffs to native nations, thus increasing obesity, one of the major triggers of diabetes. Government policies of the 1940s through 1960s encouraged Indian migration to urban areas, where the daily economic struggle entailed diets high in fat, sugar, and carbohydrates. Moving to the cities had the added effect of pulling native peoples farther away from their cultural roots, an effect that continues today. All of these factors not only impact diet, lifestyle, and health, but also pose a continuing challenge to cultural endurance and well-being for the Eastern Shoshones.

The other serious health challenges that the Shoshones are experiencing, particularly alcohol abuse, depression, and suicide, are all linked with a long history of domination, oppression, and racism from White society. It is this wider context of continued threats to culture and culture change that must be considered in dealing with health problems such as alcohol abuse. While unfair stereotypes about alcohol use, abuse, and alcoholism in native groups should be rejected, it is undeniable that alcohol abuse is quite prevalent in American Indian populations, and in many non-native populations too, with males and females, both young and old, at risk. Many other health problems stem from chronic alcohol abuse, including fetal alcohol syndrome, liver disease, depression, accidents, and crime-related injuries. While the immediate threats of this constellation of health problems needs to be addressed, the broader underlying issues of the chronic struggles of native peoples must also be considered.

Cultural Crisis: Loss of Land and the Buffalo Hunting Grounds

Another major threat to the Eastern Shoshone arrived shortly after the first epidemics, attacking the resource base upon which life depended. The threat to game animals needed for subsistence and survival began with the fur trade. The Shoshones' land was part of the fur trade territory from the beginning of the nineteenth century, and the fur trade created widespread cultural and ecological change that rapidly escalated from the 1820s.[13] By the 1840s there was a near depletion of game, and fierce competition for buffalo occurred throughout the Wyoming-Montana territory. As already noted, the heavy reliance on the buffalo initially allowed the Shoshone to expand their territory and prosper on the central plains of Wyoming; however, this dependence ultimately proved to threaten their very survival. In fact, after 1840, the buffalo hunting grounds generally were available to the Shoshone only in competition with other American Indian groups as all attempted to survive under the severe resource limitations brought about by white encroachment and the decimation of game. In the 1870s, subsistence activities in northwest Wyoming ended for the Shoshone when government officials stated that all Indians were banned from using Yellowstone National Park. By the 1880s, game animals were very scarce and could not be depended on to provide the major portion of food, and the people suffered extreme hardships of hunger and malnutrition.

Under such dire circumstances, the Eastern Shoshone were forced to consider farming as a new subsistence practice. In fact, the U.S. government was very keen on transforming the Shoshone, and many other American Indians, into settled farmers, a goal reflected in the 1887 Dawes Act. However, the climate and character of the land placed a severe limitation on this plan. Ranching, not farming, was better suited for this area. Attempts to farm the land were soon abandoned, and ranching became the major economic strategy for landowners on the reservation. The almost complete disappearance of the buffalo meant that the importance of the buffalo as a resource was necessarily replaced by cattle, though horses continued to be important for ranch work and transportation.

While coping with the devastation of disease and loss of game animals, the Eastern Shoshone also faced the loss of a great deal of their territory, the very land that sustained their way of life. In the 1860s, a treaty with the Eastern Shoshone, signed by Washakie and other leaders, officially designated the Eastern Shoshone territory as the area between the Wind River, the Uintah and Wasatch Ranges, the Snake River, and the headwaters of the Sweetwater River. The 1868 treaty between the Eastern Shoshone and the U.S. government created the Wind River Reservation. This reservation area was reduced in size in 1872 with the Brunot Agreement and then with the McLaughlin Agreement of 1898. Yet, although they were confined to the reservation, the Eastern Shoshone still were under the threat of traditional Indian enemies; raids upon the Eastern Shoshone were frequently made by the Arapaho and the Cheyenne during the early 1870s. The harshness and poverty of reservation life for the Eastern Shoshone was increased when the U.S. government allotted some of the best grazing and irrigation land in the eastern reservation to the Arapaho.

Today, the more fertile land on the reservation is used for making hay to feed horses and cattle during the winter, and the sagebrush country is utilized for open grazing. However, for the last century, making a living from the land has not been easy. The current poor profits from cattle present a serious threat to the whole ranching way of life. Of course, similar problems are faced by the Arapaho and white ranchers, and the long-term drop in cattle prices and the escalating costs of the ranching are forcing many to reconsider their livelihoods.

The Eastern Shoshone have been able to maintain many of their traditional connections with the land through game hunting, horse riding, gathering of berries, and visiting sacred sites. Although the Wind River Reservation provides some land upon which to pursue these activities, the traditional culture of the Eastern Shoshone is based on a much larger territory, including several important areas that now are national parks in the state of Wyoming. The Eastern Shoshone, together with many other American Indian groups, have been struggling in recent years to gain proper access to Yellowstone National Park and to Devils' Tower National Monument, known as *Mato Tipi* or Bear's Lodge. According to Plains Indian oral tradition, *Mato Tipi* was named for the rough crags in the rock, which look like the clawings of a bear. It was also thought to be a lodging place of bears. Mato Tipi, made famous by its use in the movie *Close Encounters of the Third Kind*, has received much media attention recently. Rock climbers have clashed with American Indians who wish to use the site for important ceremonies. The Lakota and Cheyenne, in particular, have experienced difficulties in gaining uninterrupted use of Mato Tipi to hold important cultural rituals, such as the Sun Dance.

The Eastern Shoshone have faced significant threats to their cultural continuity because of their limited access to Yellowstone National Park, which was part of their traditional territory. Yellowstone is important for the Shoshone not only because sacred sites are located there, but also because it is a place where the Eastern Shoshone wish to pursue subsistence activities. They currently have very limited rights, specifically relating to berry

Mato Tipi: American Indian sacred site. Photo: Fred Altaffer, Altaffer Photography.

picking, to the park. Rights to fishing and game remain problematic. An example of the low priority given to Shoshone rights can be seen in the distribution of meat from the buffaloes that stray outside of the park into Montana and are killed. Although the buffaloes are distributed to Indian groups in Montana, the Eastern Shoshone of Wyoming have not been included in the allocation of this culturally significant resource. The Eastern Shoshone's use of this area for traditional hunting is a strong argument for their eligibility in receiving a share of such buffalo meat.

Environmental Crisis

The Eastern Shoshone, and most other American Indian groups, face serious environmental threats as well. An overall disregard for Shoshone lands by the government and developers is a common theme; for example, the Western Shoshone of the Newe Sogobia Nation, a group closely related to the Eastern Shoshone, have had to cope with hundreds of nuclear weapons and nuclear devices being stored and deployed on their territory since the 1960s. The temptation to receive money in return for allowing for nuclear waste storage is another general threat that always lurks on the horizon for Indian nations in need of monetary resources. For the Eastern Shoshone, a more immediate and real threat is found with use of the natural forest resources on the Wind River Reservation and adjacent to the reservation. Water is another critical natural resource, and in 1997 the Eastern Shoshone's environmental management staff identified the degradation of water quality, especially for the Boulder Flats community, as the primary environmental crisis facing the tribe. The irrigation demands by nonreservation, white farmers and ranchers up stream cause annual stream flow problems for the Wind River environment. The U.S. Fish and Wildlife Service, the National Wildlife Federation, and tribal leaders are very concerned about the loss of fish and other wildlife because of the lack of stream flow, water pollution, and increased water diversion for irrigation.

Unemployment

The environmental threats only add to the serious economic problems. The current situation continues to be one in which there are not enough resources from the land to support the membership of the reservation. At present there is an 80 percent unemployment rate on the reservation, and this forces many people to migrate to such cities as Salt Lake City, Laramie, or Denver in order to find employment. The relative geographical isolation of the Wind River Reservation from major urban centers means that most Eastern Shoshones must move off of the reservation for employment, limiting their connection to the reservation to powwow celebrations and family visits. However, job opportunities are restricted for those with limited formal education, and this has been a serious problem for tribal members seeking off-reservation employment.

Unemployment and underemployment are clearly linked to crime rates and juvenile delinquency. Teenage delinquency has been a problem at Wind River, and recently the situation has worsened. Despite its very rural context, the unexpected problem of youth gangs surfaced recently on the reservation after young people encountered gangs in cities and brought these influences back to the Wind River Reservation. The Shoshone Tribal Council has recently developed a juvenile code, which includes curfews on the reservation and parental involvement in counseling and rehabilitating troubled youths.

RESPONSE: STRUGGLES TO SURVIVE CULTURALLY

Shoshone Tribal Cultural Center

Despite the many threats and challenges to their vitality, the Eastern Shoshone have worked actively as a tribe to protect their lands and treaty rights and to revitalize their culture. One example of this is the Shoshone Tribal Cultural Center, located at Fort Washakie on the Wind River Reservation. The center, which houses both a museum and a library, provides a space where Shoshones and others can learn about their culture, history, language, and current issues. The Shoshone Tribal Cultural Center organizes educational activities for the public by offering workshops on drumming, women's saddle making, and cradle board construction. Cradle boards, made from a basketry frame covered with skins, are used to carry and hold children. Often they are elaborately decorated with beads and feathers.

The center is also making great efforts to ensure the continued viability of the Shoshone language, which is regarded as a key barometer of cultural endurance, especially when spoken by young people. For those who want to improve their language skills, the Shoshone Tribal Cultural Center offers Shoshone language courses several times a year, taught by native speakers. The two-month class is divided into different proficiencies, with basic, intermediate, and advanced levels. In the basic level, participants learn names for common items, such as animals, numbers, and colors. Pronunciation improvements are stressed in the intermediate level, and full conversational competence is the goal of the advanced class. To make these classes more accessible to people who work during the day, the center offers many of its courses in the evening.

Improved Living Conditions and Transportation

Improving living conditions on the reservation is another response. The construction of adequate modern housing has been a major project for the Wind River Tribal Government. Approximately 3,000 Indian homes are located on the Wind River Reservation, the majority of which were constructed or improved with Tribal Housing Authority subsidies. There is still much to be done, but there have been vast improvements over the past few decades in providing comfortable and safe shelter for Eastern Shoshone Nation members. In addition to housing, access to transportation is important because shopping is limited on the reservation and may need to be supplemented with trips to such off-reservation Wyoming towns as Lander, Thermopolis, and Riverton, which entails a trip up to an hour and a half in length. The Shoshone and Arapaho Nation Transportation Authority (SANTA) provides public transportation on the reservation, and to towns such as Lander and Riverton. Public bus lines connect the reservation to Casper, Cody, Sheridan, and other locations in Wyoming. Access to off-reservation resources is not only important for shopping, but also for special health care needs, although there are facilities located on the Wind River Reservation, including the Fort Washakie Health Center. The Eastern Shoshone Tribe operates the Community Health Representative Program which provides services and outreach care for local communities. In addition, the reservation houses the Wind River Dialysis Center, which provides care for people with severe diabetes and also functions as an important employer on the reservation.

Employment Opportunities

The tribal government and community are committed to improving employment opportunities on the reservation. Some tribal members are fortunate enough to be employed on large ranches and farms, in tribal government offices, at the Bureau of Indian Affairs (BIA), or at the Indian Health Service. Other sources of income include tourism, private businesses, and gas and oil leases organized through the Shoshone-Arapaho Oil and Gas Commission. There are also a number of nation businesses, including gas stations, the Morning Star Manor (a hotel), and the Wind River Dialysis Center.

Environmental Focus

Good schools, health care facilities, and transportation systems are fruitless, however, if the environment is not protected for the safety and health of reservation residents. With this in mind, the tribal government takes part in the Mini Sose (Lakota for Missouri River) Intertribal Water Rights Coalition, a nonprofit organization founded in 1988 to protect Indian water rights and to develop viable economies that rely on such rights.[14] The Eastern Shoshone environmental management staff has identified inadequate and unsafe water as one of the biggest environmental threats currently facing the Nation. Thus far, the quality of life for all twenty-eight Indian nations within the Missouri River Basin has been compromised by federal public works projects and water pollution which threaten the availability of water for these tribes.[15] The coalition's response to this threat has been hindered, however, by lack of funding, technical consultants, and information on water resource technology.

Spiritual and Religious Continuities

Despite all of the challenges and changes imposed on the Eastern Shoshone, there are many important spiritual and religious continuities, such as in traditional ceremonies and dance. The Sun Dance, Peyotism, and the powwow represent dynamic and meaningful traditions in which Indian identity can be expressed and through which the Eastern Shoshone can reaffirm their bonds to other American Indian groups. The flexibility of these rituals allows them to continue to enrich the culture; for example, the Eastern Shoshone Sun Dance has become infused with some Christian elements. The powwow is an excellent example of combining the old with the new in a context of a pan-Indian expression of contemporary native identity. The Eastern Shoshone host an annual powwow and treaty celebration at the end of June, called the Eastern Shoshone Indian Days and

Treaty Day Celebration. These festivities, held on the reservation at Fort Washakie, are very important to cultural revitalization among the Eastern Shoshone and the other American Indian groups who attend. Powwows, in fact, contain elements such as dances, regalia, and storytelling, from tribes all over North America.

The Eastern Shoshone also continue to revere the role of sacred dreams, personal songs used to heal sickness, and the veneration of such sacred symbols as eagle feathers and eagle bone whistles.[16] The Eastern Shoshone's important role in the general revival of the Sun Dance and the tribe's participation in regional powwows are two examples of support for pan-Indian cooperation. In addition, the Eastern Shoshone have shown solidarity with other groups, such as the Lakota and Cheyenne, in fostering respect for sacred ceremonies and the preservation of their sacred sites.

The Eastern Shoshone have joined a coalition of tribes petitioning for native use of Mato Tipi, or Devil's Tower National Monument, a sacred site and place of pilgrimage for almost two dozen American Indian groups. The National Park Service, which currently administers the site, has attempted to accommodate the need for Native American access to Mato Tipi through its policies of asking hikers and climbers not to use the area during several months of the year, especially in June when sacred rituals, such as the Sun Dance, are performed there. Beginning in 1995, the Park Service banned commercial climbing and instituted voluntary restrictions on individual climbing during the month of June. This policy also sought to ensure the protection of the birds of prey that nest during this time at Mato Tipi.

Since 1995, more than 6,000 climbers per year attempt to climb the challenging vertical rock surface of Mato Tipi. Both the voluntary and mandatory restrictions were met with resistance by climbers, especially commercial climbing groups, who claimed that protecting the site for native religious use was an infringement on *their rights* to climb in a federally owned public park. Some of these groups organized under the names Friends of Devil's Tower and, ironically, Bear Lodge Multiple Use Association. These groups were instrumental in challenging the bans in court. This led to a ruling by the United States District Court on June 8, 1996, that the commercial climbing ban instituted by the Park Service was unconstitutional. This ruling was reaffirmed on April 2, 1998.[17] Currently, the Park Service continues to ask respectfully that people refrain from climbing activities during the month of June. For American Indian groups, this is just the latest chapter in a long struggle to practice native religions and ceremonies. Despite the 1978 American Indian Religious Freedom Act passed by the U.S. Congress, there continues to be a fundamental lack of understanding how many native spiritual practices are rooted in the land and connected to specific sacred sites.[18]

FOOD FOR THOUGHT

It is easy to see that the Eastern Shoshone have faced many challenges over the past few hundred years, especially since contact with non-native Americans. Clearly, adjustment to living with treaty agreements, adaptation to reservation life, management of the difficulties of coexistence to a significant white settler population, and acceptance of shared resources within the Wind River region with Arapaho and white neighbors have all presented great obstacles to survival.

Through all of these struggles, the Eastern Shoshone have sustained a vital connection to the land. Star Weed, a leader for the Eastern Shoshone people, notes the unbroken religious, economic, and social ties to the land and natural environment.[19] This connection has been shown to be particularly evident in the Sun Dance tradition, in reverence for sacred sites such as Mato Tipi, and in other religious practices embedded in the landscape of the Wind River Reservation and surrounding areas.

Current challenges for survival are numerous. The rural, arid natural environment continues to make agriculture a risky, unrewarding enterprise. Life on the reservation continues to be one of poverty for many, and the high rate of migration out of the region in order to get jobs and survive economically will continue to dissipate the strength of the Eastern Shoshone community. On the positive side, great strides have been made by the tribal government to provide for the growing educational needs of Eastern Shoshone people as they continue to cope with the challenge of a changing economy in Wyoming and bordering states.

Perhaps most significant has been the struggle to protect the environment. As described earlier, this is indeed an enormous challenge since this struggle involves land and people outside of the Eastern Shoshone Nation. It is important to note that the Eastern Shoshone, in fact, are leading the way in an attempt to save the Wind River environment for the benefit of wildlife, fisheries, and all the people of Wyoming and the United States who enjoy this important area located in close proximity to national forests and park lands.

These are the kinds of challenges the Eastern Shoshone will continue to face, and with their long history of strong leadership, adaptability, and forging alliances with others to further their cause, their cultural vitality and endurance as a people undoubtedly will be sustained.

Questions

1. How has the Eastern Shoshone's long history of strong leadership, adaptability, and forging alliances with others helped to ensure their cultural vitality? How do you think the Eastern Shoshone will succeed in meeting the coming challenges

of the twenty-first century, including continued struggles over native rights to resources, threats to environmental preservation, and conflicts over the access to sacred sites and the expression of native spirituality?

2. Why is the land important? How is their endurance as a people linked with their continued possession of a territory? How are reservation and nonreservation areas involved with cultural traditions?

3. How important is the continued respect for ceremonies and sacred sties? How do ceremonies like the Sun Dance keep the sacred aspects of the culture alive?

4. In what different ways are the Eastern Shoshone working to revitalize their culture? Why is language instruction thought to be so important to cultural identity? How can non-natives be supportive of cultural revitalization in American Indian groups?

5. How does pan-Indian cooperation in regard to water rights and religious freedom reveal the strength in unity in common cause efforts? How can the problems about access be resolved at Mato Tipi and Yellowstone National Park?

6. How are pan-Indian activities and groups important for the Eastern Shoshone?

NOTES

1. Trudy Griffin-Pierce, *Native Americans: Enduring Cultures and Traditions* (New York: MetroBooks, 1996).

2. Demitri Shimkin, *Handbook of North American Indians*, vol. 2, *Great Basin* (Washington, D.C.: Smithsonian Institution, 1986), 308–35.

3. Ibid.

4. Further information on Washakie is found in Virginia Trenholm and Maurine Carley, *The Shoshonis: Sentinels of the Rockies* (Norman: University of Oklahoma Press, 1964).

5. Fred Voget, *The Shoshoni-Crow Sun Dance* (Norman: University of Oklahoma Press, 1984).

6. Ibid.

7. Further information on the Sun Dance can be found in Voget, *Shoshoni-Crow Sun Dance*.

8. Griffin-Pierce, *Native Americans*.

9. Shimkin, *Handbook*.

10. Data from the Eastern Shoshone Culture Center, 2001.

11. See T. Kue Young, *The Health of Native Americans: Toward a Biocultural Epidemiology* (New York: Oxford University Press, 1994).

12. Ibid.

13. Shimkin, *Handbook*.

14. See http://www.mnisose.org/25.html.

15. William B. Lord, Mary G. Wallace, and Thomas McGuire, eds., *Indian Water in the New West* (Tucson: University of Arizona Press, 1993).

16. Voget, *Shoshoni-Crow Sun Dance*.

17. See the following two web sites: *http://web/hamline.edu/law/lawrelign/sacred/dev.phot/html*, and http://www.dcomp.comm/sundance/dtower.htm.

18. Further information on Native American sacred sites can be found in Christopher Vecsey, ed., *Handbook of American Indian Religious Freedom* (New York: Crossroad Publishing, 1991).

19. Star Weed's views on the spiritual character of the environment are presented in the video, *Wind River* (Oley, PA: Bullfrog Films, 2000).

RESOURCE GUIDE

Published Literature

Griffin-Pierce, Trudy. *Native Americans: Enduring Cultures and Traditions.* New York: MetroBooks, 1996.

Lord, William B., Mary G. Wallace, and Thomas McGuire, eds. *Indian Water in the New West.* Tucson: University of Arizona Press, 1993.

News from Indian Country: The Nations Native Newspaper. Rt. 2, Box 2900-A. Hayward, Wisc. 54843.

Shimkin, Demitri B. *Handbook of North American Indians,* vol. 2, *Great Basin.* Washington, D.C.: Smithsonian Institution, 1986), 308–35.

Shurts, John. *Indian Reserved Water Rights: The Winters Doctrine in Its Social and Legal Context, 1880s–1930s.* Norman: University of Oklahoma Press, 2000.

Trenholm, Virginia, and Maurine Carley. *The Shoshonis: Sentinels of the Rockies.* Norman: University of Oklahoma Press, 1964.

Vecsey, Christopher, ed. *Handbook of American Indian Religious Freedom.* New York: Crossroad Publishing, 1991.

Voget, Fred. *The Shoshoni-Crow Sun Dance.* Norman: University of Oklahoma Press, 1984.

Young, T. Kue. *The Health of Native Americans: Toward a Biocultural Epidemiology.* New York: Oxford University Press, 1994.

Video

Wind River. Bullfrog Films. Box 149, Oley, Pennsylvania 19547.

WWW Sites

Eastern Shoshone Tribe
This site provides general information about the tribal government of the Eastern Shoshone and gives phone numbers for the cultural center.
http://www.mnisose.org/25.html

Mni Sose Intertribal Water Rights Coalition
http://www.mnisose.org/profiles/eshoshone.htm

Devil's Tower Controversy
http://www.hamline.edu/law/lawrelign/sacred/lodge2.htm

http://www.hamline.edu/law/lawrelign/sacred/devphot.html
http://www.NEWyoming.com/DevilsTower/

Organization

Eastern Shoshone Tribe
John Washakie, Tribal Chairman
P.O. Box 538
Fort Washakie, Wyoming 82514
(307)332–3532/4932

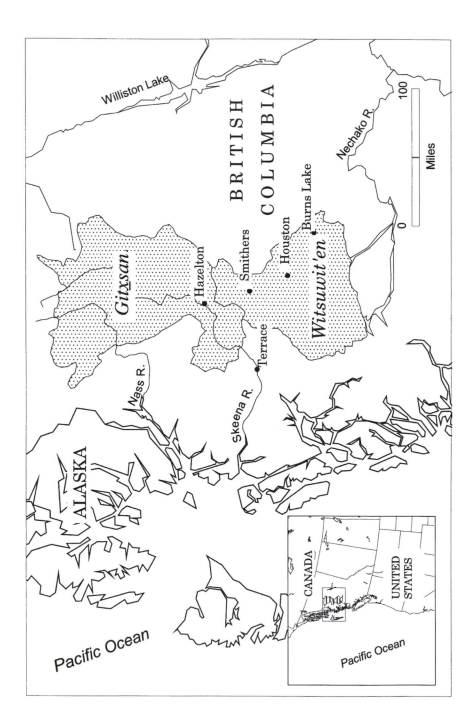

Chapter 4

The Gitxsan and Witsuwit'en in British Columbia

Antonia Mills

Before I leave I'd like to apologize to the industrial people and governments and the federal government for being a thorn in your paw. We
are used to that feeling. We grew up, we traveled for hundreds of miles
in devil's club and we are used to it. Thank you.

Alfred Joseph, Chief Gisday Wa[1]

The Witsuwit'en people and the Gitxsan people do not see themselves as
endangered, if endangered is understood to mean peoples who are disappearing or giving up their distinct identities and resources. The Gitxsan and
Witsuwit'en have worked resolutely and consistently to change the expectation that they, as well as other Native or First Nations people in the
province of British Columbia and the country of Canada, would dwindle
and disappear or assimilate so that they are indistinguishable from the general Euro-Canadian population. There are today approximately 5,000 Gitxsan and 3,000 Witsuwit'en[2]. The Gitxsan and Witsuwit'en have made
sure that their presence is felt by taking their land claims case, known as
Delgamuukw v. R (R for regina meaning the queen), first to the provincial
court of British Columbia (beginning in 1984), then through the provincial
court of appeal (in 1991), and finally to the Supreme Court of Canada.
There, on December 11, 1997, they were given the important decision that
aboriginal title to land does exist, that it is an exclusive right, that it includes rights to subsurface resources such as minerals, and that it includes
the right to use their traditional territory in ways that were not known to
their ancestors prior to contact with the settler society. This decision has
potential to impact other aboriginal peoples, endangered or otherwise, not

only in Canada, but around the world. Indeed today some of the Euro-Canadian settler society feels endangered by the Delgamuukw decision, a decision fought for strenuously by the Witsuwit'en and Gitxsan, lest they become endangered peoples.

CULTURAL OVERVIEW

The People

The Gitxsan and Witsuwit'en are two aboriginal peoples who have been neighbors at least since the end of the last ice age, perhaps 10,000 years ago. They have influenced each other and intermarried over a very long period, yet they speak unrelated languages. The Witsuwit'en are sometimes called the Bulkley River Carrier, or the Western Carrier. The language they speak, Witsuwit'en (pronounced, roughly "wit-So-wit-tain"), is part of the Athapaskan or Dene language stock. The Carrier to their east, as well as many of the peoples to the northeast up into the subarctic part of Western Canada, speak Dene languages, as do the Navaho and Apache, who are known as the Southern Athapaskans. The Gitxsan (pronounced "git-san"), on the other hand, who speak a language that is part of the Tsimshian family, are most closely related to the Nisga'a on the Nass River (who have also pursued their land claims through court and treaty negotiations). The Nisga'a and Gitxsan languages are related to the Tsimshian who live downstream from the Gitxsan on the Skeena River, and south along the coast from where the Skeena River enters the Pacific Ocean. The name Gitxsan means "People of the Skeena River"; Skeena means the "River of Mists." The Gitxsan are a classic Northwest Coast people although they do not live on the coast.[3] The Witsuwit'en fit into this pattern as well.

The Gitxsan and Witsuwit'en are both matrilineal potlatching (ceremonial feast marked by reciprocal gift giving) peoples. Because each Gitxsan and Witsuwit'en person is a member of a house and clan, and each person's membership in that house and clan comes from one's mother,[4] the peoples are both matrilineal. The term Delgamuukw (pronounced "dell-gah-MOO-hk"), made famous through their land claims court case, is the name of the head chief of one of thirty-nine Gitxsan houses or matrilines, who with the Witsuwit'en houses took the issue of ownership and jurisdiction over their traditional territories to court. Gisday Wa, quoted at the beginning of this chapter, is one of the twelve Witsuwit'en head chiefs of his house or matriline. For obvious reasons, the list of these fifty-one head chiefs has been shortened to Delgamuukw. Every inch of the Gitxsan and Witsuwit'en territory belongs to one or another of these matrilineal houses. The houses refer to the members of a matriline, who previously lived in longhouses with its identifying totem pole erected in front of it, by the river's edge.

The Setting

The Gitxsan and Witsuwit'en traditional territory, some 22,000 square miles in north central British Columbia, is made up of spectacular mountains which level off on the Witsuwit'en eastern boundary into a high plateau. The Gitxsan territory is prime northwest coast cedar rainforest territory in the Pacific Coastal or Cordilleran mountain range, southeast of the Alaskan panhandle. The Gitxsan territory is located in the watersheds of the Upper Skeena and Nass Rivers. The Witsuwit'en homeland is upstream to the east of the Gitxsan territory, along the Bulkley River and its tributaries, which spill into the Skeena River. The western part of the Witsuwit'en territory shares the northwest coast environment. The eastern part of the Witsuwit'en territory extends into the western portion of the Nechako and Fraser River watersheds which form an interior plateau with a colder climate and few cedar trees. The rivers abound in salmon, and the land is rich with berries, plants, and wildlife. Although most of the people continue to live in traditional villages, a number have moved to urban centers such as Vancouver, Smithers, Prince George, and Prince Rupert.

Traditional Subsistence Strategies

The economies of the Gitxsan and Witsuwit'en were and are based on harvesting the rich salmon resources, as well as the various resources their vast territories, with their shifting climates, support. The partnership of the Witsuwit'en and Gitxsan was and is based on a shared and slightly differing traditional economy, as well as on sharing and trading the resources of the peoples on either side. The eulachan (candlefish) of the Nisga'a on the Nass River, the copper of the Tlingit, and the furs and hides of the east were all part of an intense trade network before contact, as well as after.

Both the Witsuwit'en and Gitxsan economies were and are based on catching and preserving the many species of salmon that abound in all the rivers (the Bulkley, the Upper Skeena, the Upper Nass, the Upper Nechako); gathering and preserving berries and plants (such as the thorny devil's club referred to by Chief Gisday Wa) and hunting the animals that inhabit their land: mountain goat, bear, deer, moose, caribou, rabbit, marmot, fox, cougar, ermine, wolverine, and mink. Traditionally mountain goat fur and dog hair were spun into yarn and used to make Chilkat blankets (intricately woven ceremonial regalia) which showed the crests or totems of the wearer. Cedar bark was made into neck rings for the healers. Furs and hides were used for clothes and robes. Food from the territories was and is distributed at feasts, or potlatches. Both the Witsuwit'en and Gitxsan were (and are) deeply identified with their land, and they regulate carefully who uses the resources and when.

Over time the pre-contact economy expanded to include more than the

Hereditary Chief Lelt, the late Fred Johnson. Photo: Stephen Bosch. Copyright by Gitxsan-Witsuwit'en Hereditary Chiefs.

commercial fur trade. By the twentieth century, commercial fishing and canning on the coast, some farming and haying, and some small-scale logging and mining were all pursued. Today the Gitxsan and Witsuwit'en are taking over administration of the educational, health, and social services provided to their people, and they are creating new businesses such as a value-added wood plant (Witsuwit'en) stock market ventures (Gitxsan), and working for non-native logging outfits. Despite the shift to a cash economy, salmon and the resources of the territories remain central to their subsistence.

Social and Political Organization

The key to the Gitxsan and Witsuwit'en social and political structures, and to their economies as well, is that the right to harvest fish, plants, and animals was and is based on matrilineal house control over the fishing sites and the different territories. The head chief, with the wing chiefs of each house, oversees the use of the fishing sites and their specific territories and they are the ones who say who can fish at the sites and use the resources on the territories. The main responsibility of a head chief is as guardian of the fishing sites and territories and the life-forms on them; he or she must make sure they are used for the sustenance of the members of their house. Since one of the key principles of the matrilineal system is that one must marry outside of one's house and clan, rights through one's father and spouse also play an integral part in one's life.

The rights over the territories are passed on through ceremonial feasts called potlatches. Potlatches were and are the keystone of both the Gitxsan and Witsuwit'en political organizations. They are their form of governance, dispute resolution, and empowerment. During these feasts the succession of names or hereditary titles is announced, witnessed, and ritually recognized by one's own house and clan and by the chiefs of the other houses.[5] Today a potlatch occurs every time a Gitxsan or Witsuwit'en dies, but the most significant potlatches take place when a head chief passes away, and the title and its associated territory and fishing rights are passed on to a successor; or when a totem pole is erected to mark the succession of the rights to the new holder. When a chief dies, his or her house and clan affirms the successor and pays the chief's father's house and clan for helping in the burial. The father's clan is also hired to carve the totem pole, which is placed in front of the longhouse of the head chief of a house. Totem poles reference the history of the house by featuring clan and house crests, whose meaning is revealed in the house's oral traditions.

The Gitxsan clans were and still are the Eagle, the Fireweed, the Wolf, and the Frog. The Witsuwit'en Beaver clan relates to the Eagle clan; the Fireweed, to the Fireweed; the Wolf, to the Wolf; and the Witsuwit'en Big Frog and Little Frog, to the Gitxsan Frog. The Gitxsan and Witsuwit'en clans also link with their neighbors through marriage, which produce a system of interlocking clans. The Frog clan is the equivalent of the Coast Haida Eagle clan, to the Raven clan of the Tlingit, for example.

The variation in the Gitxsan and the Witsuwit'en habitats is reflected in the differences between their traditional types of village settlement and their potlatching seasons. In pre-contact times the Gitxsan wintered in seven villages (Kitwancool, Kitwanga, Gitsegukla, Gitanmaax, Kispiox, Kisgegas, and Kuldo) along the Skeena River or its tributaries. Each of the cedar plank longhouses in each village belonged to a particular group of matrilineally related people. During the summer salmon run, members of the house would move from the village to their fishing sites to catch and dry the salmon. At other times of the year, house members traveled from the longhouse into its territories to harvest other resources as seasonally appropriate.

Traditionally the Witsuwit'en seasonal pattern was somewhat different: in summer the Witsuwit'en gathered at their longhouses at their two major village sites for the salmon runs in the summer. The summer villages were Kya Wiget, the ancient village (later called Moricetown) and Tse Kya (also called Hagwilget). Tse Kya was founded after the 1820 rock slide created excellent fishing sites to be formed at this location.[6] Each fall, after drying their salmon, the Witsuwit'en would disperse and winter on fish lakes from which they could catch other types of fish and hunt and trap from these distantly scattered winter houses.

The Gitxsan held most of their potlatches or feasts in the wintertime while they were in their villages; the Witsuwit'en held most of their potlatches or feasts in the summer while they were congregated in their longhouses at the salmon fishing villages. The name Carrier (*porteur* in French) came from the custom of having a widow carry the cremated bones of her husband, particularly if he was a head chief, back from the territory where he died to the summer salmon village where a potlatch was held to commemorate his passing and to pass on his title and the rights to the territory. In the summer fishing villages, this chiefly succession was witnessed by people from all the clans.

Today the villages of both the Witsuwit'en and Gitxsan are occupied year-round because schools and services are concentrated there. Groups or individuals use the natural resources as seasonally appropriate. Members of a house or matriline no longer live in longhouses, and the totem poles erected today are placed in front of the individual house of the head chief. Despite the changes, the matrilineal houses and the potlatch remain crucial to the governance of both the Gitxsan and the Witsuwit'en. Today, commodities purchased in the non-native town of Smithers on Witsuwit'en territory form a major part of the gifts distributed at feasts, as well as a major part of the economy.

Religion and World View

The religion and world view of the Witsuwit'en and Gitxsan are based on the premise that all life-forms are imbued with spirit that must be respected. The opening statement made by Chief Delgamuukw and Chief Gisday Wa for their land claims court case is called the "Spirit in the Land." The Witsuwit'en and Gitxsan oral traditions typically relate how a village or house was founded with the supernatural help of the crest or totem animal.[7] The sacred relationship of the totem animals to the houses and clans remains the foundation of Gitxsan and Witsuwit'en religious experience and ritual. Respecting life-forms and honoring them, as well as the relationship of the chiefs to their territories and the life-forms on them, are at the heart of the Witsuwit'en and Gitxsan philosophies, political acts, wars, and healing rituals.

Christian missionaries typically opposed much of the traditional world view. The Witsuwit'en were missionized by Catholics. Father LeJacq arrived in 1869 and stayed until he was replaced by Father Morice eleven years later. Father Morice renamed Kya Wiget Moricetown after himself, and like his predecessor, forbade potlatching. The Gitxsan were missionized by Protestants. Reverend Collinson and Bishop Rigley arrived in 1880; Tomlinson first preached in the Tsimshian village of Kitsumkalem, downriver to the Gitxsan, in 1874 and founded Cedarvale, an alternate village modelled after the Tsimshian Metlakatla, near the Gitxsan village of Kit-

wanga in 1888. The Salvation Army similarly founded Glen Vowell between the Gitxsan villages of Kispiox and Gitanmaax, hoping that the
removal of people from a village with totem poles would remove their
traditional beliefs. Despite the overlay of Christianity, the Gitxsan and Witsuwit'en religions and world views retain a great deal of their traditional
beliefs. The belief that salmon, as well as all animals and people, reincarnate is deeply seated among the Gitxsan and Witsuwit'en, as well as among
many other North American Indian peoples.[8] One of the reasons the Gitxsan and Witsuwit'en feel so strongly about their land is that they experience it as being theirs not only since time immemorial, but they experience
themselves as coming back, being reborn on it, lifetime after lifetime. For
example, the Gitxsan and Witsuwit'en continue to act respectfully toward
the animals and fish they take so they will want to reincarnate, and they
continue to relate the knowledge of small children reincarnated from an
ancestor in their house and clan. The identity of the Witsuwit'en and Gitxsan is based on the expectation that the people alive today are reincar-
nations of their grandparents and so on back to their founding ancestors.
The oral traditions, now as in the past, are passed along by telling the
traditional stories, in and out of potlatches. These oral traditions relate that
both the Gitxsan and the Witsuwit'en in ancient times lived in a village
which has ceased to exist. According to the Gitxsan the ancient village of
Temlahan was destroyed by a rock slide after an earthquake which occurred after some youths mistreated mountain goats; the Witsuwit'en accounts relate how Dizkle was abandoned after a portent of danger.

THREATS TO SURVIVAL

Aboriginally the threats to survival came from warring neighboring peoples or the wrath of spirit beings. The Gitxsan and Witsuwit'en experienced
new threats to their survival with the coming of Euro-Canadian settlers and
their assumption that Indian land was free for the taking and belonged not
to Natives but to the crown. More recently the threats stem from the intense exploitation of the fish and timber resources by multinational companies, and from the opposition among some Euro-Canadians to
Aboriginal rights to land. The Witsuwit'en and Gitxsan have to contend
with the continued racism on the part of many people who now live on
their traditional territories, and who prefer to think that Indians have no
rights to their traditional lands and should assimilate and become "good
white men and women."

Historical Overview

Initially the Witsuwit'en and Gitxsan accepted and assisted the European
strangers who arrived on their peripheries. Traders had arrived on the coast

west of the Gitxsan by 1790, and a fur trade post had opened to the east of the Witsuwit'en by 1812. The Gitxsan and Witsuwit'en entered enthusiastically into the fur trade and took over and regulated much of its activity. By 1862, however, smallpox had spread up the coast and reduced the Gitxsan and Witsuwit'en population by a third.

In 1876 the Indian Act was established in Ottawa, Canada's national capital, with the purpose of assimilating Indian peoples. The act's intent was (1) to establish small reserves for Indians, relegating the rest of their traditional territories to the Crown; (2) to create a new form of band council government to supplant traditional tribal governments; and (3) to define who was an Indian. The Gitxsan and Witsuwit'en are still battling this imposition on their territory, their way of governance, and their definition of membership against persistent opposition.

In the late 1800s more and more prospectors came through Gitxsan and Witsuwit'en territory, followed by more settlers. As long as their number was small, they did not pose a problem, but relations were not always easy. In 1872 miners burned twelve Gitxsan houses and six totem poles in the Gitxsan village of Gitsegukla. The Gitsegukla chiefs then blockaded the Skeena River to all trading and supply boats. The colonial government sent gunboats to the mouth of the Skeena, but the Skeena Rebellion was settled peaceably when Lieutenant Joseph Trutch met with Gitsegukla chiefs and agreed to make compensation for the burning. Some Gitxsan villages, not already fortified, fortified themselves. Trutch stated, "Indians have really no right to the land they claim, nor are they of any actual value or utility to them, and I cannot see why they should . . . retain these lands to the prejudice of the general interest of the colony."[9]

After 1872 the Gitxsan and Witsuwit'en found themselves repeatedly confronted with a long succession of threats to the survival of their way of life. In 1884 the Indian Act outlawed the Sun Dance and the potlatch and the Gitxsan and Witsuwit'en form of governance. In 1884 Gitxsan chief Gyetim Galdo'o of Gitanmaax openly held a potlatch and was arrested by the Royal Canadian Mounted Police. This did not cause potlatches to cease, but did cause them to be practiced in greater secrecy. In 1900 Father Morice burned the Witsuwit'en potlatch regalia in honor of Bishop Augustin Dontenwill's visit. Nonetheless, the Witsuwit'en and Gitxsan continued to hold potlatches, and do so today, to settle disputes, to witness the succession of head chiefs, and to regulate their affairs.

In 1888 the Indian Act was amended to prohibit Indians from trading, bartering, or selling fish. This did not stop the traditional trade among themselves, nor did it stop clandestine sale to non-Indians. Negotiations are *still* ongoing between the Department of Fisheries and Oceans and the Gitxsan and Witsuwit'en about their right to regulate fishing in their rivers, to use their traditional fishing sites and methods of fishing, and to sell the fish.

At the same time the Witsuwit'en and Gitxsan as other First Nations were denied timber leases and the right to buy land.[10] The settler society and its government denied their right to exist except on small reserves, and continues to disregard their rights to participate in allocation of resources on their traditional land. They, as all Native peoples in Canada, were denied the right to vote provincially until 1949, and federally until 1959.[11] Until the same time period, educated First Nations people lost their status as Indians, since in the settler society's eyes, Western education was considered sufficient to eradicate the indigenous world view. Again until 1959 disenfranchised Indians (those who lost status through education, or often through serving in the army) were not allowed to spend the night on Indian reserves. In short the settler and government goal was "assimilate or cease to exist."

In 1901 returning Boer War veterans were given rights to land in the Witsuwit'en Bulkley valley. There the head chiefs of the matrilines had typically cleared and fenced fields and built log cabins and barns. When the Witsuwit'en head chiefs returned to their homesteads after drying their winter's supply of salmon at Hagwilget or Kya Wiget/Moricetown, they found to their dismay that their homesteads had been taken over by war veterans. When they protested they were often put in jail. With one exception their homesteads were not returned.

In 1912 the Canadian National began forging a railway from Prince George to Prince Rupert, right through Witsuwit'en and Gitxsan territory, opening up the area to more and more settlers, who clustered particularly in the less mountainous Witsuwit'en area. In 1912–1924 the McKenna-McBride Treaty Commission conferred small reserves at the Witsuwit'en and Gitxsan village sites. The Gitxsan and Witsuwit'en restated that their territories are much more extensive and rejected the concept of reserves. They made it clear that they did not agree with this unilateral action on the part of the government. Indeed, in 1908, the Gitxsan sent a delegation to Ottawa to speak to the Prime Minister about white incursion into their territories. The same year three Witsuwit'en were convicted and fined for threatening at gunpoint white settlers who had taken over Kya Wiget/Moricetown reserve land. In 1909 Kispiox chiefs stopped the road building in their valley; seven were arrested. At Kitwanga surveyors were stopped at gunpoint, and the Gitxsan invoked the Royal Proclamation of 1763 as part of the basis of their rights. The next year Kitwancool and Kitwanga chiefs quoted the Royal Proclamation and pinned notices of their land claims along the trails. The Royal Proclamation, which is still in force, says that the Crown must make treaties with the indigenous peoples, as they have prior right to their land. In 1921 Witsuwit'en Jean Baptiste sent his family away from his homestead and threatened to kill anyone who tried to remove him. Grudgingly, the Department of Indian Affairs registered his homestead into the Jean Baptiste reserve.

Consistently, both Witsuwit'en and Gitxsan chiefs made it clear that their territories were far larger than these small reserves. In 1927 the government responded by making it an offense punishable by imprisonment to raise money to press for land claims in Canada.

In 1893 residential schools were established with the intent to destroy Indian languages and world views.

Further serious threats to the Gitxsan and Witsuwit'en continued to come in the form of foreign diseases to which they had no resistance. Small-pox, diphtheria, measles, tuberculosis, and influenza brought back by veterans of World War II wreaked havoc on the population. By 1924 Witsuwit'en people had been reduced to less than a third of their aboriginal numbers, prompting a visiting anthropologist Diamond Jenness to predict their eventual total demise. The Gitxsan population was similarly decimated. Father Morice, using fear as a conversion technique, explained to the Witsuwit'en that they were dying in droves because God was angry at them for not embracing Christianity.

The Gitxsan and Witsuwit'en were determined to repopulate their villages. While traditionally they limited family size, after the frightening drop in population they consciously sought to increase their numbers. Their numbers now may approximate pre-contact population. Many Gitxsan and Witsuwit'en people lost status (their classification as native) through the Indian Act policy, which defines any woman who marries a non-native and her children as non-status. In 1983 Bill C31 partially changed this part of the Indian Act, and many Gitxsan and Witsuwit'en were reinstated. The Witsuwit'en and Gitxsan continue to define membership through matrilineal house membership.[12]

With some recognition that First Nations were here to stay, they were given the right to vote in provincial (i.e., British Columbia) elections in 1947. The right to vote in federal elections did not come until 1960. In 1951 the Anti-Potlatch Law was repealed, as well as the prohibition on raising money for land claims. Yet this in no way led to land security. In 1952 the Witsuwit'en neighbors to the east, the Cheslatta Carrier, were driven from their traditional lands and their village when their land was flooded by a dam built without their consent and consideration. In 1967 the territory of the Sekanni Indians to their northeast was flooded—by another dam, again without consultation and consent. In 1969 Jean Chrétien, the Minister of Aboriginal Affairs, and Prime Minister Pierre Trudeau sought to change Indian policy so that Indians would no longer have rights to their reserves, let alone their traditional territories.

In the 1950s the Gitxsan Eagle Clan began to block logging on their territory done without their consent. Since then logging corporations have been augmenting the size of the blocks of timber they control and instituting clear cutting (in which the land is stripped bare of all trees and brush) to the grave concern of the chiefs. At the same time, the chiefs were becoming increasingly concerned about the salmon stocks, which were dwindling as a result of excessive harvesting by fishing boats from many countries off the coast. The Department of Fisheries and Oceans mistakenly attributed the decline to rocks in the Bulkley and Skeena Rivers which, they thought, were impeding the salmon from returning up the rivers to spawn. In 1959 the Department of Fisheries and Oceans blasted a major rock from the Hagwilget Canyon, as well as rocks in the Kya Wiget/Moricetown Canyon, destroying the fishing at Hagwilget and the fishing sites of many chiefs at Kya Wiget. These actions were taken without consultation with the Gitxsan or the Witsuwit'en.

Today out-migration continues. Since television has entered every home, fewer children are learning their native language. Loss of language is recognized as serious. At the same time, the Witsuwit'en and Gitxsan find the ability to speak and read and write English has also been necessary, equipping them to make effective responses to the threats the government and settlers pose to them.

RESPONSE: STRUGGLES TO SURVIVE CULTURALLY

The response to the decimation of the salmon sites was to readjust where the affected houses could get their fish. But there was a larger sense that something had to be done to secure recognition of their rights to their territories following the lead of their neighbor, the Nisga'a. The Nisga'a challenged the government in the famous Calder case, regarding their rights to their traditional territory. In 1973 the Supreme Court of Canada ruled in the Calder case that First Nations rights to land have not been extinguished and must be considered.[13] The Nisga'a Treaty was finally ratified on April 13, 2000, long delayed by a filibuster supported by right-wing coalitions and politicians hopeful of making political capital from the resistance of some part of the population to conclude modern-day treaties creating a "third order of government."[14]

In 1977 the federal government accepted the Gitxsan and Witsuwit'en declaration for land claims negotiation. In 1982 the Canadian Constitution, in Section 35 (1), established that aboriginal title exists, but it still remained to be seen how that would be interpreted. Therefore, in 1984, the Gitxsan and Witsuwit'en filed their statement of claim to demonstrate ownership and jurisdiction over their traditional territories. Witsuwit'en and Gitxsan had used their education in western traditions well; they were aware of the rights they had from the Royal Proclamation of 1763 before the courts ruled on this issue. Thirty-nine Gitxsan head chiefs and twelve Witsuwit'en head chiefs took this action on behalf of their house members and their traditional territories, encompassing 22,000 square miles and all the people except the people of Kitwancool, who opted to negotiate separately. In May

1987 the testimony of the Gitxsan and Witsuwit'en chiefs began in the courthouse in Smithers, the largest town in Witsuwit'en territory.

The court case was an epic. The Witsuwit'en and Gitxsan were certain that this would be their chance to have their hereditary chiefs tell their story. To do this they established their own translation school to prepare bilingual Gitxsan and Witsuwit'en speakers to translate for the chiefs who gave their testimony in their own language. Three years later the testimony ended, and on March 8, 1991, Chief Justice Allan McEachern rendered his decision: aboriginal title had been extinguished at the time of confederation. To add insult to injury he said that the lives of the Witsuwit'en and Gitxsan were, as English philosopher Thomas Hobbes said, "nasty, brutish, and short."[15] In fact the full quote from McEachern is, "It would not be accurate that even pre-contact existence in the territory was in the least bit idyllic. The plaintiffs' ancestors had no written language, no horses or wheeled vehicles, slavery and starvation was not uncommon, and there is no doubt, to quote Hobbs [*sic*], that aboriginal life in the territory was, at best, nasty, brutish, and short."[16] The Gitxsan and Witsuwit'en immediately filed an appeal. In 1993 the provincial court set aside the McEachern decision, declaring that the Gitxsan and Witsuwit'en have "unextinguished non-exclusive aboriginal rights other than the right of ownership to their traditional territory."[17] The Gitxsan and Witsuwit'en then entered into treaty negotiations to determine whether they could hammer out acceptable treaties. British Columbia withdrew from negotiations with the Gitxsan because some head chiefs had set up blockades to stop clear-cut logging in their territories. The Gitxsan and Witsuwit'en therefore took their case to the Supreme Court of Canada.

On December 11, 1997, the Supreme Court of Canada ruled that aboriginal title exists and includes subsurface mineral rights and rights to modern activities (e.g., logging). The Delgamuukw decision established criteria for demonstrating title including the use of oral traditions. That decision also said that Chief Justice McEachern was in error when he refused to accord legal validity to the oral traditions of the Gitxsan and Witsuwit'en. The court ruled that, in the absence of historical documents, oral traditions must be considered as evidence of occupation at the time of confederation. The decision stated that if McEachern had listened to the Witsuwit'en and Gitxsan oral traditions, he might have ruled differently; since he did not, the Gitxsan and Witsuwit'en must go back to the treaty negotiating table or go back to court to get a declaration that the traditional territories they claim are theirs. Although the decision specified conditions that could infringe on the exclusive right of ownership, such as using the land in an environmentally unsustainable way, the decision itself represents a major victory and breakthrough in recognizing that the Gitxsan and Witsuwit'en, as all aboriginal people, have unextinguished rights to their territory, not simply to tiny parcels relegated as reserves.

By autumn 2000 the Gitxsan were on the brink of returning to court despite the cost, because they have found the Crown unwilling to entertain what they are asking for based on the Delgamuukw decision. The Gitxsan house chiefs have been forging sustainable development plans for their territories with the province and with Canada. The Witsuwit'en are continuing treaty negotiations and have signed a political accord concerning land and resources with the province and Canada, with particular reference to forestry.[18]

Immersion pre-schools and kindergarten classes are currently trying to stem the tide of language loss. The Witsuwit'en and Gitxsan have each taken over the administration of alternate justice systems which are applied in many instances, based on House affiliation and instructing offenders in the traditional means of settling disputes and compensating the injured party.

FOOD FOR THOUGHT

Since 1997, when the Supreme Court of Canada rendered its decision in the Delgamuukw case, affirming that aboriginal title exists and is an exclusive right to land, both the Witsuwit'en and Gitxsan have tried to advance their land claims through the treaty negotiation process, to little avail. On the first anniversary of this important decision, the Gitxsan decided to take their case back to court because they had made no progress in moving the province in treaty negotiations, yet continued some negotiations. In the first year of the Supreme Court decision, the Witsuwit'en succeeded in getting one of the several district ministry of forests offices to acknowledge that there are hereditary chiefs in charge of the territories who must be consulted regarding any timber licenses granted on their territory. Small as this advance was, it was a major concession on the part of the Ministry of Forests. It does not solve the problems of the colonial divide-and-conquer policy: both the Gitxsan and Witsuwit'en have to contend with the bureaucracy that has them dealing separately with the Department of Fisheries and Oceans regarding rights to fish stocks, fishing sites, and rights to sell fish; separately with the Ministry of the Environment about concerns with timber licenses; separately with provincial and federal treaty negotiators; and so on. By 1999 the Witsuwit'en had reestablished five clan cabins out on their territories.

In 1998 Witsuwit'en Herb George, Chief Satsan, who is also the vice chief of the National Assembly of First Nations, stated that nothing had changed since the Delgamuukw decision a year before. The province of British Columbia acted as though the decision had not come down, meanwhile urging ratification of the Nisga'a Treaty, which was written before the Delgamuukw decision. The Nisga'a Treaty grants the Nisga'a ownership to only 8 percent of their claimed traditional territory, following the policy the Province of British Columbia had established *before* the Supreme Court Delgamuukw decision. Among Euro-Canadians, opposition even to the Nisga'a Treaty has been vociferous. The official opposition to the party in power in the province claimed (without legal authority) that all the citizens of the province should have the right to vote for or against the Nisga'a Treaty. Interest groups held extralegal (meaning they have no official status) plebiscites to demonstrate opposition to the Nisga'a Treaty.[19] Nonetheless, the Nisga'a Treaty was finally ratified on April 13, 2000.

It gives one food for thought when two legally binding decisions have come down in the form of the Supreme Court Delgamuukw decision and the Marshall decision regarding Micmae fishing rights but neither Canadian federal officials nor the provincial ones seem to have any will or interest in abiding by them apparently because they fear that they will not be reelected if they act in accordance with the rulings, which recognize First Nations as having ownership rights and decision-making powers over their traditional territories. Both the Gitxsan and Witsuwit'en have been attempting to work out comanagement agreements, which would place decisions about what resources would be extracted from the Gitxsan and Witsuwit'en territories jointly in the hands of the head chief of the affected territories and the relevant government agency (Forestry, Fisheries, and so on). What is becoming apparent, however, is that it is very difficult for the government, at any of its levels, to acknowledge that the Witsuwit'en and Gitxsan chiefs have relevant and valid authority and knowledge over these matters. The colonial mentality that assumes that it is best for native peoples to be ruled by others is tenacious.

The Gitxsan and Witsuwit'en chiefs remain concerned about the degradation of their territories and the endangered quality of the salmon and the environment. They have a strong sense of having lived in their homelands for a very long time, and they are committed to keeping their homelands intact. They are willing to negotiate in good faith and to share many aspects of their territories with outsiders and settlers. But they also remain adamant that they will do whatever it takes, whether blockades or legal action, to ensure that their communally held house territories survive.

The challenges are not small. They must demonstrate that the territories were held by the hereditary chiefs in 1845, and they must do this by using oral traditions which the courts, though compelled to accept as evidence, are ill equipped to comprehend. Questions of overlap between neighboring First Nations must also be resolved, to each party's agreement. To resolve such issues so that eagle down, a traditional symbol of accord, can be distributed between the neighboring aboriginal peoples and the Gitxsan and the Witsuwit'en, and between the federal and provincial government and the Canadian citizenry will require a dismantling of the colonial mentality that assumes "white people know best." To conduct meaningful cross-cultural communication based on the concept "we are all here to stay," stated in the final Delgamuukw decision, requires a conceptual leap. The provincial and federal governments and their citizenry must acknowledge that they need to respect the Witsuwit'en and Gitxsan people, rather than assuming or demanding their assimilation or extinction. In the meantime, the question of who has rights to their traditional territories and their resources remains unresolved.

Questions

1. What impact do you think the Delgamuukw Supreme Court ruling will have on (a) the way in which the Gitxsan and Witsuwit'en will be able to control what happens in their traditional territories, (b) the way in which timber and mining companies will consult with aboriginal peoples, (c) land claims cases by aboriginal peoples in other parts of Canada, and (d) land claims cases in other parts of the world?

2. Do you think the Delgamuukw decision will make non-native citizenry and multinational corporations respect aboriginal peoples, now recognized as having aboriginal title to their traditional territories? Why or why not?

3. How do you think respect can be promoted between people with different visions of what is the best use for the territories?

4. The Delgamuukw decision gives the Gitxsan and Witsuwit'en exclusive right to the resources on their territories. Do you think that big commercial interests, such as mining companies and timber companies, will continue their effort to negate the two groups' exclusive rights and use of these valuable assets? What tactics might the companies use?

5. How would you recommend the Delgamuukw decision be implemented now and in the future?

NOTES

This chapter was prepared with the consent and assistance of the Gitxsan and Witsuwit'en nations. Their assistance is gratefully acknowledged.

1. James A. McDonald, Janice Tollefsen, and Barbara Milmine, eds., *Delgamuukw: We're All Here to Stay: Forum on the Implications of the Delgamuukw Decision for Northern British Columbia* (Prince George: University of Northern British Columbia, 1998), 31.

2. Data from the Office of the Gitxsan and Office of the Witsuwit'en.

3. The Northwest Coast societies are found on the Pacific Coast of North America from northern California through Oregon, Washington, British Columbia (Canada) to southern Alaska. Northwest Coast societies are noted for having the highest population density of any nonagricultural society, based on their use of the rich resources of salmon, other fishes, and sea mammals, as well as plants and animals on the land. Each of the distinct Northwest Coast societies had settled villages by the ocean or along salmon-rich rivers. Typically in Northwest Coast villages a number of large longhouses were located along the shore, each with the

design of the house's crests carved and painted on the front, and also often with a totem or crest pole placed in front. Such crests or totem poles are the most dramatic examples of the distinctive Northwest Coast artistic tradition. For illustrations of Northwest Coast art, see Doreen Jensen and Polly Sargent, *Robes of Power: Totem Poles on Cloth* (Vancouver: University of British Columbia Press, 1987) and Gary Wyatt, *Mythic Beings: Spirit Art of the Northwest Coast* (Vancouver: Douglas and McIntyre, 1999). The Northwest Coast is also famous for having lavish potlatches in which a person, who was taking a new hereditary title with associated rights over a particular territory, distributed gifts to the people from the surrounding villages who were invited to witness this succession of titles, the erection of totem poles, and the funeral potlatch for deceased chiefs.

4. The Northwest Coast peoples, and particularly the northern Northwest Coast peoples, are typically made up of clans, such as Raven, Eagle, Wolf, and Killer whale. Membership in clans is determined by different principles in the southern, central, and northern regions. In the northern Northwest Coast region, clan membership is based on one's matriline, or one's mother's clan. The totems for the clans typically relate to the oral traditions about the founding of the villages. Clans too large to live in a single longhouse divided long ago into a series of distinct houses each with a separate line of chiefs with rights to different fishing sites and territories. The houses of one clan work together and are seated together at potlatches. For a chart that shows the relation of the Haida, Tlingit, Tahltan, Tsimshian, Nisga'a, Gitxsan, Witsuwit'en and Carrier clan systems, see Antonia Mills, *Eagle Down Is Our Law: Witsuwit'en Laws, Feasts, and Land Claims* (Vancouver: University of British Columbia Press, 1994), 104. For a table that shows how the Witsuwit'en houses fit into the clans, see Mills, *Eagle Down*, 108.

5. Readers interested in knowing more about the Northwest Coast potlatch traditions will find Mills, *Eagle Down*, a useful resource for the Witsuwit'en. For a detailed depiction of Gitxsan potlatches of the 1940s, see Margaret Anderson and Marjorie Halpin, eds., *Potlatch at Gitsegulka: William Benynon's 1945 Field Notebooks* (Vancouver: University of British Columbia Press, 2000). The U'Mista Society's 1979 video *Potlatch: A Strict Law Bids Us Dance* depicts the suppression and resurrection of the Kwakiutl potlatch, but each of the northwest groups practiced the potlatch in their own ways.

6. Don Monet, and Skanu'u (Ardyth Wilson), *Colonialism on Trial: Indigenous Land Rights and the Gitksan and Wet'suwet'en Sovereignty Case* (Gabriola Island, British Columbia: New Society Publishers, 1992), 13.

7. Totem animals are supernatural beings who assisted the founders of a clan, as related in the clan's oral traditions. See Diamond Jenness, "The Carrier Indians of the Bulkley River: Their Social and Religious Life," *Anthropological Papers*, Bureau of American Ethnology Bulletin 133, no. 25 (1943): 469–586, for accounts of the Witsuwit'en oral traditions that depict these totem or ancestral creatures, such as Frog, Bear, Wolf, and Beaver. For examples of Gitxsan and Tsimshian oral traditions, see Marius Barbeau, *The Downfall of Temlaham* (Toronto: Macmillan, 1928); Franz Boas, *Tsimshian Mythology, Thirty-First Annual Report of the Bureau of American Ethnology for the Years 1909–1910* (Washington, D.C.: Smithsonian Institution, 1916); John Cove and George MacDonald, eds., *Tsimshian Narratives, Vol 1: Tricksters, Shamans, and Heroes*, Mercury Series no. 3 (Hull, Quebec: Canadian Museum of Civilization, 1987); Wilson Duff, ed., *Histories, Territories and*

Laws of the Kitwancool (Victoria, British Columbia: Royal British Columbia Museum, 1989); George MacDonald and John Cove, eds., *Tsimshian Narratives, Vol 2: Trade and Warfare*, Mercury Series no. 3 (Hull, Quebec: Canadian Museum of Civilization, 1987); and Kenneth B. Harris, *Visitors Who Never Left: The Origin of the People of Damelahamid*, translated by Kenneth B. Harris in collaboration with Frances M.P. Robinson, Vancouver, British Columbia: University of British Columbia Press, 1974).

8. For accounts of the nature and prevalence of reincarnation concepts not only for the Gitxsan, but also particularly for the Inuit and subarctic peoples, see Antonia Mills and Richard Slobodin, *Amerindian Rebirth: Reincarnation Belief Among North American Indians and Inuit* (Toronto: University of Toronto Press, 1994).

9. Joseph Trutch, "Report on the Lower Indian Reserves, 28 August 1867," in *Papers Connected with the Indian Land Question, 1850–1875* (Victoria, British Columbia: Government Printing Office, 1875), p. 42.

10. James A. McDonald, and Jennifer Joseph, "Key Events in the Gitksan Encounter with the Colonial World." In *Potlatch at Gitsegukla: William Beynon's 1945 Field Notebooks*, edited by Margaret Anderson and Marjorie Halpin (Vancouver, British Columbia: University of British Columbia Press, 2000), 199.

11. Paul Tennant, *Aboriginal Peoples and Politics: The Land Question in British Columbia, 1849–1989* (Vancouver, British Columbia: University of British Columbia Press, 1990), 16.

12. Many formerly disenfranchised Gitxsan and Witsuwit'en have sought to be reinstated as being status Indians, and some have returned to their home communities. The government, however, has established a procedure which allows the children of the sons of a reinstated woman to have Indian status (but not their children) and disallows the children of the daughters of a woman who is reinstated.

13. The term "First Nations" is used particularly in Western Canada today to refer to Native or Indian or aboriginal peoples. The Assembly of First Nations was founded in the 1950s with this title to emphasize that the First Nations/Indians were on the continent first and also to make people more aware that treaties had not been made with the vast majority of the native peoples of British Columbia, Canada.

14. Both the Liberal Party of British Columbia, Canada, the Conservative Party, and the new Alliance Party of Canada at times question whether there is a constitutional right to establish treaties with the First Nations of Canada, despite the entrenchment of aboriginal rights in the Canadian Constitution Act of 1982. They claim that the government is establishing a third order of government, independent of the federal and provincial governments, in part based on the rights of the Nisga'a to establish their own judicial system based on Nisga'a tradition. The opposition to taking First Nations or Native rights to their land seriously is what delayed the making of treaties in British Columbia from the middle 1800s until 1999. Despite this opposition, there are approximately fifty First Nations in British Columbia currently in the process of negotiating a treaty with the provincial and federal governments of Canada.

15. Thomas Hobbes, *Leviathan* Part 1 Chapter 13, John Bartlett, *Familiar Quotations* (Boston: Little, Brown and Co., 1955).

16. *Delgamuukw v. British Columbia 1991. Reasons for Judgment*, no. 0843, Smithers Registry [Reasons for Judgment of Chief Justice Allan McEachern].

17. Supreme Court of Canada, Delgamuukw Decision, File no. 23799, p. 3.

18. Antonia Mills, "Three Years after Delgamuukw: The Continuing Battle over Respect for First Nations Interests to their Traditional Territories and Rights to Work their Resources," *Anthropology of Work Review* vol. 21, no. 2 (summer, 2000): 21–29.

19. The Delgamuukw decision was cited in the Marshall decision of September 1999, which gave the Eastern Canadian Mi'kmaq of Nova Scotia rights to make a modest living by selling eels and, by extension, other fish and lobster without being subject to Department of Oceans and Fisheries regulations. Despite the Delgamuukw and the Marshall rulings, in fall 2000 the minister of fisheries and oceans, finding it expedient to side with the irate non-native fishermen rather than the Supreme Court ruling, ordered the seizure of Mi'kmaq lobster traps and the ramming of two lobster boats. See *National Post* [Toronto], September 22, 2000, 1; *CBC Newsworld Online*, August 30, 2000; "Hundreds of Lobster Traps Seized in Latest DFO Raid" http://cbc.ca/cgibin/templates/view.cgi?/news/2000/08/29/burnt churcha000829; Chris. August 29, 2000, "Two Indian Boats Sink During Dispute with Canadian Fisheries Officials." The Associated Press State & Local Wire. http://www.ap.org/

RESOURCE GUIDE

Published Literature

Anderson, Margaret, and Marjorie Halpin, eds. *Potlatch at Gitsegukla: William Benynon's 1945 Field Notebooks*. Vancouver: University of British Columbia Press, 2000.

Asch, Michael, ed. *Aboriginal and Treaty Rights in Canada: Essays on Law, Equality, and Respect for Difference*. Vancouver: University of British Columbia Press, 1997.

Barbeau, Marius. *The Downfall of Temlahan*. Toronto: Macmillan, 1928.

Boas, Franz. *Tsimshian Mythology, Based on Texts Provided by Henry Tate*. Thirty-First Annual Report of the Bureau of American Ethnology for the Years 1909–10. Washington D.C.: Smithsonian Institution, 1916.

Cassidy, Frank, ed. *Aboriginal Title in British Columbia: Delgamuukw v. the Queen*. Lantzville, British Columbia: Oolichan Books and the Institute for Research on Public Policy, 1992.

Cove, John, and George MacDonald, eds. *Tsimshian Narratives*, vol. 1, *Tricksters, Shamans & Heroes*. Mercury Series no. 3. Hull, Quebec: Canadian Museum of Civilization, 1987.

Culhane, Dara. *The Pleasure of the Crown: Anthropology, Law and First Nations*. Burnaby, British Columbia: Talon Books, 1998.

Delgamuukw v. British Columbia, Reasons for Judgment, No. 0843, Smithers Registry [Reasons for Judgment of Chief Justice Allan McEachern], 1991.

Duff, Wilson, ed. *Histories, Territories and Laws of the Kitwancool*. Victoria: Royal British Columbia Museum, 1928.

Fife, Robert, "All Signs Pointing to Fall Election: From Gas to EI to Fisheries,

Chrétien Government Tries to Curry Favor with Voters." *National Post* [Toronto], September 22, 2000, 1.

Gisday Wa, and Delgam Uuk. *The Spirit in the Land: The Opening Statement of the Gitxsan and Wet'suwet'en Hereditary Chiefs in the Supreme Court of British Columbia* Gabriola, British Columbia: Reflections, 1989.

Harris, Kenneth B. *Visitors Who Never Left: The Origin of the People of Damelahamid.* Trans. and arr. by Kenneth B. Harris in collaboration with Frances M. P. Robinson. Vancouver: University of British Columbia Press, 1974.

Jenness, Diamond. "The Carrier Indians of the Bulkley River: Their Social and Religious Life. *Anthropological Papers, Bureau of American Ethnology Bulletin* 133, no. 25 (1943): 469–586.

Jensen, Doreen, and Polly Sargent. *Robes of Power: Totem Poles on Cloth.* Vancouver: University of British Columbia Press, 1987.

MacDonald, George, and John Cove, eds. *Tsimshian Narratives*, vol. 2, *Trade and Warfare.* Mercury Series no. 3. Hull, Quebec: Canadian Museum of Civilization, 1987.

McDonald, James A., and Jennifer Joseph, "Key Events in the Gitksan Encounter with the Colonial World." In *Potlatch at Gitsegukla: William Beynon's 1945 Field Notebooks.* Margaret Anderson and Marjorie Halpin, eds., Vancouver, BC. UBC Press, 193–214.

McDonald, James A., Janice Tollefsen, and Barbara Milmine, eds. *Delgamuukw: We're All Here to Stay: Forum on the Implications of the Delgamuukw Decision for Northern British Columbia.* Prince George, British Columbia: University of Northern British Columbia, 1998.

Mills, Antonia. *Eagle Down Is Our Law: Witsuwit'en Laws, Feasts and Land Claims.* Vancouver: University of British Columbia Press, 1994.

———. "Three Years After Delgamuukw: The Continuing Battle over Respect for First Nations Interests to Their Traditional Territories and Rights to Work Their Resources. *Anthropology of Work Review*, vol. 21, no. 2 (summer 2000): 21–29.

Mills, Antonia, and Richard Slobodin. *Amerindian Rebirth: Reincarnation Belief Among North American Indians and Inuit.* Toronto: University of Toronto Press, 1994.

Monet, Don, and Skanu'u (Ardyth Wilson). *Colonialism on Trial: Indigenous Land Rights and the Gitksan and Wet'suwet'en Sovereignty Case.* Gabriola Island, British Columbia: New Society Publishers, 1992.

Morris, Chris. "Two Indian Boats Sink During Dispute with Canadian Fisheries Officials." Associated Press, August 29, 2000. http://www.ap.org/.

Sterritt, Neil J. "Gitksan and Wet'suwet'en: Unflinching Resistance to an Implacable Invader." In *Drum Beat: Anger and Renewal in Indian Country*, edited by Boyce Richardson, 265–94. Toronto: Summerhill Press, 1989.

Tennant, Paul. *Aboriginal Peoples and Politics: The Land Question in British Columbia, 1849–1989.* Vancouver, British Columbia: University of British Columbia Press, 1990.

'Wii Muk'willixw (Ardyth, Wilson). *Heartbeat of the Earth.* Gabriola Island, British Columbia: New Society Publishers, 1996.

Wyatt, Gary. *Mythic Beings: Spirit Art of the Northwest Coast.* Vancouver, British Columbia: Douglas and McIntyre, 1999.

Films & Videos

Blockade: It's About the Land and Who Controls It. Montreal: National Film Board, 1993. *On Indian Land: Gitksan and Wet'suwet'en History.* Gixtsan-Witsuwit'en Tribal Council, 1987.
Potlatch: A Strict Law Bids Us Dance. U'Mista Society. Video: Alert Bay, 1979.

WWW Sites

Delgamuukw
http://www.droit.umontreal.ca/doc/csc-scc/en/rec/html/delgamii.en.html

Witsuwit'en
http://otaku.unbc.ca/bc_aboriginal/

Organizations

Office of the Witsuwit'en
RR 1 Box 25 Site 15
Moricetown BC V0J 2N0

Office of the Gitxsan
P.O. Box 115
Hazelton BC V0J 1Y0

Chapter 5

The Hopi in Arizona

Miguel Vasquez

CULTURAL OVERVIEW

The People

In the midst of the remote and rugged high desert of northeastern Arizona, just east of the Grand Canyon, lives one of the most traditional Native American groups in the United States. The Hopi, a tribe of about 10,000 people today, live in thirteen villages on or around the three flat-topped mesas that make up most of their reservation. They are descendants of the Anasazi (or *Hisatsinom*, as they prefer), the ancestral Pueblo people who built many of the famous ruins throughout the Four Corners area that visitors come to see today. For much of their long history, the Hopi have lived in relative isolation, protected by a vast desert landscape which, until recently, held little appeal for outsiders. Today, encircled by the much larger Navajo Reservation and the rapidly growing populations of the Southwest, they are no longer alone.

Perhaps nowhere else in North America has a native people been so closely associated with a specific natural landscape over so long a period of time as the Hopi. Their small, densely populated villages, or pueblos, are among the oldest continuously inhabited communities on the continent. Pueblo, a Spanish word meaning village, town, or people, has been applied to Hopis and other Southwest Indian groups living in multistoried stone or adobe farming communities. As much as any other native group in the country, most of the 10,000 Hopi have maintained much of their ancient culture in the midst of the rapid and constant change of modern, mainstream American life. Now, however, while their way of life continues to

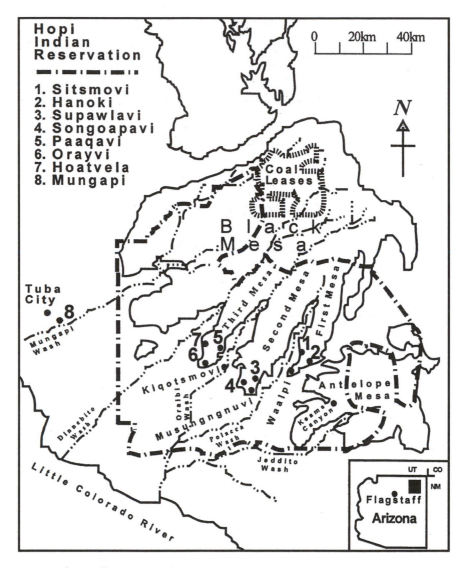

Hopi Indian Villages in northeastern Arizona. Map: Javier Guerrero.

provide a meaningful and important guide to living for most Hopi, the pressures of the mainstream society threaten it more than ever. These pressures are environmental, economic, social, and cultural. Although the Hopi have survived many outsiders' predictions of their cultural destruction over the past 150 years of contact with the dominant American culture, the pressure for change today is even more intense.

Recently a tribal chairman explained why the Hopi, as ancient agriculturists, with all the fertile and abundant farmland available in North America, had chosen to live here, in the Four Corners, "on top of a pile of rocks." The Hopi settled where they did because here they encountered Ma'saw, the Caretaker of the Earth. With him, he had only a gourd of water, a planting stick, and a pouch of corn seed. This for the Hopi signaled the humility and hardship that they had chosen in the previous world as the path to living in the right way. They knew that it would force them to live close to the earth, in small villages, and with good hearts, which would protect them from the corruption they had escaped in the lands to the south. If they had settled in a lush, fertile, desirable place, other groups would always be after their land and their wealth; if they lived in a place no one wanted, they would be left alone. This isolation, hundreds of miles from major population centers, has, in fact, played an important historic role in protecting and maintaining the Hopi culture for generations.[1]

The Setting

It appears to an outsider that the Hopi could not have chosen a worse place for farming. This high desert environment is a harsh land. Spring is cool and windy, summers are hot and dry, fall is short and cool, and winters are cold and long. Rising from a sea of sand and sage and rabbit brush, three massive sandstone ridges—First, Second, and Third Mesa—point south from Black Mesa, the high pinyon and juniper-studded plateau that dominates much of northeastern Arizona. On or around these mesas are the thirteen compact, densely settled stone villages that are home to the Hopi. This land, though beautiful in its stark vastness, is barren, rugged, rocky, and apparently poor in any kind of resource except sunshine, sand, and rock. Surprisingly however, deep beneath the mesas, are two resources that are vital in the rapidly growing Southwest: water and energy. The N-aquifer, a vast underground reservoir, which underlies this area, stores a huge quantity of water. This "fossil" water, so-called because it has collected there in the sandstone bedrock over millions of years, has only recently been tapped for coal-mining operations on Black Mesa.

Traditional Subsistence Strategies

This high desert environment, between 5,000 and 6,000 feet in altitude, with a short growing season, less than ten inches of rainfall per year, and frequent drying winds, would challenge the best farmers anywhere. Traditionally, the Hopi grew corn, beans, squash, melons, and other crops here without irrigation; they also hunted and gathered many plants for food, medicinal, and ceremonial purposes. At small perennial springs on the sides of the mesas, they undertook intensive, irrigated terrace gardening. When the Spanish colonists came north from Mexico into the Southwest, beginning in the seventeenth century, the Hopi saw new opportunities and began to grow fruit trees, chiles, onions, and other new crops. They also learned how to raise sheep, cattle, horses, goats, and burros on the rangeland around their villages. Still, the Hopi are best known as dry farmers who can grow plants with minimal amounts of moisture. Over the centuries, their way of saving seeds and planting them deeply into the moisture remaining from winter snows in the clay subsoil beneath the sand has allowed the Hopi to develop a culture centered on the production of corn.

Social and Political Organization

Although Hopi men are the ones who grow the corn, the cornfield, the family home, and almost everything else of importance traditionally passes through the woman's line. The Hopi are a matrilineal society—family and inheritance are traced and transmitted through the mother's line. A baby is born into its mother's clan, and much of its life will be centered on this clan. Hopi clans are closely associated with elements of nature (e.g., Bear, Sun, Reed, and Sand) and signify to the Hopi their place among the members of the natural world. As children grow, they come to learn more of the responsibilities that are a part of their place as Hopis. These lifelong responsibilities to the clan begin at birth, become more numerous at initiation into adulthood, and never cease. Hopi society is focused on responsibilities: to immediate family, to extended family, to clan, to religious societies, to the village, and to the tribe. This view is very different from the emphasis on civil, individual, or property rights, which are dominant in the Euro-American society.

It was not until 1936, when the U.S. government imposed the Hopi Tribal Government as part of the Indian Reorganization Act, that any Hopi government larger than independent villages existed. The legitimacy of this alien, centralized authority is still questioned by some Hopi. Two villages refuse to recognize the council's authority but regard it as a creation and a tool of the *pahana* (white man), and do not send representatives because they regard it. Villages are governed either by a *kikmongwi* (traditional religious leader) or by a governor and a village board adapted from the Anglo system. The reservation, although ultimately controlled by the U.S. Secretary of the Interior, is governed day to day by the Hopi Tribal Council, which has representatives from each village and a chairman and a vice chairman.

Religion and World View

For the Hopi, as for many native peoples, it is wrong to separate religion from the rest of life. They are understood as one and the same. In fulfilling the promise of stewardship—their agreement to care for the land given to them—their religion is necessarily an active rather than passive part of their lives. Farming, for example, is not only an economic activity. In the midst of a desert, without irrigation or modern technology, it becomes an act of faith. As part of the lesson of the need for hard work and humility in life, farming is something that Hopi families have done for generations to identify anew with the earth and with the teachings of their ancestors. Throughout the summer months, people gather in the village plazas to witness *katsina* ceremonies, when Hopis pray to be blessed with rain. Hopis dance for rain, sing for it, and pray for it in many different ways. Rain and snowmelt replenish the earth's waters so that all of life will benefit, be in balance, and, as the Hopis say, "be happy." The natural world here is not one of spiritless, unconscious plants and animals, as taught by Western science, but one in which the Hopi inhabit with all organisms the same natural and moral world. Hopis have, so to speak, "both a moral ecology and an ecological morality."[2] This ancient and holistic orientation to nature is worlds apart from modern, mainstream America, which, to the Hopi, often seems out of balance and moving much too fast.

THREATS TO SURVIVAL

The word "Hopi" can be translated as "one who follows the path." It not only signifies a people, but also a place and connection of the people to that place. Hopis regard this path as a vital, extremely practical guide to the difficulties of human existence. While community identification with this tradition remains relatively strong, both economic and ecological changes have occurred, especially since World War II, which continue to erode Hopi's direct experience of nature and their connection to tradition. Hopi agriculture generally experienced a major decline during the 1960s and 1970s as more and more families turned to wage work for their livelihoods, away from even small-scale farming. New cash income opportunities for Hopi people have been created. Road construction, ending centuries of physical isolation, and dramatic expansion of the tribal bureaucracy during the 1970s have transformed the local economy. So too have new federal programs, tribally sponsored development projects, and blossoming national and international markets for Indian arts and crafts. Yet, although most Hopis recognize the need for economic development if they are to have any control over their lives, they refuse to give in to the dominant influences of mainstream America. Cultural survival—the capacity to weave ancient traditions and modern lifeways—is a constant concern for the Hopi, and current threats include controversies over the environment and resources, joblessness, and the erosion of culture and language.

Environment and Resources

To the Hopi, nature and the land are much more than sources of wealth, as property or real estate, to be bought or sold. As Chairman Wayne Taylor, Jr., has explained

Our home is a place of destiny, a place where we belong and where we are free to work out our lives as we choose. Finally, it is the place where we keep our obligations to the Creator, who gave us this land on the condition that we care for it as part of a sacred stewardship. In exchange for this commitment, the land shares with us the blessings of its beauty and the blessings of life itself.[3]

It is ironic that part of the threat to the Hopi land base has come from another Native American group—the Navajo—who regard the land in much the same way. Events over the past three centuries have laid the foundations for what is now known as the Navajo-Hopi land dispute. Latecomers to the Southwest, the Navajo, like the Apache, are an Athapaskan people who migrated south from Canada over generations, probably arriving in the Four Corners area just after A.D. 1500. The Navajo, an extremely adaptive hunting and gathering group, learned to take advantage of what they found on the landscape. From the pueblos in New Mexico they learned farming and weaving. From the Spanish they acquired sheep, cattle, and horses. But it was not until Euro-American aggression drove them westward that Navajos began to occupy the Hopi homeland in disruptive numbers. As part of the 1868 peace treaty, Navajos were given reservation land to homestead, along with tools, seeds, and sheep. This reservation, however, included traditional land long claimed by the Hopi. In 1882, with little understanding of who was living where, the U.S. government drew lines on a map and declared a Joint Use Area (JUA) for both tribes to use. This arrangement imposed alien ideas of legalistic ownership and sovereignty instead of the traditional use patterns that were known and accepted locally. From the beginning, both Navajo and Hopi found the JUA unsatisfactory, and many lawsuits have been filed. In 1974 Congress called for the partition of the JUA into Hopi and Navajo areas and the relocation of those Indians living on the opposite side of the partition line. More than 8,000 Navajo and about 100 Hopi were affected. Most moved, but neither group was happy about it. This controversy continues today, with minor daily conflicts on the range between cattlemen and farmers on both sides and intense intertribal politics over various issues. Now surrounded by the Navajo Reservation and outnumbered roughly twenty to one by the Navajo, the Hopi consider their opportunities limited in terms of land base, economy, and political clout relative to their neighbors. Because both tribes need more land for growing populations, the land struggle continues.

In the 1960s, the opening of coal strip-mining operations by the Peabody Coal Company on Black Mesa, in the JUA, increased tremendously the value of what many outsiders had regarded as a wasteland. The land dispute intensified. Hopis had used coal for hundreds of years as a local source of fuel to heat their homes and fire their pottery, but this was the first time industrial exploitation and use had been attempted here. While some object to coal strip-mining as the "raping of Mother Earth," most Hopis consider it necessary to help finance tribal programs. Although the mines also provide well-paid employment, most of the jobs are held by Navajos who live in the area, or by non-Indians from outside the reservation area.

The rich coal deposits of the Four Corners area also play an important role in the sustainability of another, even more vital resource—water. With fewer than ten inches of rainfall per year, water has always been scarce, and Hopis have had to learn over the years to carefully conserve what little moisture there is. These days, however, industrial mining, together with a growing population, has created a serious problem. The tribe is very much dependent on coal revenues from their leases to Peabody Coal Company; as much as 80 percent of the tribal funds now come from this and are used for many programs which provide goods, services, and jobs for tribal members.[4] At the same time, the below-market price, which the tribe receives for high-quality coal from these operations, shortchanges the Hopi but provides cheap energy for the rapidly growing Southwest. The coal mining also presents several major environment versus economy dilemmas for the Hopi that have no easy answers.

The first problem is water. Coal from the mine is finely ground, mixed with water, and transported in a slurry line through a pipeline across northern Arizona to a coal-fired electrical generating plant near Las Vegas, Nevada. The process consumes as much as 4,000 acre feet of water per year. By comparison, the entire population of the Hopi and Navajo reservations (approximately 250,000 people) consumes less than this amount in a typical year, and the Hopis' consumption of water now averages between 10 to 40 gallons per day, compared with the 200 gallons per day average for the Southwest.[5] As tribal populations grow, demand increases for indoor plumbing, and a higher standard of living. As a result, the need for water is expected to increase by six times in the next fifty years. The Hopi worry that the ancient aquifer may not be able to supply both the mine and their future communities.

A second dilemma from the coal operations involves the generating plant and the pollution of the once crystal-clear air over the nearby Grand Canyon. Smokestack scrubbers to clean up these emissions are very expensive and, when pressed by tribes and environmentalists, the plant's owners threaten to sell or close down the plant rather than clean up the emissions. Yet, both the Hopi Tribe and the Navajo Nation need the coal revenues in the short term to overcome the rampant poverty on both reservations. Their dilemma is whether to push hard for lowered pollution and risk plant closure.

Other threats to traditional Hopi lands are occurring off the reservation in the vicinity of Flagstaff. Expansion of both ski runs and an open-pit pumice mine (to provide stone for "stone-washed" jeans) threaten the home of the *katsina* spirits, the sacred San Francisco Peaks. The Hopi, and every other tribe in the Southwest, view these activities as completely inappropriate for this holy place. Recently, a coalition of tribes and local environmentalists was able to negotiate successfully a government buyout of the pumice mine and arrange for eventual restoration of the site. Locally, this has strengthened the resolve to work for the removal of federal use permits in sacred sites. It has also forced the U.S. Forest Service to reassess its perspective on appropriate land use. Traditionally focused on resource extraction—mining, logging, and grazing—population growth, the changing economy of the West, and federal Indian law are all forcing the U.S. Forest Service to reconsider its definition of "mixed use" to include both recreational and traditional cultural uses.

Joblessness

The opportunity to make a decent, meaningful living and be able to live close to one's family and culture on the "res" (short for reservation) are what parents repeatedly express as their most important needs. This is difficult. While many families continue to farm or garden on a limited basis, all but a few aged Hopi have traded the traditional subsistence economy for the modern wage economy. Unfortunately, few long-term jobs exist on or near the reservation. The average family income is still less than $10,000 per year, and local jobless rates are around 50 percent.[6] While it took most of the United States some 200 years to replace its rural, agrarian lifestyle with the wage economy, the Hopi economy has made this change only since World War II. Lacking capital to invest, political connections, or an understanding of the competitive world of the free enterprise system, they were pushed to the margins of the economy as unskilled, short-term employees and recipients of government subsidies. There are some who now work as administrators, nurses, teachers, truck drivers, social service workers, or office workers, and others have adapted traditional arts and crafts activities to tourism or gone into construction work. But for many, employment consists of seasonal, temporary, and mixed income from several sources through the year, or working in tribal public works, or other very modest local employment possibilities. Some families also receive unemployment or some form of welfare payment.

A major question for the Hopi is how to combine valued native traditions with the lifestyle and career changes demanded by modern life. Because most people are under age twenty-five, Hopi numbers will continue to increase. More land, water, and opportunities for education and employment will be needed. As the population grows, resources will become even scarcer, forcing many to leave the Hopi reservation. The frustration that many experience in struggling with this issue leads to what are relatively new problems for the Hopi: hopelessness, alcoholism, and domestic abuse. These difficulties will likely increase as population numbers grow.

The Erosion of Culture and Language

One Hopi prophesy explains much of the dilemma the Hopi face in dealing with mainstream America. "One day a Hopi will wake up, open his door, and realize that *pahaana* (white men) have rained down all around him." It turns out though, that these *pahaana* are not necessarily white people, but rather fellow Hopis who have been influenced by the dominant culture and lost their Hopi values.[7] The prophesy captures very well the concern and misgivings of many elders about young Hopis going "off the res" where they will become educated and trained in the white man's ways. Then they return home, having lost their grounding in Hopi culture, and become influential in tribal affairs, running things in a way that is *ka'hopi* or not respectful of the Hopi way. This is the dilemma of leaders who feel the urgency for economic development. On the one hand they are strongly aware of the fact that education and training are necessary, and that those who do not have the skills and the knowledge needed to understand and manipulate the technology of the new century will be economically impoverished and politically powerless. At the same time, they are reluctant to move too quickly to make the accelerated changes if the reservation economy is to be viable in the years ahead. The task in the next decade will be for the Hopi to develop, with education, planning, and determination, ways to achieve an acceptable standard of living without destroying their culture in the process.

From the time of the Spanish, outsiders have attempted to change the Hopi. These newcomers had little understanding of the people or the land the Hopi had successfully lived on for so long. They set about to change Hopi in the Euro-American image, regarding any traditional Hopi customs as "pagan," "uncivilized," or "backward." There are important differences between Anglo and Hopi culture: attitudes about time, competitiveness versus cooperation, spirituality, family ties, decision-making processes, and responses to the pressures of modern life generally. While these ways are regarded by some today as curious or quaint cultural "survivals," in fact they are practical strategies to cope with the realities of native life in America: low and unstable incomes, limited job opportunities, prejudice, and lack of control over their own resources. In many ways, these survival strategies resemble those observed among impoverished groups anywhere.

The fact that the Hopi have lived so long in this desert area leads the Hopi to believe that the old ways have value. Although adopting and integrating contemporary technology as fast as possible might seem attractive and logical, they have not done so. The Hopi path—of clan and extended family, religion, farming, and language—is a disciplined and demanding one. It has had to be that way for people to survive in this rugged landscape. With the temptations of modern life, many Hopis wonder how many new directions the path can take before Hopi culture is lost. "Once it is gone," they say, "we will never get it back."[8]

The decline of farming and gardening is an area of special worry. For the Hopi, growing and caring for plants and working in nature not only provide food and sustenance, but also foster the development of both the inner soul and social relations. The feeling of working with nature, rather than against her; the readiness to do what is necessary without complaint; a lifestyle oriented to what nature gives, to family collaboration, and to the rhythms of the sun and the seasons—these are ways and lessons that come from working one's family's lands. But today, no more than 30 percent of the Hopi farm any longer, and parents increasingly fear that, in their search for meaning and identity, children are now looking beyond the Hopi to the dominant society.[9] They fear that "community memory" and, ultimately, Hopi culture will gradually erode.

With language the situation is even more precarious. Fewer than 5 percent of the students at Hopi High School speak their language fluently.[10] At one time earlier in this century, boarding schools punished Hopi children for speaking their language and forced them to speak English. The effects of that history are now compounded by television, the lack of Hopi teachers, and the lack of fluency in Hopi on the part of many parents. The question could be asked; "Why is Hopi language important these days if everyone speaks English?" Its importance is best understood in the ceremonies and prayers that are so much a part of Hopi life. They cannot be performed in English; English has no words to express the richness and understanding of an ancient culture that has co-evolved with this particular world of nature and spirit. Yet, how to restore the strength of the language is not clear. For example, while many are very concerned about it, there is an ongoing controversy over which of the three Hopi dialects should be taught, and whether they should be taught in a school at all.

The weakening of language is part of a larger social challenge. When children can no longer understand these ancestral ties in their full meaning, their connections to past and people and place begin to unravel. Social problems that were never a part of Hopi life, such as laziness, apathy, and selfishness, as well as drug and alcohol abuse, mistreatment of elders and children, and gang membership, become more common. Faced with all these problems, how are the Hopi responding?

RESPONSE: STRUGGLES TO SURVIVE CULTURALLY

Weaving the Threads of Ancient and Modern

In the past Hopi people have used their culture and their sociopolitical structure to deal successfully with the changes and threats they have encountered. They are still here, and despite all of the pressures, the Hopi are among the most successful of all native people in the United States in maintaining their aboriginal roots. Many tribes across the country look to the Hopi for innovative leadership and inspiration in strengthening their own traditions. Despite their difficulties over coal, water, and corporate involvement in their economy, the Hopi themselves want to be a part of the larger global culture. They want to do it, however, on their own terms.

At the heart of the tribe's initiatives to deal with these issues and bring about an improvement in the quality of life for Hopi people are their efforts to develop a sustainable tribal economy over the long term. The current tribal chairman, Wayne Taylor, Jr., has described this strategy as one that focuses on (1) securing a land base with the infrastructure (roads, utilities, sewage, and water) to support economic development, (2) education and skill building for growing the tribal economy, (3) diversifying the tribal economy beyond dependence on coal revenues, and (4) accomplishing this in a way that respects and protects the Hopi culture as a resource and guide.[11]

Environment and Resources

Establishing a secure land base has been a priority of the last several Hopi administrations. By actively battling in federal courts to recover land lost to the Navajo Tribe in the Joint Use Act, and by purchasing almost 400,000 acres of traditional lands off the reservation, the Tribe has moved to develop a land base that can sustain future population and economic growth. Through its Hopi Office of Lands, the Tribe has also implemented state-of-the-art Global Information Systems (GIS) satellite technology to develop databases allowing them effectively to map, assess, and manage these areas and the resources they can provide. This land base, which includes rangelands and some potential commercial/industrial, timber, and agricultural lands along the Interstate 40 corridor (across northern Arizona east of Flagstaff), enables the Tribe to begin to move their economy away from its dependency on coal mining. The coal operations are only expected to last about another forty years. After that, alternative sources of wealth and employment must be found.

The Tribe has also given high priority to developing an alternative water source on which to base development. Their proposed solution is the construction of a ninety-mile pipeline from Lake Powell, Arizona, to the Hopi Reservation, with a spur line built to the mining operation for use in the coal slurry line. This pipeline, similar to several others already built around the country, would supply water for use throughout parts of the Navajo Reservation and to all of the villages of the Hopi Reservation. According to tribal officials, construction of this pipeline would provide three major benefits to the Hopi, the Navajo, the Peabody Coal Company, and the United States. First, it would bring a halt to the pumping of water from the N-aquifer, thus preserving it as a future water source for the tribes, while allowing continued operation of the mines—an integral part of the tribal economy. Second, it would enable the Tribe to limit future use of the aquifer so that it could be preserved as a source of drinking water and seepage for the springs that are an important part of Hopi traditional ways. Third, it will add an additional source of domestic water supply for a growing Hopi population that will not always be able to rely on the aquifer for drinking supplies. This additional source would not only allow the Hopi to survive, but to develop a viable economy, and help them to attain some level of equality with most American communities, who often take adequate water supplies much more for granted.

The obstacle to this proposal, as with the still-unsolved cleanup of airborne pollution from the generating plant and expanded skiing and mining operations on the San Francisco Peaks, is the opposition of corporations who object to the significant increased costs or loss of profits that would result. Seemingly endless legal maneuvering by corporate lawyers and negotiators, with the short-term focus of profitability, become part of a strategy calculated to wear down and discourage tribal initiatives. What corporations may underestimate is the Hopi perspective on time, their commitment to this place, and their willingness to persist in protecting it.[12]

Joblessness

Building a strong local economy that can provide meaningful and well-paying work for tribal members has also been established as an important Hopi priority. There are few retail businesses on the reservation, and not many places to spend what money is earned locally. As a result, as much as 90 percent of all income is spent off the reservation, and there is very little of what economists call a "multiplier effect."[13] Rather than circulating within the reservation economy, money paid out in salaries goes to benefit businesses in nearby border towns, including Flagstaff and Winslow, Arizona, and Gallup, New Mexico. In order to correct this situation and "build" a local economy, the Hopi have taken an approach that can best be described as building from the inside out. Hopi leaders now look at each Hopi individual as an asset bringing certain gifts to the community, and they view Hopi culture as a unique strength in building solutions that will be appropriate and acceptable to Hopi culture over the long run. Local leaders have moved away from more conventional economic development plans, which too often have nothing to do with local needs and aspirations. Instead of repeating earlier (failed) attempts at establishing manufacturing plants, which were oriented to an industrial model very alien to their cultural values, Hopis are now working to develop more culturally appropriate training programs and employment opportunities. Some of these include cottage industries like Gentle Rain, a workers' cooperative that employs homebound women on the reservation as seamstresses to produce and market outdoor clothing, with a tribal motif, made from recycled plastic milk jugs. The Tribe is currently negotiating to bring this work and other Hopi arts and crafts into the Olympic market for the 2002 Salt Lake City Winter Games.

Economic development activities are not limited to the Hopi reservation. In its attempts to diversify the tribal economy, the Tribe has purchased two small, strategically located shopping centers in Flagstaff and has purchased four ranches totaling 17,500 acres of Hopi ancestral lands (including one ranch that once belonged to John Wayne). These will be developed as "dude" ranches for tourist visits.

Other job initiatives have included the reconstruction and restoration of important historic buildings and traditional terrace gardens. Further, the Hopi are working to preserve and restore ancestral sites in the nearby Flagstaff area. They now provide training and employment in ruins preservation, through a joint partnership among the Hopi Cultural Preservation Office, the Hopi Foundation, the National Park Service, and Northern Arizona University. The partnership provides training for Hopi young people for careers in hands-on restoration techniques and further education in cultural preservation.

What is perhaps surprising to many outsiders is that, unlike many other Native American groups, the Hopi have not built casinos and moved into Indian gaming as a means of generating income. So far, Hopi voters have twice turned down gaming initiatives, citing their cultural values and concern about introducing another kind of addictive behavior into their communities.

Combating Erosion of Culture and Language

While full-time traditional dry farming by the Hopi has just about disappeared, much smaller scale gardening has captured the interest of Hopis in several communities, especially young people, and it holds out promise for revitalizing the Hopi agricultural tradition. In 1990 a terrace restoration project was begun at one of the Third Mesa villages, which has since spread to three other villages. The projects employ local young people to restore the terraces, some of which have been in use for up to 600 years, to safe and productive use. As children, village leaders had played in the canyon terraces below the villages, and worked the gardens with family and friends. After 1975, however, most of these spring-fed gardens fell into disuse because of new household water systems and television. People made individual gardens next to their houses and stayed close to home. Pained to see that their own children no longer had the community gardens as a place to play, work, and learn Hopi customs, songs, stories, and gardening practices, these leaders sought to restore the gardens to their former importance

Passing it on: the next generation. Photo: Miguel Vasquez.

in village life. Other parents who supported the project commented that a generation gap had developed. Children brought up without the activities and the interactions provided by the gardens were being denied an important means of learning Hopi culture and its base in the land. As one grandmother, an avid gardener and a fan of Oprah Winfrey put it, "This is quality time with my grandchildren."[14] Many people in these communities seem to understand that the lessons learned in the community gardens are not the kind to be found in schools or modern lifestyles. Instead, the gardens provide a means of cultural transmission to the next generation that is meaningful, productive, and fun.

Language renovation for the Hopi remains an open question. There is growing agreement that the language must not be lost—that schools must play an active part, and that recent controversies over which of three dialects should be taught are really secondary to the issue of language survival. As one Hopi High School student put it, "If the *pahaana* [white authorities] could force us to speak English, and our language is so important, why can't we force ourselves to speak Hopi—as a requirement for graduation from Hopi High?"[15] Toward this goal, several important initiatives have begun: bilingual school programs, starting from Head Start and going through high school; and KUYI, the new Hopi language radio station. Whether these efforts prevail, in the face of the constant onslaught of mainstream media and persistent English-only initiatives in Arizona schools, remains to be seen. What is evident from other successful language preservation programs across the globe is that, to be successful, the Hopi must attack the problem on all fronts—home, school, and work.

FOOD FOR THOUGHT

Embedded in Western cultures is a deep feeling that those people who do not follow the mainstream ways are misguided. From the time of first contact between Euro-Americans and native people the vast differences in values, attitudes, beliefs, and ways of life have made conflict inevitable. Over the past 100 years, the Western impact on the Hopi has resulted in forced changes in livelihood, forced assimilation (without real acceptance) by the larger society, 50 percent unemployment, family incomes of less than $10,000 per year, poor housing and nutrition, dismal high school dropout rates, and chronic alcoholism. In short, mainstream America has brought little benefit to the Hopi. Their isolation has protected them somewhat up until now, and they have been among the most successful of Native American groups in passing on their cultural traditions. Now that isolation is disappearing. Although Hopi people have used their culture successfully to deal with the changes and threats, it remains to be seen how well they will succeed in the future—weaving the threads of the ancient and the modern.

Questions

1. In today's modern globalized culture, why is the passing on of their culture and language to the next generation so important to the Hopi?
2. What do you think are the primary factors in the remarkable success of the Hopi in determining their own path?
3. Why is it so difficult for "mainstream" American society to accept the validity and worth of other cultural traditions, especially those of indigenous peoples?
4. What potential lessons might "mainstream" American society learn from Hopi culture, especially in the area of the environment versus economy debate?
5. Modern American mainstream culture is very focused on rights: property rights, individual rights, civil rights, human rights. Hopi culture, even now, is much more focused on responsibilities: to family, clan, community, tribe, and the Creator. How does this difference in world view shape how the Hopi react to social, environmental, and economic problems?

NOTES

D. Taylor, member of the Hopi Cultural Preservation Office's Cultural Resource Advisory Team, checked facts in the course of preparing this chapter. His help is much appreciated.

1. Ivan Sidney, former Tribal Chairman, was a visitor to my course on Peoples of the Southwest at Northern Arizona University, October 3, 1989.

2. Peter M. Whiteley, *Rethinking Hopi Ethnography* (Washington, D.C.: Smithsonian Press, 1998), 196.

3. Wayne Taylor, Jr., "The Hopi Tribe and Water: Preserving the Future Through Sustainable Development." Address to EPA of Tribal Chairman: In *Tutuveni: Newspaper of the Hopi Tribe*, December 11, 1998, 3.

4. Vernon Masayesva (former Tribal Chairman) personal communication: April 1997.

5. Wayne Taylor (current Tribal Chairman) personal communication: April 2000.

6. Ferrell Sekacucu (former Tribal Chairman) personal communication: June 1998.

7. Leigh Kuwanwisiwma (Director, Hopi Cultural Preservation Office) interview: July 1994.

8. Personal communication with former Tribal Chairman Ivan Sidney, October 3, 1989.

9. Leigh Kuwanwisiwma (Farmer and Director, Hopi Cultural Preservation Office) interview: July 1994.

10. Anita Poleahla (Director, Hopi Language Project) personal communication: March 2000.

11. Taylor, "The Hopi Tribe and Water."

12. See R. Clemmer, *Roads in the Sky: The Hopi Indians in a Century of Change* (Boulder, Colo.: Westview Press, 1995); J. Loftin, *Religion and Hopi Life in the Twentieth Century* (Bloomington: University of Indiana Press, 1991); Taylor, "The Hopi Tribe and Water"; tutuveni@hopi.nsn.us; http://www.nau.edu/~hcpo-p/.

13. Gail Poley (former Community Development Administrator, Bacavi Village) personal communication: August 1991.

14. Mary Lahlo (Grandmother) personal communication: July 1992.

15. Anonymous personal communication: May 1997.

RESOURCE GUIDE

Published Literature

Clemmer, Richard O. *Roads in the Sky: The Hopi Indians in a Century of Change.* Boulder, Colo.: Westview Press, 1995.

Loftin, J. *Religion and Hopi Life in the Twentieth Century.* Bloomington: University of Indiana Press, 1991.

Sekaquaptewa, H. *Me and Mine: The Life Story of Helen Sekaquaptewa. As told to Louise Udall.* Tucson: University of Arizona Press, 1969.

Vasquez, M., and L. Jenkins. "Reciprocity and Sustainability: Terrace Restoration on Third Mesa." *Practicing Anthropology* 16, no. 2 (Spring 1994): 14–17.

Whiteley, Peter M. *Rethinking Hopi Ethnography*. Washington, D.C.: Smithsonian Press, 1998.

Whiteley, Peter M. *Bacavi: Journey to Reed Springs*. Flagstaff: Ariz.: Northland Press, 1988.

Films and videos

Broken Rainbow, Earthworks 1986.

The 4 Corners: A National Sacrifice Area, Bullfrog Films 1996.

Hopi Songs of the Fourth World. Distributed by New Day Films, 1984.

In The Light of Reverence, The Sacred Land Film Project, P.O. Box, C151, La Honda, CA 94020.

WWW Sites

Site of *Hopi Tutuveni*: newspaper of the Hopi Tribe. It includes current events on the Hopi Reservation and official tribal information.
tutuveni@hopi.nsn.us

Official Hopi Cultural Preservation Office site. It provides updated information on research guidelines and general cultural information.
http://www.nau.edu/~hcpo-p/

Organization

Hopi Cultural Preservation Office
P.O. Box 123, Kykotsmovi, AZ 86039
or P.O. Box 15200, Flagstaff, AZ 86011

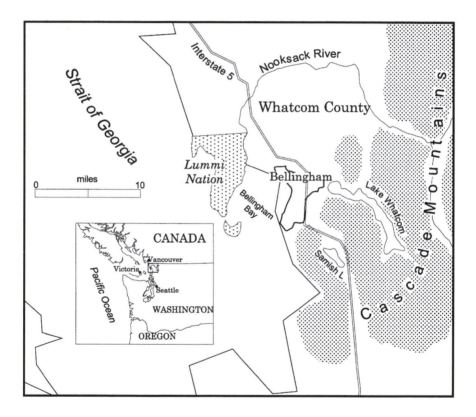

Chapter 6

The Lummi in Washington State
Kurt Russo

The Time Before Time . . .

In the beginning the world was quite different from what it is today. The First People lived then. They looked like us but were called Deer, Raven, Mink, Wolf, and such names, and could use the forms that we now associate with those names. There were also then many dangerous Beings. Then a powerful Being, Xales (the Transformer) came through the world and transformed things. He transformed the dangerous Beings into rocks and other natural features, and he transformed Deer, Raven, and the others into their present forms. Then the Second People appeared. They were the Indians. To them, the Transformer taught the essential arts of life, and to a few of the First Men of these Second People He taught secret words and songs giving supernatural power. To all He taught that the power might be obtained from nature—from animals, plants, and natural objects, by bathing, and fasting. The Transformer then went away and came back no more.

Lummi Indian Oral History[1]

CULTURAL OVERVIEW

The People

Since time immemorial the forebears of the Lummi lived on the mainland and in the archipelago of islands in present-day Whatcom and San Juan Counties in northwestern Washington State. Their unique way of life, customs, and beliefs developed in a landscape formed by successive periods of glaciation which, at its zenith, covered Whatcom County and the Puget Sound trough with ice over a mile thick. Over the millennia, the landscape

97

was slowly transformed to become part of an unbroken coastal temperate rain forest that extended from British Columbia to northern California. This unimaginable aboriginal landscape teemed with wildlife and dozens of species of waterfowl, and its streams, creeks, and rivers were so thick with salmon it was said you could walk on their backs.

Up through the late-nineteenth century, Lummi, like other Coast Salish peoples, lived in longhouses that could accommodate one or more extended families. The typical winter village might consist of a half-dozen or more cedar plank longhouses clustered together in sheltered bays or coves. The use of the longhouse was largely abandoned by the late 1890s in favor of European-style single-family houses. The reasons for this change in lifestyle are varied and complex but, in large part, trace to a sociocultural disorganization resulting from disease, dislocation, political and military coercion, and the impact of forced Christianization.

During the historic period and up through the mid-nineteenth century, the Lummi Indians lived throughout the San Juan Islands, with large, permanent winter villages on Lopez Island, Lummi Island, San Juan Island, Waldron Island, Sucia Island, and Orcas Island. In present-day Whatcom County, additional villages on the mainland were located along Bellingham Bay including village sites on what would later become the Lummi Indian reservation. Intermarriage was common between the Lummi Indians and other aboriginal groups in the area, including the Swinomish and Samish Indians to the south, the Nooksack Indians to the east, Native bands in the Frasier River delta to the north, and communities located in the southern portion of Vancouver Island to the west.

Today, the majority of Lummi live on the Lummi reservation located at the mouth of the Nooksack River. The 18,000-acre reservation is home to 3,200 of the 4,000 enrolled Lummi. It is a young community, with a median age of just under twenty-two years.[2] In a pattern repeated throughout Washington State, non-Indians constitute a significant proportion of landowners on the reservation. Despite the terms of the Treaty of Point Elliott, which reserves the Lummi reservation as the exclusive homeland of the Lummi, approximately 45 percent of the reservation land is now under non-Indian ownership.[3] This alienation of tribal lands bears witness to the failure on the part of the United States to enforce the terms and conditions of the treaty.

Traditional Subsistence Strategies

Aboriginal life was a rhythmic repetition, a seasonal round, and salmon was its centerpiece. Each spring the Lummi would leave their winter villages in search of camas roots and shellfish, or troll for spring chinook salmon and halibut, gather herring eggs, and collect fresh sprouts and other vegetal material. Summer was the busiest season, when they trolled for chinook salmon and gill net in the bays, along the mainland, and in the islands. In August, at the height of summer, they conducted their First Salmon Ceremony and gave thanks for their good fortune. In the fall they fished in the streams and went fowling. In October and November they picked up the camas roots they had stored; fished for cod, chum salmon, pink salmon, coho salmon, and steelhead; and went to the mountains to hunt deer, elk, and bear. With the coming of winter, they devoted themselves to relaxation, tended to their fowl nets, traded, and took part in the winter ceremonial cycle of the potlatch (a ceremonial feast featuring reciprocal gift giving) and spirit dancing.

The precipitous decline of the salmon fishery over the past decade has resulted in a severe economic and social dislocation in the Lummi community. The Lummi were among the first to operate a successful aquaculture program and salmon hatchery, but even these efforts have been hampered, most notably by logging practices taking place in the upper Nooksack River basin.

Social and Political Organization

Typically, the village was located in a protected cove, inlet, or bay and consisted of several cedar longhouses that could measure well over 200 feet in length. The longhouse, home to the extended family or clan, was presided over by headmen who spoke on behalf of their immediate family. Rank was important, and class was a factor, but so were social systems and structures that distributed power throughout the families. For example, decisions that affected the village were seldom made by one person. Rather, decisions were most often based on a consensus among the ranking headmen.

Significantly, this preference for consensus is still evident in the Lummi community. This cultural orientation, however, can collide with the Western political systems imposed on the Lummi and other tribes by the U.S. government. Under the current system, the Lummi Nation is governed by an eleven-member Business Council whose members serve a three-year term and which is elected by enrolled tribal members over the age of eighteen. The elected body, in turn, elects its officers including the chairman of the tribe. The Business Council has final authority over all of the various governmental agencies, including Natural Resources, Self-Governance, Health and Human Services, Law and Order, Administrative Services, Planning and Economic Development, and Education.

The principle of majority at the heart of the electoral process can, and often does, collide with the community's overriding belief that credible decisions must be based on a consensus. But consensus takes time in a community of interrelated families, and time is often in short supply. Consensus also requires an informed political body in a time of increasingly complex technical, economic, and legal problems. It is this clash not only of core values but of cultural forces—the mad rush of modernism versus the cautious approach of collaterality—that is a common occurrence among many native communities throughout the United States.

Religion and World View

The entire aboriginal region of the Lummi was a veritable garden, ideally suited for human habitation. Like indigenous peoples everywhere, the ancestors of the Lummi evolved, or had revealed to them, a way of life that solved the most basic human problems: how to organize themselves as a social community, how to organize work, and how to relate to the natural and supernatural forces around them. This way of life, or *chalangen* in the Lummi language, survived for uncounted generations.

While much has changed over the past hundred years, many of the beliefs, customs, and traditional practices have endured. Today, as in the past, Lummi women and men novitiates between puberty and middle age are initiated into the longhouse winter ceremonial tradition. As in the past, some of these initiates are taken to the forest to undergo a rigorous initiation into a way of life, and world view, that is unique to the aboriginal peoples of the region. Known to outsiders as the Guardian Spirit Complex, these practices and beliefs unite the community, link the deep cultural past to the present, and provide healing for the individual and the group.

Still, today, Lummi elders pass on to the younger generation the story of the Transformer, Xales (pronounced Hals), who passed through the land long ago to change things forever. The Lummi, like other native groups around them, still follow the tradition of the *sxwaixwe* (masked dancers who bring a blessing), used in conjunction with the winter ceremonials, Indian namings, marriages, funerals, or other important social occasions. Most important, many Lummi still believe that they are the salmon people, and they learn at a young age the significance of the story of the Salmon Woman. At the level of deep culture, the Lummi still believe that native peoples have both a historic right and obligation to protect the children of Salmon Woman.

The Lummi and other Coast Salish peoples have been greatly impacted by the forces of Christianization. One often hears from tribal members that much has been lost and that the knowledge of tradition has passed with the loss of the elders. This is certainly understandable among a people who have suffered for 150 years under the yoke of political and economic oppression, military coercion, and relentless Christianization. Still the aboriginal beliefs and practices persist side by side with the Christian, and especially the Roman Catholic, tradition. The ultimate measure of the meaning and value of these aboriginal beliefs is not in what has been lost but rather what has endured, largely unchanged, to the present day.

THREATS TO SURVIVAL

The Chronicle of Contact

The arrival of non-Indians in Lummi territory began in the 1830s, largely as a result of trading activity at Fort Langley, located in present-day British Columbia. Indications are that the early years of contact were characterized by peaceful and harmonious relations between the Lummi and the new arrivals. Intermarriage was fairly common, and strife between these two profoundly different cultures was infrequent. This era of relatively peaceful relations provided an opportunity for each to share with, and learn from, the other. This all began to change in 1850 when a resurgence in missionary activity occurred, the rate of settlement throughout Lummi territory accelerated, competition for resources increased, and the Lummi both on the mainland and on the San Juan Islands were decimated by introduced diseases.

In a pattern repeated throughout the Americas, the Lummi, falling victim to new diseases, witnessed their numbers decline. Between the mid-fifteenth century and 1910, the population of native North Americans shrank from 15,000,000 to just over 200,000.[4] Foremost among these diseases in this era of the Great Dying was smallpox, the most harrowing of many European pathogens, which devastated Lummi villages throughout the nineteenth century.

After a brief lapse of activity in the 1840s, the process of governmental consolidation and Christianization began in earnest in the early 1850s and continued apace for more than seventy years. In the 1850s, coincident with the first major influx of settlers into the area, the forebears of the Lummi were forced to abandon their villages in the San Juan Islands and were resettled on the mainland. Later in the decade, a Father Chirouse established the first missionary boarding school for young Indians in the area, and church and governmental authorities took steps to discourage or, in many cases, prohibit traditional native religious practices and the use of native languages. The attitude of the authorities regarding native culture was expressed by one federal agent in the Puget Sound area about 1900.

I am satisfied that the greatest obstacle to progress of the young Indian is the old Indian. He still clings to his old superstitions and cherishes secretly the old traditions and teachings. With his disappearance, a more rapid advance will take place among the younger Indians.[5]

As Long as the Sun Rises and Sets

It was during these deeply troubled times that Isaac Stevens arrived to take up his post as governor of Washington Territory. His task was to bring together the various tribes in Washington Territory as parties to a series of treaties with the United States. In large part, the format for the treaties resembles that found in other peace treaties made with other native communities west of the Mississippi River. Some unique provisions, however, were included in the arrangement based on the cultural and social context of the Lummi and other native peoples in the territory.

The consultations that later resulted in the Treaty of Point Elliott were conducted in Chinook jargon—a cryptic trading language spoken by many of the participating native groups. It is difficult to imagine what this process might have meant to the forefathers of the Lummi who participated in the negotiations. There were conflicts in meanings and language, and new concepts of ownership were imposed upon the native participants who came on behalf of their family, household, or clan.

In signing the treaty, one thing is certain: the Lummi would not have given away what they knew their descendants would need to continue their way of life, their *chalengen*, which had been theirs from the beginning. Furthermore, the U.S. Supreme Court has upheld the position that whatever rights the tribes did not expressly *grant* to the United States were *reserved* by native peoples.[6] The obligation to honor the dual principles of original intent and reserved rights are part of the promises referred to at the conclusion of the treaty signing by Isaac Stevens when he stood to call his three witnesses:

There will be witnesses. These witnesses will be the tides. You Indians know that the tide goes out and comes in, that it never fails to go in or out; you people know that streams that flow from the mountains never cease flowing, flow forever; you people know the sun rises and sets and never fails to do so. Those are my witnesses and you Indians, your witnesses, and these promises will be carried out, and your promises to me and the promises the Great Father made to you will be carried out as long as these three witnesses continue—the tide to go in and out, the streams to flow, and the sun to rise and set.[7]

The most ancient and basic injunction of international law—and of personal relations, too—is *pacta sunt servanda*: promises are to be kept. It would not be long, however, before this injunction would be violated. By the 1880s, the Lummi were denied access to areas that they had used for generations. Conflicts between the Lummi and non-Indians increased with the emergence of competing claims on the land, its resources, and the fisheries. By the late nineteenth century, most of the lowland aboriginal forests were gone, the lower valleys drained, and the channel of the Nooksack River changed as a result of logging and associated activities. The once abundant wild salmon began a spiral into extinction that continues to this day.

The Fiction of Conquest

At no time during this long and harrowing period did the United States take steps to honor the promises made to the aboriginal people in the treaty or to uphold the sovereign status of Indian nations acknowledged in the United States Constitution. The U.S. Constitution contains only two bases for the United States to have authority in dealing with Indian nations. One is the treaty clause, which allows the federal government to make treaties with Indians as with any other nation. The other is the commerce clause, which empowers the federal government to regulate commerce with foreign nations, and among the several states, and with the Indian tribes. Neither of these provisions allows the United States to intervene in the internal affairs of Indian nations any more than it allows the United States to intervene in the internal affairs of Great Britain or China. Just as significantly, in the absence of a tribal agreement, there is no legitimating constitutional ground for any tribal loss of land or jurisdiction or for any corresponding federal or state gain of land or jurisdiction.

If neither the treaty nor the commerce clauses provide for U.S. authority in Indian country, on what basis is that authority exercised? One answer is that tribal sovereignty has been violated through a series of legal fictions.[8] Some Lummi believe that many of the rulings of the court employ insulting language, invent history, abandon legitimacy, and represent a fiction of conquest invented by the modern U.S. Supreme Court in an attempt to mask U.S. lawlessness.

Current Events and Conditions

Despite decades of neglect, discrimination, dislocation, and disingenuous legal fictions, the Lummi have persisted in their struggle for cultural survival. Like many other native communities, it struggles against a high rate of joblessness; 79 percent of the households are below the median income for a family of four in Whatcom County.[9] The threat to survival, however, is not primarily economic. Rather, the severest challenges faced by the Lummi today can be placed in three broad categories: threats to tribal sovereignty and home rule, threats to the environment, and threats to spiritual and cultural beliefs.

Threats to Tribal Sovereignty and Home Rule

In a historical pattern repeated in native communities across the United States, the Lummi Nation must contend with opposition from local, state, and national interests on a range of issues that touch on tribal sovereignty. One of the most significant issues today is the exercise of the Nation's senior water right. Water law in the western United States is based on the principle of prior appropriation (i.e., first in time, first in right). The first person, organization, or community to put water to beneficial use has the right to as much water as necessary for this use. This right must be fully satisfied before any other water use is accommodated.

There is no questioning the senior status of the Lummi Nation's water right, which dates back to the signing of the Treaty of Point Elliot of 1855, or that the nation has the right to sufficient quality and quantity of water to fulfill the purposes of the reservation. The Treaty of Point Elliott clearly reserved the tribe's right to sufficient water flows to support fishing, hunting, domestic, and economic and cultural rights in the usual and accustomed areas. This senior status is recognized by state as well as federal authorities. Just as important, Indian reserved water rights are not forfeited if they are not used.

Many tribal communities in the United States face conflicts from within, where non-Indians hold title to lands on the reservation. The legacy of the fiction of conquest and, by extension, the General Allotment Act and successive legislation has resulted in a jurisdictional puzzle throughout much of Indian country. On the Lummi Indian reservation, non-Indians hold title to 45 percent of the reservation upland area and account for approximately 45 percent of the water consumed by the reservation population.

Sadly, the efforts of the Lummi Nation to exercise its senior water right and establish a more just and equitable distribution of water have met with the opposition of several nontribal water associations on the reservation, among them the Sandy Point Improvement Company (SPIC). The members of this water association live in the northwestern portion of the reservation where almost two-thirds of the area is owned by tribal members. A joint federal, state, and tribal technical team has determined that the underground water supply on Sandy Point is insufficient to meet future tribal needs. As a result, the Lummi Nation opposes any new development in the area. Fearful of the potential impact on present and future property values, and resentful of the Lummi Nation's home-rule authority, the members of SPIC rejected the building moratorium.

In 1994 the conflict between SPIC and the Lummi Nation was brought to the attention of then Senator Slade Gorton (R-WA). Senator Gorton has a well-documented history of antagonism toward the tribes in Washington State. In response to intense lobbying by SPIC, Gorton attached a legislative rider in 1995 to the appropriations bill that provided the authority to eliminate *at least* 50 percent of the Lummi Nation's self-governance funding if it failed to accommodate non-Indian water claims on the reservation.

The Lummi Nation found itself between a small, but vocal, minority of non-Indian in-holders on the reservation and a U.S. senator with a long history of hostility for what he mistakenly characterizes as special rights afforded Indians. Seemingly lost in this debate were the promises made in the treaty and well-established legal principles of Western water law. Also lost to the debate was the legacy of neglect by the federal government and the history of how the lands on the reservation were taken out of tribal ownership and conveyed into the hands of non-Indian in-holders.

Another water-related area of contention is the use of the tidelands on the Lummi reservation. Once again, this issue brought the Lummi Nation into conflict with SPIC. The treaty and court rulings leave no doubt of the Lummi Nation's ownership of the tidelands. In 1965 SPIC acknowledged the Nation's ownership and entered into a lease of the tidelands with the Bureau of Indian Affairs (BIA) which was acting on behalf of the Lummi Nation.

In 1963 the lease value for nontribal use of the tidelands on Sandy Point was $2,000 per year. By the late 1970s, the lease was raised to $7,500 per year. In 1984 both the Lummi Nation and SPIC appealed the BIA's proposed lease increase to $26,000 per year; the former argued it was too low, and the latter asserted the assessment was too high. To resolve the matter, an independent appraisal was conducted at the direction of the assistant secretary of the BIA. This appraisal determined that the fair market tideland lease value was $186,000 per year. What followed was a classic example of how an individual group can work the system to oppose the legal rights of tribal home rule and sovereignty.

SPIC refused to pay the higher annual rent until a judgment was entered against them in federal court. As a result of this ruling, in 1988, SPIC paid on the final three years of the lease, but has refused to make any additional payments since that time. It should be understood that the lease is for several miles of tidelands and, based on current occupancy, the assessment of $186,000 amounts to approximately $18 per lot per month. Nor has SPIC made any payments since 1988 for use of the entrance to the Sandy Point marina, an artificial channel dredged over thirty years ago to provide homeowners with direct marine water access.

In explaining their position, SPIC stated that its members no longer use the beach and thus do not have to pay the lease. This seems unlikely, given there are multiple and obvious access points to the beach from non-Indian residences in addition to multiple bulkheads built on the tribal tidelands by non-Indian landowners. They offer no reasonable defense for the lack of payment for use of the entrance channel.

In response to this violation of the agreement and the continuing illegal trespass, and to the damage of tribal property, the Lummi Nation has stated that it reserves the right to remove the bulkheads and close the channel to Sandy Point. Their legal right to do so is self-evident. They must contend, however, with political reality in the fact that SPIC is assisted in its efforts by a close associate of Senator Gorton.

The significance of such groups as SPIC reaches beyond the boundaries of Whatcom County and the borders of Washington State. There is a historical and ideological bond between SPIC and such nationally prominent organizations as the Wise Use movement. This movement is the modern-day equivalent of the "sage brush" revolution, which pitted influential land-holders in the American West against federal land management agencies as well as Indian tribes.

In 1992, in a meeting organized by Wise Use, an organization known as CLUE was formed in Washington State.[10] More ominously for the Lummi, in 1995 CLUE endorsed and financed the successful campaign of a candidate running for the member-at-large position on the Whatcom County Council. The councilwoman, a former board member of SPIC, owns over $500,000 of real estate on the Lummi Indian reservation. Recently elected to a second term, she uses the power of her position to oppose any and all efforts of the Lummi Nation to exercise its senior water right or assert its inherent right of home rule.

Threats to the Environment

It is impossible to overstate the importance of nature to the Lummi people. It has been, and remains, a source of economic, as well as social, cultural, and spiritual, sustenance to the community. This relationship to nature and its bounty is perhaps best expressed in their regard for the salmon. The causes and consequences of the steady decline of the salmon populations have been a long-standing concern of the Lummi Nation.

The degradation of the salmon habitat is one of the factors that has driven the once-abundant salmon to the brink of extinction throughout the Pacific Northwest. The impact of logging and forest-related activities is the most visible threat. Throughout the United States, commercial forests are treated as crops to be clear-cut, then replanted with a single species (monoculture forestry), with little consideration given to the needs, limitations, and natural conditions of these unique and fragile ecosystems.

Clear-cutting, monoculture forestry, and chemical treatment have caused irreparable harm to many of the salmon-bearing streams and rivers in the Pacific Northwest. Clear-cutting increases the amount of silt (the silt load) in the streams, which buries salmon eggs or covers over the fine gravel salmon require for spawning. The elimination of trees also reduces shade along the stream, dramatically increasing water temperature and further degrading salmon habitat. In the South Fork of the Nooksack River, for example, water temperatures of over 70 degrees Fahrenheit have been recorded. Water temperatures of over 60 degrees are known to be lethal to salmon. Another culprit is the construction of roads, which may promote silt runoff into adjacent streams and rivers, further increasing the silt load. The cumulative effects of forest-related activities have devastated many of the once-abundant salmon streams throughout Whatcom County, Washington State, and the Pacific Northwest.

Logging is not the only threat to the salmon. The rapid growth of Whatcom County has resulted in the elimination of innumerable salmon-bearing creeks and streams. Just as important, many wetland areas which nourish and sustain the Nooksack River have been drained or paved over to make room for agriculture, industry, golf courses, and houses. No one suggests that growth should not occur. It is evident, however, that the manner of growth that has occurred in Whatcom County has proceeded without any serious consideration for the impact on the salmon. Sadly, when population growth arrives, the salmon disappear.

In the span of a few generations, the Lummi people have witnessed a radical change in their aboriginal homeland. The vast forests have vanished from the lowlands and the foothills. The intricate web of creeks, streams, and wetlands has all but disappeared. The Nooksack River, which traverses Whatcom County, is greatly reduced in flow and is increasingly polluted with both industrial and agricultural waste. Meanwhile, the growth of Whatcom County continues, driven by the engine of commerce rather than the principles of sustainable development.

Threats to Spiritual and Cultural Beliefs

The religious and cultural beliefs of the Lummi people are tied to the land that gave birth to their people. Long before the arrival of the first European, the ancestors of the Lummi participated in spiritual practices that gave expression to their sacred relationship to the land, to each other, and to past and future generations. Despite persecution by the Christian churches and later by the U.S. government, these beliefs are still present, and practiced, today.

It is neither proper nor necessary to describe these practices, which are sacred and therefore private. It is enough to say that many of these practices must take place in a natural setting that is pure, private, and secluded. Before the arrival of the non-Indians, the aboriginal homeland of the Lummi people offered countless natural sanctuaries for the spirit. Each of these sanctuaries had its own gift to bestow and lessons to teach for the benefit of both the person and the Lummi people.

The greatest threat to the continuation of these beliefs is neither the church nor the government; rather, it is the degradation of the natural environment. The destruction of the forest; the degradation of the streams, creeks, and rivers; and the rapid development of Whatcom County have eliminated all but a few of these ancient sanctuaries. The need and the beliefs remain, but access to these sacred sites continues to diminish with the passing of time. This threat is a dagger aimed at the heart of a cultural and spiritual way of life unique to the Lummi.

RESPONSE: STRUGGLES TO SURVIVE CULTURALLY

Issue of Tribal Sovereignty

In the spring of 1995, conflicts with nontribal landowners of SPIC reached a critical juncture over competing water withdrawals from the limited ground water aquifer. The Lummi Nation made a request to the Department of the Interior to appoint a team to negotiate a fair and equitable settlement of this issue. Several months later, the Department of the Interior appointed a federal team to negotiate a solution to the Lummi reservation ground water conflicts outside of litigation. Negotiations began in August 1995, and the federal, state, and Lummi Nation teams have been meeting frequently since that time. It is now anticipated that, the objections of SPIC notwithstanding, negotiation of a solution to reservation ground water issues will lead directly into negotiations to resolve water conflicts on the reservation.

There remain, however, other unresolved issues over the senior water rights of the Lummi in the greater Nooksack River basin in Whatcom County. In addition to having the senior right to water in their aboriginal territory, the Lummi are also guaranteed sufficient water quality and quantity to ensure the viability of the salmon fishery. At the center of the conflict is the health of the Nooksack River which runs the width of Whatcom County, as well as its innumerable tributaries which are being threatened with pollution from agriculture and industry.

The threat posed by such groups as SPIC is a symptom of a deeply rooted problem facing American Indian tribes and nations. Indian tribes have long been acknowledged by the United States as separate and distinct societies with original, natural (inherent) rights. The famous 1832 case of *Worcester v. Georgia* was one of only a handful of cases in which the tribes were parties and tribal interests were immediately at issue. In that ruling, U.S. Supreme Court Chief Justice John Marshall wrote,

Indian Nations had always been considered as distinct, independent, political communities, retaining their original natural rights. . . . The words "treaty" and "nation" are words of our language, selected in our diplomatic and legislative proceedings, by ourselves, have in each a definite and well-understood meaning. We have applied them to Indians, as we have applied them to the other nations of the earth; they are applied to all in the same sense.[11]

The Lummi Nation, like other native communities, still considers itself a "distinct, independent, political" community with the inherent right to govern itself without external interference. The denial of this fundamental right, whether by non-Indians on the reservation or by external authorities, subverts the responsibility of the Court, subverts constitutional government, and subverts law, justice, and decency. This inherent right of self-governance was not established by the Treaty of Point Elliott; rather, the treaty rests upon the self-evident and inherent right of aboriginal home rule, autonomy, and self-determination.

In order to address the deeper issue of inherent rights, the Lummi Nation was one of a small vanguard of tribes to promote federal recognition of the concept of true tribal self-governance. In response to this tribal initiative, in 1988 the U.S. Congress initiated the Self-Government Demonstration Project, made permanent in 1994 under congressional legislation. This program recognizes greater autonomy and home rule in the allocation of federal resources, reduces bureaucratic waste and inefficiency, and increases the responsiveness of tribal programs to tribal needs, values, and priorities.

Self-governance is a growing point not only in the Lummi Nation, but also the non-Indian community. As a result of economic growth inspired by the self-governance initiative, the Lummi Nation is among the top twenty employers in the area contributing millions of dollars to the state and local communities. Progress in partnership, however, is measured in more than jobs, dollars, and economic growth. For the Lummi people, it is measured by an acknowledgment of their inherent right to preserve their way of life for future generations. For the larger community, this partnership is an opportunity to heal past wounds, to honor the obligations made in the treaty, and to enter into a new, more enlightened era of relations with native peoples. In the final analysis, progress will be measured by the ability to transcend fear and hostility, to embrace differences, and to open up to others thereby strengthening the fabric of society.

Educational Growth

The Lummi Nation has also entered a new era of educational growth and opportunity. In a dramatic turnaround from the days of the church and government-run boarding schools, the Lummi Nation, in 1982, chartered Northwest Indian College (NWIC). Since that time NWIC, a two-year, fully accredited institution, has established seven satellite campuses throughout Washington State to serve native educational needs within a framework of native values. With over 800 full-time equivalent students drawn from two hundred tribes across the United States, it represents one of the fastest growing of the thirty-three Indian colleges in the United States. The college, which is open to both Indian and non-Indian students, offers programs in such areas as health, education, business, tribal administration, cultural arts, and natural resource management. The college is now engaged in a five-year capital campaign to construct new campus facilities and expand to a four-year institution.

Aquaculture Program

In response to the potential loss of the salmon, the Lummi people initiated programs to restore the wildstock salmon and to enhance these populations through a salmon aquaculture program. The Lummi aquaculture program began in 1968, when the Lummi Nation began operating what has since become one of the most successful programs of its kind in the Pacific Northwest. Each year the Lummi Nation releases over 17 million salmon raised in their hatchery in the foothills of Mount Baker in the North Cascades Mountains. In addition to benefiting the Lummi people, the harvesting of the returning salmon adds millions of dollars to the local and regional economy.

The aquaculture program is designed to augment, not replace, the highly endangered wildstock salmon populations. The decline of these populations can be traced directly to the degradation of the 860-square-mile Nooksack River watershed. In response, the Lummi Nation has, for more than twenty years, participated in a vigorous campaign to restore and enhance the salmon habitat throughout their aboriginal territory. The Lummi Nation's Natural Resource Department includes scientists, specialists, and technicians with expertise in fisheries, hydrology, geology, wildlife, and forestry who are dedicated to conserving and restoring the watershed. The Lummi Nation works in close cooperation with private landowners, local government, and state and federal agencies in programs designed to prevent further degradation of the watershed and restore critical habitat areas.

Economics and Education

While continuing its efforts to restore the salmon fishery, the Lummi government has begun to diversify its economy through tribal business ventures and business training for tribal members. In 1993 the Lummi opened a casino that closed three years later, largely as a result of the legalization of casino-style gambling in British Columbia. Of greater significance is the Northwest Indian College, located on the Lummi Indian reservation. The college represents the best hope for tribal members to maintain their cultural identity and to expand their economic opportunities.

Spiritual and Cultural Initiatives

The Lummi Nation has responded at many different levels to the threats posed to their spiritual and cultural beliefs. On one level, it has helped to usher in a new era of relations with the Christian community. As an example, in 1985, the Lummi Nation formally pressed for an apology from the Church Council of Greater Seattle (CCGS) for past and present persecutions of traditional native spiritual practices and beliefs. The CCGS processed the request through its Native American Liaison Group, which was responsible for communicating the request to other tribal communities in the region. As a result, in 1987, a Public Declaration of Apology to all the native peoples of the Pacific Northwest was issued by ten bishops and denominational leaders, in care of Jewell James of the Lummi Nation. The opening paragraph of the public declaration captures the spirit of this un-precedented acknowledgment of injustice:

This is a formal apology on behalf of our churches for their long-standing partic-ipation in the destruction of traditional Native American spiritual practices. We call upon our people for recognition and respect for your traditional ways of life and for protection of your sacred places and ceremonial objects. We have frequently been unconscious and insensitive and have not come to your aid when you have been victimized by unjust Federal policies and practices. In many other circum-stances we reflected the rampant racism and prejudice of the dominant culture with which we too willingly identified. . . . We ask for your forgiveness and blessing.[12]

The apology was taken to many different native communities to be read aloud to tribal members in both the United States and Canada. In some tribal communities, the apology was greeted with disbelief. It would later be made clear to the most ardent disbelievers, however, that the apology was more than a symbolic gesture.

Over the past ten years, the Lummi Nation has stepped up its efforts to preserve the few remaining sacred sites in their original territory. Two such efforts are especially worth noting: the protection of Madrona Point and the preservation of the Arlecho Creek basin. Madrona Point is a pristine, thirty-two-acre headland located on Orcas Island, in the San Juan Islands. Madrona Point has long been recognized as a sacred site to the Lummi. Situated between two registered archaeological sites, it is known to contain numerous burial sites that predated the arrival of the Europeans. In 1987 the Lummi Nation was informed that plans were being made to develop an exclusive, gated community on Madrona Point.

Responding to this threat, the Lummi Nation, in association with the CCGS, launched a national campaign to bring attention to the issue and halt the proposed development. In what was often characterized as a David and Goliath battle, the Lummi struggled against one of the largest land development companies in the Pacific Northwest and eventually brought the issue to the U.S. Congress. Thankfully, in 1989, Congress appropriated $2.25 million to the Lummi Nation for the purchase and acquisition of the site by the Lummi Nation. This victory was due in no small part to the patience and persistence of the Lummi Nation, and to the support of a broad-based coalition organized and coordinated by the CCGS.

Another example of the response of the Lummi Nation is its efforts to preserve the old-growth forests of the Arlecho Creek watershed. The 2,250-acre watershed, located in the foothills of the North Cascade Mountains forty miles from the Lummi reservation, contains the largest remaining stand of mid-elevation old-growth forest on private lands in western Wash-ington State. Generations of Lummi have used the Arlecho Basin (known as Tseq to the Lummi) for cultural and spiritual purposes and practices. In addition, the cool, clear waters of Arlecho Creek are of vital importance to both hatchery-raised and wildstock salmon populations.

In 1989 clear-cutting in the Arlecho Basin was brought to the attention of the Lummi Nation. In response, the Lummi Nation developed a five-year plan to secure permanent protection of the watershed. In 1990 it filed the first of several legal injunctions which successfully halted the logging operations for almost two years. In 1992 the nation initiated a regional and national public relations campaign to expose questionable forest practices in the basin. In 1993 the Lummi Nation succeeded in its efforts to have a comprehensive biological inventory completed in the basin. This inventory would later establish the Arlecho Creek basin as primary habitat for the marbled murrulet, a federally protected endangered seabird that nests in old-growth forests.

In 1995 the Arlecho basin was sold to Crown Pacific, along with 85,000 acres in the surrounding watershed. Soon after acquiring the land, Crown Pacific and the Nature Conservancy of Washington proposed an unprecedented partnership that would eventually transfer title of the Arlecho basin to the Lummi Nation. Under the terms of the partnership, the sale price of the basin was reduced from $11.1 million to $7.1 million. By September 2000, the Lummi Nation had successfully raised over $5 million from a variety of sources including the Paul G. Allen Forest Protection Foundation, the David and Lucile Packard Foundation, the Panaphil Foundation of New York, the Oregon Climate Trust, the Flintridge Foundation, the M.J. Murdock Charitable Trust, the National Fish and Wildlife Foundation, and $625,000 in donations from individuals in Washington State. Once the acquisition is completed, the site will be owned by the Lummi Nation and permanently preserved as a cultural sanctuary and as a living laboratory to advance our understanding of the highly endangered mid-elevation old-growth forest systems.

Relations Without Borders

The Lummi Nation's efforts to promote true tribal sovereignty, to protect the environment, and to preserve indigenous values and culture reach well beyond the borders of the United States. Over the past ten years, the Lummi Nation has led the way in raising awareness of these issues in both international forums and in indigenous communities in Central and South America. In 1992 the Lummi Nation organized the largest indigenous delegation to attend the United Nations Earth Summit, held in Rio de Janeiro, Brazil. It has also initiated programs that continue to this day in support of indigenous communities in the rain forests of Mexico, Guatemala, Peru, Bolivia, and Ecuador. In each community, the goal is the same: to assist indigenous communities in their efforts to preserve their aboriginal homeland and protect their unique way of life.

Postscript

In the elections of November 2000, Senator Slade Gorton was defeated by political newcomer Maria Cantwell in the narrowest of margins (approximately 2,000 votes). The defeat of Senator Gorton can be traced to many factors, not the least of which was his relentless attack on environmental laws such as the Endangered Species Act and his open enmity toward Indian tribes.

Senator Gorton was not alone in his attacks on tribal sovereignty and treaty rights. There are indications that President George W. Bush is opposed to tribal self-determination and may seek to diminish the federal trust responsibility. Other members of Congress, such as Congressman George Nethercutt Jr. from Washington State, will eagerly take up the campaign to unilaterally change the rights and status of Indian nations.

Then, as now, the outcome ultimately will be determined by the courts and by the willingness of the American people, and their representatives, to stand by the promises made to the original peoples of this land.

FOOD FOR THOUGHT

In 1682 the French explorer Sieur de La Salle, standing at the mouth of the Mississippi River, proclaimed the entire midsection of the continent, from the Alleghenies to the Rockies, to be the possession of Louis XIV. History shows that non-Indians have never stopped making such proclamations about the tribes and their lands. Indeed, these proclamations continue to this day in the aboriginal homeland of the Lummi.

In 1855 the U.S. government entered into a sacred agreement with the ancestors of the present-day Lummi. These treaties reserved to the Lummi rights and resources in perpetuity, regardless of the social, economic, or political winds of change that might blow across the land. Despite these promises, the Lummi now struggle against local, regional, and national interests on such key issues as the meaning of tribal sovereignty, the ownership and management of natural resources, and the fundamental right of the Lummi to practice their traditional spirituality. In each case, the Lummi continue to assert their inherent rights of self-determination, autonomy, and home rule—rights embodied in the Treaty of Point Elliott. The fact that the Lummi must continue this struggle raises some troubling questions, and some food for thought, about the true face of power in the United States.

Questions

1. The Lummi, who were never conquered by the Americans (or any other European power), signed a federal treaty in 1855 in which they gave up the right to

exclude Whites from most of their lands in return for a perpetual homeland (their reservation), the right to practice their lifeway and manage their lives in that homeland forever, and certain other rights. The treaty also assured them continued access to their former lands for economic and cultural purposes in "usual and accustomed" places. Why then do Whites often react angrily when the Lummi seek to do what the treaty guarantees?

2. When Indian tribes seek adjudication of their rights, they must inevitably seek justice in a U.S. court. At the same time, the United States is often a party to the conflict. Can the United States reasonably assert that its court system is impartial, or should such cases be heard in an international court?

3. The senior water right of the Lummi Nation is well established. At the same time, any attempt to assert this right meets with political opposition at the local and national levels. What does this mean for a country that describes itself as "a Nation of laws, not of men?"

4. Few would disagree that the environment of the Lummi homeland has been severely degraded since the signing of the treaty. In view of promises made in the treaty, what role, if any, should the U.S. government play in restoring the ecological health (for instance, unpolluted water and abundant fish stocks) of the aboriginal homeland of the Lummi?

5. The Lummi, like most tribal communities, place the greatest value on the past and the beliefs and customs of their ancestors. American national society, however, is more oriented to the present and the future, preferring progress to maintaining past traditions. How is this conflict between a past and present orientation illustrated by the opposition the Lummi encounter as they attempt to preserve and protect sacred areas and cultural use sites and resources?

6. In order to protect sacred sites, the Lummi must inform the state or federal government of the location of the site or area. However, due to the nature and importance of these sacred places, tribal members are taught not to reveal their location. How would you resolve this conflict between the need to go public with the information and the cultural imperative of private knowledge?

NOTES

This chapter has been developed with the consultation of members of the Lummi Nation, whose assistance is gratefully acknowledged.

1. Author's field interviews, ca. 1982.

2. Lummi Indian Planning Department, 2001.

3. Ibid.

4. Donald A. Grinde and Bruce E. Johansen, *Ecocide of Native America: Environmental Destruction of Indian Lands and Peoples.* (Santa Fe, N.M.: Clear Light Publishers, 1995), 44–52.

5. Wayne Suttles, "Post Contact Culture Change Among the Lummi Indians," *Columbia History Quarterly* 18, nos. 1, 2 (1954): 77.

6. The principle of reserved rights underlies many decisions of the Court, including, for example, the 1974 Boldt decision (*U.S. vs. Washington*).

7. Statement made by American negotiator Isaac Stevens at the signing of the Point Elliott Treaty of 1855 as recorded by interpreter and recorder John Taylor (12 Statute 927).

8. Milnar S. Ball, "Nations, Treaties, Tribes" in *Our People . . . Our Land: Perspectives on the Columbus Quincentenary (Kurt Russo, ed.). Bellingham,* WA: Kluckhohn Center Press and the Council of Energy Resource Tribes, 22–24.

9. Lummi Indian Planning Department, 2000.

10. The meaning of the acronym, CLUE, is not known.

11. Milnar S. Ball "Constitution, Court, Indian Tribes," *American Bar Foundation Research Journal* 1987, Winter (no. 1): 35.

12. "A Public Declaration to the Tribal Councils and Traditional, Spiritual Leaders of the Indian and Eskimo Peoples of the Pacific Northwest," c/o Jewell Praying Wolf James, Lummi Tribe. Church Council of Greater Seattle. December 1987.

RESOURCE GUIDE

Published Literature

Ball, Milnar S. "Constitution, Court, Indian Tribes." *American Bar Foundation Research Journal* 1 (Winter 1987): 3–140.

Grinde, Donald A., and Bruce E. Johansen. *Ecocide of Native America: Environmental Destruction of Indian Lands and Peoples.* Santa Fe, N.M.: Clear Light Publishers, 1995.

Onat, Astrida. *Inventory of Native American Religious Use, Practices, Localities, and Resources: Study Area on the Mt. Baker–Snoqualmie National Forest in Washington State.* Washington, DC: United States Department of Agriculture, 1981.

Russo, Kurt W. *Our People . . . Our Land: Perspectives on the Columbus Quincentenary.* Denver, Colo.: Council of Energy Resource Tribes, 1992.

Schoonmaker, Peter K. *The Rainforests of Home: Profile of a North American Bioregion.* Washington, D.C.: Island Press, 1997.

Suttles, Wayne. "Economic Life of the Coast Salish Indians of Haro and Rosario Straits." Ph.D. diss., University of Washington, 1951.

Video

A Common Destiny: Walking in Both Worlds. Environmental Media Corporation, Chapel Hill, North Carolina, 1990.

WWW Sites

http://www.nwic.edu

http://www.nwic.edu/arlecho

Organizations

Florence R. Kluckhohn Center for the Study of Values
119 North Commercial, Room 240
Bellingham, WA 98225

Northwest Indian College
2622 Kwina Road
Bellingham, WA 98226

Chapter 7

The Onodowaga (Seneca) in New York State

Robert B. Porter

CULTURAL OVERVIEW

The People

The Onodowaga (pronounced "O-no-doe-WA-ga"), or People of the Great Hill, have existed for hundreds of years in an alliance of five nations known collectively as the Haudenosaunee ("Hoe-dee-no-SHOW-nee"), or People of the Longhouse. The first European colonists who arrived in our territory called the people Senecas and called our alliance the Six Nations or the Iroquois Confederacy. These nations are distinct, with their own languages and cultures, but have developed much in common due to their long historical relationships. They called the other nations the Mohawks, Oneidas, Onondagas, and Cayugas.[1] This alliance was founded upon the *Gayanashagowa*, or the Great Law of Peace, which was brought to our peoples by a Huron known only as the Peacemaker.

For much of Seneca history, the struggle for survival was a successful one. The Great Law made it possible for our nations to unite, to grow strong, and to become the dominant power in the sixteenth and seventeenth centuries over what is now known as the northeastern United States. The Senecas have always been the westernmost nation in the confederacy, and are referred to as the "Keepers of the Western Door." As a result, a geographical buffer existed between our nation and the European colonies to the east. Thus, while there was much interaction between the nation and these settlers during the early colonial years—such as fur trading, diplomacy, and warfare—the people were able to maintain the integrity of who and what it meant to be Seneca.

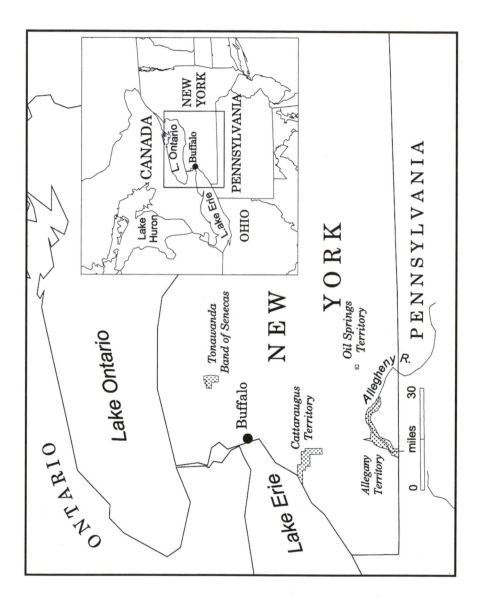

By the mid-eighteenth century, however, the Confederacy's political power began to wane and, with it, the ability to resist the forces of cultural change brought on by the colonists. The Great Law of Peace, upon which the Confederacy operated, requires that all decisions made by the Confederacy Council carry unanimous support of each of the component nations. When the American Revolutionary War came, the Confederacy was unable to agree upon whether it would support the Americans or the English. Unanimity was lost and, with it, the Confederacy's military and political power.

For over 200 years, the Seneca and the other Haudenosaunee peoples have struggled to survive as distinct societies. American colonization has resulted in the loss of almost all Seneca lands and a dramatic transformation of Seneca society. Despite these losses, Euro-American attacks on the Seneca way of life continue. These attacks, and the changes that follow from them, have been rapid, intense, and destructive. Today, the threats to Seneca survival are as great as they have ever been.

The Setting

There are about 10,000 Senecas in the world with about half living on four small territories located in the woodlands of western New York State. The Allegany, Cattaraugus, and Oil Springs Territories are under the authority of the Seneca Nation of Indians. The Tonawanda Territory is under the authority of the Tonawanda Band of Senecas. Other Senecas are scattered throughout the United States and Canada, with concentrations in the urban areas of Western New York State and Pennsylvania (Buffalo, Rochester, and Erie) and territories in Ontario (Grand River Iroquois) and Oklahoma (Seneca-Cayuga Tribe). This chapter focuses on the Seneca Nation of Indians.

The Allegany Territory comprises about 22,000 acres running for about thirty miles along the Allegheny River as it flows into Pennsylvania from New York.[2] The Cattaraugus Territory, also about 22,000 acres, is located about twenty-five miles south of the city of Buffalo, New York, and follows the Cattaraugus Creek as it flows into Lake Erie. The Oil Springs Territory is one square mile in size and is located thirty miles due east of the Allegany Territory. The Tonawanda Territory is about 7,000 acres and is located thirty miles east of the city of Buffalo.

There are about 6,000 residents in Allegany Territory, but only about 1,000 are Senecas. Since the mid-nineteenth century, a significant number of non-Indians have been living within the territory. In the course of westward expansion, these non-Indians illegally established several communities, including the city of Salamanca. Originally, these "squatters" leased their land from individual Senecas, but paid only a dollar or two a year in annual rent. Congress later approved ninety-nine-year leases with the Seneca Nation at this ridiculously low rent. In 1990, however, the old leases expired and, after bitter resistance from the leaseholders, new ones were negotiated that increased the total annual lease payments to nearly three-quarters of a million dollars.

The Cattaraugus Territory has about 3,500 residents, most of whom are Seneca. A few hundred Cayugas, who lost all of their lands following the American Revolutionary War, also live there. The Tonawanda Territory has about 800 residents, mostly Seneca. No Senecas live on the Oil Springs Territory, although a few non-Indian squatters have been living there since the early part of the twentieth century. The Seneca Nation currently is seeking their eviction in federal court.

Traditional Subsistence Strategies

Early Seneca society was based upon a subsistence economy, with men and women assuming particular responsibilities for the survival of the community on the basis of their gender. Men were the hunters and fishers, taking bear, deer, small game, and salmon from the abundant forests and waters. Women, on the other hand, were the farmers. Three of the most important crops for the Senecas were beans, corn, and squash, which were called the "three sisters." Senecas developed an efficient method of growing these three crops together in small mounds, a technique later borrowed by the colonists.

In the seventeenth century, the Seneca economy changed dramatically with the emergence of the fur trade. The colonists had a great demand for the furs and pelts of the beaver and muskrat common in Seneca territory. Senecas soon realized that these furs could be traded for such things as cooking pots, cloth, blankets, and other durable goods. The trade also allowed Senecas to obtain guns and liquor. As the Seneca economy changed, some Senecas temporarily prospered. Indeed, it was enviously said by some non-Indians that the Senecas were more affluent than the colonists.

With the loss of lands following the American Revolutionary War, the Seneca economy—as with much of the Seneca way of life—was destroyed. The now very small Seneca land base made it impossible to generate sufficient food from hunting, fishing, and farming. Moreover, it was no longer possible to trap furs in sufficient quantities. There was great despair and many Senecas fell victim to alcohol abuse and disease.

Seneca society began to revitalize in the early nineteenth century. Men were encouraged by the Quaker missionaries to take up farming, which had previously been scorned as "women's work," and farming expanded. Men also began to do wage work for non-Indians. Later in the century, farming decreased in importance as men began to work far outside Seneca territory, such as on the railroads and commercial farms. By the twentieth century, some men earned a living from logging, and many others worked away from home as tradesmen. Senecas, as well as other Haudenosaunee peoples, developed a reputation for working high steel in the construction industry. Despite these changes, however, the Seneca economy remained mostly undeveloped and dependent upon the resources that could be obtained from outside of its territory.

The Seneca economy has changed dramatically during the last thirty-five years. In the early 1960s, the United States seized one-third of the Allegany Territory for construction of the Kinzua reservoir on the Allegheny River. This taking of land resulted in the forced removal of several hundred Senecas living along the river's banks and the loss of an important part of the cultural life of the people living there. As partial compensation, the government built new homes in new relocation communities and later paid $15 million as "compensation" for the confiscation and destruction of lifestyle. In addition to this money, the Seneca Nation obtained money from the United States in the 1970s as part of the federal government's efforts to assist all Indian nations with community and economic development. These monies also thrust the colonizing nation's economic system—capitalism—into the heart of Seneca society. The change had as profound an impact on the Seneca economy as the fur trade had 300 years earlier.

In the 1980s, an economic explosion occurred. The Seneca Nation government had grown rapidly with the infusion of federal money. Services provided to the Seneca people expanded and, with it, the need for even more revenue. The Seneca government began to develop and operate its own businesses, such as a bowling alley and a campground, to generate income. Later on, however, it constructed two high-stakes bingo halls, one at Allegany and one at Cattaraugus, which attracted considerable numbers of non-Indian patrons. Perhaps the most significant development, however, was the establishment of new businesses that sold cigarettes and gasoline without collecting state sales taxes. Because of the much lower prices of these otherwise highly taxed goods, non-Indians drove for miles to buy these products (and to play bingo).[3] In addition to the nation's stores, individual Senecas entered this business. As a result, for maybe the first time ever, a few Senecas became millionaires. The inflow of wealth allowed many Senecas to gain employment and to generate small businesses of their own.

Social and Political Organization

Senecas have always had a sophisticated political and social structure. Prior to the onset of American colonization, there were multiple levels of political organization—the longhouse, the clan, the village, the Nation, and the Confederacy. The Confederacy's Great Law of Peace established a confederacy-wide council comprising fifty representatives known as *royanier*, or chiefs. Each of the *royanier* positions was designated with a particular title. When that person died or left office his successor received the same title. The presiding chief of the Confederate Council was the *ta-dodaho*, who was always an Onondaga. Each nation had only one vote in Confederate Council deliberations, even though each was represented by a different number of *royanier*. The Seneca were represented by eight *roy-anier*. For the Confederacy to take official action, all nations, as represented by their chiefs, had to be in agreement.

Women played a critical role in traditional Seneca government because they were responsible for the selection and removal of the Seneca *royanier* as well as the nation's war chief. There were eight clans in Seneca society and some, but not all, of the clan families "held" the eight *royanier* titles. The women of that family were thus responsible for choosing, and removing if need be, the *royanier* and otherwise ensuring that he represented the people wisely. A wise *royanier* would try to ensure that he made decisions with the Senecas' long-term benefit in mind—to the "seventh generation." And while it was the men who had the official decision-making responsibility, the women held much influence over what they actually decided.

As is true of much in Seneca society, the Seneca political structure changed greatly following the loss of lands after the American Revolutionary War. In 1848 these changes culminated in a revolutionary movement in the Allegany and Cattaraugus Territories that overthrew the traditional government established under the Great Law. Out of this turmoil came a new government, a constitutional republic called the Seneca Nation of Indians. Modeled after the American form of government, the Nation introduced many changes in the Seneca governing process. For example, elections, rather than selection by certain clan women, were instituted to select the new Nation officials. Women, in fact, were eliminated entirely from the governing process and could not even vote. The Senecas at Tonawanda, however, refused to accept the new form and retained the traditional government. They became known as the Tonawanda Band of Senecas.

Religion and World View

Senecas have always been a deeply spiritual people. Ceremonial activity takes place at designated times of the year to celebrate the changing of the seasons and to give thanks to the Creator.

The most dramatic change in Seneca religion came shortly after the American Revolutionary War. In 1798 a Seneca man named Handsome Lake began to have visions that eventually became the foundation of a new religion. Its basis, the *Gaiwiio*, or the "Good Word," included a social gospel which, in part, reflected the values brought by the colonists and their Christian religion. As the *Gaiwiio* spread it brought changes to Seneca society. For example, unlike the balanced gender roles that previously had been in place, men were taught to be the head of household and women were taught simply to support the man's needs.

Christian missionaries were also able during this time to sustain a presence in Seneca territory. Until the end of the eighteenth century, Senecas had been able to resist the missionaries' influence. Many Senecas, most notably the famed orator Red Jacket, rejected Christianity outright and sought to adhere to the traditional Seneca beliefs and ceremonies. But the weakening of Seneca society following the Revolutionary War made it easier for the missionaries to penetrate Seneca society, and within only a few decades, many Senecas had been converted to Christianity.

THREATS TO SURVIVAL

Historical Trends

As with all other societies, Senecas have undergone several periods of decline and renewal. During the early years of interaction with the colonists, many Senecas fell victim to the white man's diseases. Warfare also contributed to the periodic decline of the Seneca population. Nonetheless, the inherent strength and prosperity of Seneca society eventually permitted recovery and regeneration. One method by which this occurred was adoption. For example, if men were lost in war, it was frequently the practice to take captive men—both Indians from other nations and non-Indians—and incorporate them into Seneca society. This was also the case with women, and children orphaned during war. Because being a Seneca entailed certain duties and responsibilities, it was relatively easy for an outsider to be assimilated into Seneca society. Often, adopted Senecas assumed leadership positions. Because women held the property in Seneca society and were in control of the household, assimilating a foreign man was not necessarily disruptive to domestic relations.

The American Revolutionary War induced major changes in Seneca society. In 1779 General George Washington sent American armies through Haudenosaunee territories, where they burned over forty villages and all of the winter food stores. Few Senecas were killed, but the economic destruction and dislocation wrought by this military campaign precipitated a period of considerable decline. White settlers began to encroach on Seneca lands, and there were many skirmishes. These hostilities had mostly ended by 1794 when the Seneca Nation entered into its last and most significant peace treaty with the United States at Canandaigua. However, contrary to Seneca expectations, peaceful relations only brought greater pressure from Whites for them to relinquish Seneca lands. In 1797, at Big Tree, an American businessman named Robert Morris induced the Seneca leadership and women to sell more than 2 million acres of Seneca territory. This left the Seneca Nation with only about 200,000 acres of aboriginal land.

The loss of Seneca military power and land virtually ended the traditional Seneca way of life. Men were effectively rendered useless since their traditional activities—warfare, diplomacy, and extended hunting and trading forays—had been eliminated. Of course, the presence of these despondent men in the villages affected the women as well. To compound the misery, alcohol abuse proliferated. Nonetheless, Seneca society rebounded after the adoption of Handsome Lake's *Gaiwiio* and a restructuring of Seneca social life by the Quakers. This revitalization, however, eroded much of what had long been traditionally Seneca. The introduction of Christianity, Western education, the nuclear family, and single-family homes all contributed to a dramatic transformation in Seneca society. Thus, the cost of Seneca survival following the Revolutionary War was the loss of much of the traditional Seneca identity.

During the last 200 years, Senecas have continued to face various threats. These threats have focused primarily on efforts by Whites to obtain title or control over the remaining Seneca lands. In the early nineteenth century, the Seneca Nation was swindled out of the Buffalo Creek Territory and a number of smaller territories along the Genesee River. In the late nineteenth century, the white lessees in Salamanca sought to have the United States simply take the Seneca land that they had been leasing. In the early twentieth century, New York State launched an aggressive effort to obtain criminal and civil jurisdiction over all Indian lands within its borders. In 1948 and 1950, New York State finally convinced the United States to give it such authority. In the early 1960s, the United States confiscated one-third of the Allegany Territory for the Kinzua Reservoir. Because of the continuity of these threats, Senecas give particular attention to protecting the land base.

In the last thirty-five years Seneca society has been thrust into American society to a degree not experienced in over 200 years. The taking of one-third of the Allegany Territory for the Kinzua Dam and the forced removal of more than 300 Senecas by the United States greatly transformed Seneca life at Allegany. Many elders died soon after seeing their ancestral homes bulldozed and burned. The way of life of the survivors changed overnight. New homes were built in the relocation areas near the white communities of Salamanca and Steamburg, and many Senecas had electricity and plumbing for the very first time. The Kinzua land seizure thrust Seneca society into American society in more subtle but no less significant ways. The $15 million settlement paid to the Nation allowed for considerable community and economic development. This began a period of rapid economic and social change.

The infusion of money into the Seneca Nation continued in the 1970s, when the United States began to provide millions of dollars of development assistance to fund government programs and business ventures. The early 1980s saw economic development expand beyond the public sector to include widespread entrepreneurial capitalism. As a result, in a thirty-five-year period, Senecas—both as a government and in some individual cases—have made millions. For most Senecas the material quality of Seneca life has improved dramatically.

One of the paramount beliefs of American society is that money translates into happiness. Thus, one might naturally conclude that the Seneca Nation's incorporation into the American economic system would have resolved many of the ills present in Seneca society. Unfortunately, the opposite has been true. Because entrepreneurial capitalism has been thrust upon Seneca society so quickly, Senecas are now confronted with a multitude of afflictions that present grave new threats to the Seneca future. Four of these contemporary threats are economic, political, environmental, and sociocultural.

Economic Crisis

Many Senecas today have become preoccupied with pursuing excess material wealth for their own personal benefit. This reflects an assimilation of American values that runs counter to traditional Seneca values which focus on the satisfaction of family and community needs. While it is true that Seneca society has been exposed to capitalism for centuries, most of the economic activity—trade—took place far from the core of Seneca communal life. In contrast, the economic activity now taking place is much more intense because it is occurring within Seneca communities (and even in some peoples' homes). This has precipitated an interaction with Whites and White society that is unprecedented in its invasive and transformative qualities. As a result, entrepreneurial capitalism is tearing apart the fabric of the Seneca community and all of Seneca society.

To be sure, the tax-free sale of cigarettes and gasoline has allowed many Senecas to find employment. It has also allowed a few others to become millionaires. Capitalism, by definition, is premised upon individuals pursuing their economic self-interest. The growth of capitalism has contributed to the proliferation of values in Seneca society that are focused heavily on individual rather than community benefit. For example, as private business has grown, the Nation government has sought to regulate and tax this economic activity for public benefit. The Seneca entrepreneurs, however, have been successful at ensuring that these efforts have failed. As a result, while hundreds of millions of dollars have been earned by the Seneca business community during the last twenty years, none of it has been contributed directly to the Seneca government for public purposes.

This behavior has not only generated a self-destructive value system, it has also induced considerable conflict within the Seneca community. Since the late 1980s, there has been an ongoing struggle between Seneca entrepreneurs and other Senecas who believe that the entrepreneurs should pay for the opportunity to exploit collective rights for personal gain. These conflicts have been intense, frequent, and occasionally violent. For several years, the focal point has been whether the Nation should develop a casino-style gambling business. Struggle over this issue fueled a civil war that broke out in late 1994 and lasted for almost a year, leaving three men dead. Although this conflict was ignited after the election of an anti-entrepreneurial candidate to the Seneca Nation's presidency, it had been spawned by over a decade of intense economic struggle.

The Political Crisis of 1994–1995

The recent Seneca Nation civil war highlights the crisis that exists in Seneca government. In 1994 a self-styled populist was elected to the Nation presidency on an agenda of putting controls on the Seneca entrepreneurs. Once in office, he began his crusade by taking a number of provocative actions against the entrepreneurs and filing a lawsuit in the Nation's own court system seeking judicial approval of his actions. In response, his entrepreneur opponents filed suit against him in the New York State courts.

This retaliatory action violated Seneca Nation sovereignty.[4] The entrepreneurs sought to use the legal machinery of a foreign government—the State of New York—as a tool against their political enemy. This enraged many Senecas and inflamed passions. Eventually, gunfire broke out, and for many months Senecas lived in considerable danger. The entrepreneurs eventually lost their court battle when a federal judge declared the state court's actions null and void. Nonetheless, tensions had elevated to a new high. Three men were killed during an effort by one faction to take over a building that had been occupied by the other.

The Seneca Nation civil war revealed the weakness of the Nation's governmental system because it was unable to redress the underlying political disputes. Throughout the conflict, those on each side cloaked themselves in their own personal interpretations of the Nation's constitution and laws. The decisions made by the Nation's courts on these difficult questions were ignored by the losing parties. The overall effect was to render meaningless the Nation's system of law and government. In short, people simply did whatever they wanted to do regardless of the law. This lawlessness translated into violence and death, and there were no effective mechanisms within the Nation's legal or political system to keep it from escalating. Only an innate sense among most of the combatants and the whole of the Seneca community that such violence, directed toward one another, was wrong prevented this bloodshed from escalating.

While the violence of the Nation's civil war eventually subsided, the chaos associated with the Nation's weak political system has continued. In the effort to find new leadership, the Seneca people have elected four presidents in a row who have had no previous experience in government. This

Senecas in dispute. Copyright *The Buffalo News.*

has resulted in unpredictable and weak leadership that has left government operations rudderless and in disarray. In addition, the two-party political system, which for most of the Nation's history kept political affairs stable, has broken down. There are now multiple parties, and many independent candidates seek public office. Because the Nation has no runoff system, only a handful of candidates elected in the last decade have had majority support. While this multiparty broadening of Seneca democracy has had some positive effects, it nonetheless has weakened the Seneca government and political system.

Environmental Crisis

The emergence of the Seneca retail gasoline businesses has generated a new source of environmental pollution. These businesses originally were established under few regulatory controls, and few, if any, precautions have been taken to prevent spilled gasoline from contaminating the groundwater. When these spills occur, they may be only superficially cleaned up. They are thus an unknown source of danger. In the past decade, the Nation has developed a water line system for the Cattaraugus Territory which may help minimize the effect of this seepage. The long-term effects of this form of environmental pollution are unknown.

Other forms of environmental assault include the large-scale removal of gravel from Seneca lands. Gravel has been a cash crop within the Nation for at least 100 years and has benefited both individual Senecas and the Nation's government. The law within the Nation provides that an individual Seneca may obtain permanent use rights to the land's surface estate, but the Nation retains common ownership of the subsurface estate. Thus, it has been lawful to remove gravel as long as 50 percent of the proceeds were remitted to the Nation. Today, both the Allegany and Cattaraugus Territories are littered with both active and abandoned gravel pits. Many have swollen with runoff and created small lakes; others remain eyesores and lasting reminders of having sold land for profit. The long-term consequences of this activity are unknown.

Another recent environmental crisis has been the cutting of virtually all commercial-quality timber located within the Nation's territory. For the last fifteen years or so, Seneca loggers have begun to cut down most of the Nation's hardwood as a means of earning a living. These efforts have occasionally taken place with the consent of Seneca land users, but most have entailed unauthorized removal of trees from Nation common lands. Efforts made by Nation government officials to stop this activity have been thwarted by threats of violence. Today, the activity appears to be ending, not because of enforcement efforts, but because it is so difficult to find large enough trees to justify the effort to cut them down. The forest today is littered with logging roads and debris and is so damaged that some species of trees may never return.

Sociocultural Crisis

Senecas today are in the midst of a cultural crisis. The greatest evidence of this is the loss of the Seneca language. Today, it appears that no more than 350 Senecas, or less than 5 percent of the Seneca population, can speak Seneca. The loss of the Seneca language is clearly the greatest threat to the existence of the Seneca people. The Seneca language is not an easy language, but it is directly vital to the preservation of many unique aspects of Seneca society, including the traditional religious ceremonies and the Great Law of Peace.

The decline in the Seneca language is directly attributable to the efforts made by state officials and missionaries to force Seneca children to speak English. This corrosive effect has been compounded by the fairly recent development (since the 1960s) of sending Seneca children to state public schools located on or near Seneca territory, which have replaced the customary all-Seneca schools. While imperfect, the all-Seneca schools helped preserve a community of Seneca speakers. In recent years, some effort has been expended to teach the language to Seneca children in the public schools, but the trend toward fewer and fewer native speakers has not been reversed. Failure to preserve the Seneca language greatly endangers the preservation of a unique Seneca culture and identity.

Added to the loss of language has been a dramatic increase in intermarriage between Senecas and Whites in the last generation, especially of Seneca women marrying white men.[5] Because the Senecas are matrilineal, the children of such marriages have full citizen rights as Seneca even though they often grow up with little grounding in Seneca culture. Consequently, Seneca society is becoming increasingly diverse. Unlike 300 years ago, when adoptions could occur without significant effect on what it meant to be Seneca, intermarriage today and having children with non-Indians threaten what it means to be Seneca.

Today, Seneca society is being undermined by the very societal forces that most Americans generally assume are positive developments. Economic development has made some Senecas affluent, even to the point of creating a class of extremely wealthy individuals, as contrasted with the more modest economic situation of most Senecas. This, naturally, comes at the expense of traditional community values and the environment. Democracy has given more Senecas the ability to speak out on public affairs, but it has undermined the Nation's political stability. Assimilation has enabled greater participation in American society, but it has eroded Seneca identity and culture.

RESPONSE: STRUGGLES TO SURVIVE CULTURALLY

Despite the multitude and severity of the threats to Seneca society since the American Revolutionary War, there nonetheless has remained a central core of Seneca identity which has enabled the maintenance and preservation of a distinct society. Change induced accommodation, and new mechanisms were developed that redefined what it meant to be Seneca. For example, while Senecas increasingly became Christian, there always remained a functioning longhouse community that followed the *Gaiwiio* and preserved the ancient ceremonies. Some Senecas, in fact, adapted by following both religions. This was also true with respect to language; many Senecas became bilingual in English and Seneca. Thus, while colonization resulted in the assimilation of American values and culture, there remained many Senecas who continued to perpetuate key aspects of the traditional way of life.

One reason for this ability to endure was the relative isolation of Seneca territory. Despite the development of some large cities like Buffalo and other much smaller communities, western New York State has long been a largely rural, undeveloped area. Aside from the now defunct railroad and steel industries, there has not been any significant economic activity to precipitate large, non-Indian population movements into the rural areas. Moreover, there has long been a racial divide between Whites and Senecas living in the area. This social barrier, combined with geographic isolation, served to some extent to insulate Seneca society from much of the assimilating influence of the larger American society. As a result, while changes have certainly occurred during the period of American colonization, at its core Seneca society has been able to remain largely intact.

Education

The primary effort taken in recent years to promote strength in Seneca society has been a commitment to education. Seneca children are educated primarily in the state public schools located on or near the Nation territories. The Nation government, however, has spent millions to develop an education infrastructure that targets every sector of the Seneca population for assistance. Day care and preschool educational programs focus on basic skills but also include lessons in the Seneca language. There are in-school and after-school programs for youth. And there is also support for adult education, including scholarship support for postsecondary education.

It is unclear at this time whether these efforts to improve Seneca education are having any appreciable effect. Senecas continue to drop out of high school in very high numbers. Few Senecas raised in Seneca territory go to college. Senecas learn little in school about their own nation's government and history. No Seneca youth are becoming fluent in the Seneca language in the public schools.

These educational efforts appear to be failing for at least two reasons. First, Seneca education programs are not well configured to inculcate Seneca culture. Instead, the efforts over the last twenty-five years have fallen primarily along the same path as that taken by the state and missionary "educators" of the nineteenth century—the promotion and assimilation of American values and culture. Accordingly, while there has been some emphasis on teaching the Seneca language and culture in the preschool and in-school programs, this effort has been subsidiary to the general public school education and its focus on such things as reading, writing, and proficiency with computers.

Obviously these basic skills are important for survival in the modern world, but Senecas attending the state public schools receive more instruction about how to survive in American society than they do about how to survive in Seneca society. In short, current Seneca educational efforts are directed primarily toward providing only one-half of the education that Senecas need to survive as a distinct people—how to live in the dominant society. Success in promoting education will occur when Seneca language, culture, history, and government have achieved equal treatment in the classroom.

Second, Seneca educational efforts fall short of their intended goals because the Nation has abandoned its responsibility for educating Seneca children to the state of New York. The fact that all Seneca children attend the state public schools ensures that the educational focus and method of instruction will always fall short of the educational content necessary for

Senecas to survive. The part-time language programs will never succeed in the face of having most instruction offered in the English language. Seneca educational failure will continue until there is a complete resumption of Seneca responsibility for educating Seneca children.

Economic Development

Some Senecas take the view that the recent efforts to promote economic development will redress many of the ills of Seneca society. While it is unclear to what extent this is a well-thought-out approach for Seneca rejuvenation or whether it is just a rationalization for profiteering, the belief is that as individual Senecas become wealthier, there will be a commensurate strengthening of Seneca society.

Unfortunately, there is little evidence that promoting entrepreneurial capitalism will promote a stronger Seneca society. The development trend thus far has been for a handful of Senecas to generate excessive profits for their own personal benefit. While it is true that these businesses have generated additional employment opportunities that had not previously existed, there has not been any appreciable focus on promoting the overall public good. An effort made several years ago to capture some business profits to build a tribal school—the only realistic counterbalance to the corrosive social influence of economic development—was stopped by the entrepreneurial community. Economic development will continue to undermine community relations until some mechanism is developed to induce the entrepreneurs to contribute some of their profits directly to the community.

Spiritual Direction and Political Activism

Despite the almost uniform inability to develop a response to the threats facing Seneca society, at least two significant developments should be noted. One factor militating against the loss of Seneca culture has been the recent increase in the number of Senecas attending ceremonies at the longhouse. In the face of recent problems and conflict, it seems that Senecas are increasingly turning toward the spiritual foundation of Seneca society. It remains unknown whether this trend will be sufficient to overcome the current disintegrative pressures.

The second factor has been a resurgence of political activism in recent years. In 1992 Senecas engaged in a mass act of civil disobedience by blocking the two interstate highways running through Nation territory. The state had long sought to require Seneca retailers to collect state sales taxes on sales of these products made to its citizens doing business in Nation territory. After many years in court, the state finally succeeded, and the supply of cigarettes and gasoline to Seneca territory was cut off. Both public and private businesses were shut down, throwing hundreds of Senecas out of work and jeopardizing government revenues.

In response, hundreds of Senecas joined the newly unemployed and began to protest the state's actions. Using signs, speeches, marches, and bonfires, the protests focused on notifying the outside world that the state had destroyed the Nation's economy to protect its own business interests. Spontaneously, the people—from all walks of life—shut down the interstate highways and blocked access to western New York State for almost two days. Thousands of state police surrounded Nation territory, but Senecas were unarmed and there was thus no justification for violence. In the face of this mass resistance, the state quickly backed down from its taxation efforts.

This momentous act of resistance and strength unified the Seneca community in a way that most likely had not occurred for hundreds of years. In 1997 the state (led by a new and different governor) again sought to tax Nation economic activity. This time, for six weeks, Senecas resisted the state's efforts. Protests were launched and roads were blocked periodically, but again there was no submission. The state even entertained the possibility of sending in National Guard troops to suppress this defensive action. Eventually, however, the new governor acceded to the Seneca's assertion of sovereignty and abandoned his efforts to tax Seneca commerce. Together, these efforts have unleashed a political confidence that could one day translate into a sustained, comprehensive effort to redress internal problems.

Perhaps the greatest obstacle preventing a more sustained response to the threats facing the Seneca people is a failure to appreciate the magnitude of the threats and the lack of a mechanism to redress them. Many Senecas are becoming increasingly comfortable with—in fact, passionately desirous of—becoming more assimilated into American society. As a result, there is a wide failure to appreciate the unique nature of Seneca society and the need to take action to protect it. Moreover, even if this appreciation materializes, the chances of Seneca revitalization are bleak given that the primary mechanism for generating sustained collective action—the Nation's government—is extremely weak. The Seneca constitution was initially supported by only about half of the Seneca people; a considerable number have always rejected its authority. Moreover, there is no tradition of having a strong constitutional government. The Kinzua Dam crisis triggered the need for a more active government, and the increased resources of the past thirty-five years have fostered one. Unfortunately, the Nation's enlarged governmental functions have occurred on the back of a constitutional structure that is ill equipped to deal with the multitude of problems that must now be addressed.

Accordingly, power under the Seneca Nation's constitution can become too concentrated and unaccountable. In an era when Seneca politics have become more democratic, this tendency has prevented broad-based political alliances from forming. Indeed, just the opposite has occurred: feuding and political infighting have crippled the ability of the Seneca Nation's government to function effectively. As a result, Senecas today generally do not perceive that their government is legitimate and do not place the necessary faith in it to redress common problems. This is a disastrous weakness because, despite everything that has happened over the years, Seneca society retains many strong attributes: a land base, language, and culture. There is some form of government and economy. And there remains an intense Seneca spirit which values both freedom and responsibility to one another. All of the raw materials necessary for a Seneca renaissance are in place. The only thing missing is an organizing mechanism.

FOOD FOR THOUGHT

The Onodowaga (Senecas) are now an endangered people primarily because of the actions taken by Euro-American colonizers during the last 300 years to take our land and destroy our unique way of life. Because our first 100 years of interaction with the colonists occurred against the backdrop of relative military parity, Seneca society evolved naturally as any society might have when confronting newcomers. But the demise of Seneca military power following the American Revolutionary War allowed the United States and its citizens to prey upon the Seneca people and to embark upon a 200-year crusade to obtain the remaining Seneca lands and wipe out Seneca society. While this effort has not yet succeeded, Euro-America has been able to infect the Seneca people with its values and way of life. This is a more subtle, and thus a more dangerous, threat because it undermines the very core of what it means to be a Seneca. Foremost of these recent threats is capitalism, which has undermined the interconnectedness of the Seneca community through an increasingly aggressive and violent quest for excess individual wealth.

Questions

1. What can Senecas do to perpetuate their existence as a distinct people?
2. How might the Seneca develop more effective political institutions?
3. Can the process of colonization be reversed? By the colonizing power? By the colonized people?
4. Is the power of the American melting pot so strong that Senecas will eventually be assimilated and absorbed into American society?
5. Should the United States affirmatively end its recognition of Seneca sovereignty and treat Senecas just like any other ethnic or racial minority in the United States?

NOTES

1. The Haudenosaunee were known by the first British colonists as the "Five Nations." In the early eighteenth century, the Tuscaroras relocated from the Carolinas to Seneca Territory. They affiliated with the Haudenosaunee, and the Confederacy became "Six Nations."

2. The spelling of "Allegany" differs because Seneca and Euro-Americans spell the word differently. In Seneca, the term for the Allegany River is *Ohiyo* which means "beautiful river."

3. This commerce arises because of the sovereign status of Seneca Territory. State laws, including tax laws, generally do not apply. The Senecas are able to sell tobacco products and motor fuel without the very high New York State taxes associated with these goods. This naturally creates a very favorable market opportunity that has generated considerable friction with the surrounding white business community and New York State.

4. Sovereignty is a term referring to the power of a people to exercise authority over their own lives.

5. While exact figures for the Seneca Nation do not exist, according to the U.S. 1990 census, 71 percent of Indians nationally marry non-Indians.

RESOURCE GUIDE

Published Literature

Bilharz, Joy A. *The Allegany Senecas and Kinzua Dam*. Lincoln: University of Nebraska Press, 1998.

Fenton, William N. *The Great Law and the Longhouse*. Norman: University of Oklahoma Press, 1998.

Hauptman, Laurence M. *The Iroquois Struggle for Survival*. Syracuse, N.Y.: Syracuse University Press, 1986.

Morgan, Lewis H. *League of the Iroquois*. New York: Citadel Press, 1962.

Parker, Arthur C. *Parker on the Iroquois*. Syracuse, N.Y.: Syracuse University Press, 1968.

Porter, Robert B. "Building a New Longhouse: The Case for Government Reform Within the Six Nations of the Haudenosaunee." 46 *Buffalo Law Review* (1998): 805.

Wallace, Anthony F.C. *The Death and Rebirth of the Seneca*. New York: Alfred A. Knopf, 1970.

Wallace, Paul A.W. *The White Roots of Peace*. Saranac, N.Y.: Chauncy Press, 1946.

WWW Sites

Seneca Nation of Indians Homepage
http://www.sni.org/

Haudenosaunee: People Building a Longhouse Homepage
http://www.sixnations.org/

Oneida Indian Nation Homepage
http://www.oneida-nation.net/

Mohawk Nation Council of Chiefs Homepage
http://www.slic.com/~mohawkna/home.html

St. Regis Mohawk Tribe Environment Division
http://www.northnet.org/earth/index.html

Six Nations of the Grand River Homepage
http://www.geocities.com/Athens/Olympus/3808/

Video

Lands of our Ancestors/Seneca Nation of Indians. New York: Post Central, 1997.

Organizations

Seneca Nation of Indians,
Allegany Indian Reservation
P.O. Box 231
Salamanca, SNI, NY 14779

Seneca Nation of Indians,
Cattaraugus Indian Reservation
1490 Route 438
Cattaraugus Territory
via Irving, NY 14081

Chapter 8

The Wanapum of Priest Rapids, Washington

Julia G. Longenecker, Darby C. Stapp,
and Angela M. Buck

Along the banks of the Columbia River in eastern Washington State live the Wanapum Band, a small Native American group with ancient ties to the area. Life since the Euro-Americans arrived has been very difficult. The salmon, the resource on which their life is based, have all but disappeared. Other traditional foods and resources are disappearing or getting harder to find. Their land base has shrunk from millions of acres to forty acres. The burial grounds of their ancestors, now mostly on other people's land, are unearthed regularly by looters digging for arrowheads and developers during construction projects. Through it all, the Wanapum have remained living in their homeland and will continue to do so into the future.

CULTURAL OVERVIEW

The People

The Wanapum (meaning "River People" and sometimes referred to as the Priest Rapid Indians) are a Native American band of about 100 people who live at Priest Rapids, Washington. Their oral traditions, or teachings as they call them, tell the Wanapum that they have always lived in this area. The Wanapum are one of many tribes who live along the Columbia River in a geographical region known as the Columbia Plateau. The Columbia Plateau region ranges from present-day northern British Columbia in Canada, to southern Oregon in the United States, and from the coastal mountain ranges to the Rocky Mountains.

The Wanapum speak a Sahaptian language. Other languages included in the Sahaptian family include several Yakama dialects and Nez Perce.

Through marriage the Wanapum have become closely related to their neighboring groups including the Nez Perce, Palus, Yakama, Cayuse, Umatilla, Walla Wallas, and Warm Springs. Wanapum men tend to stay at Priest Rapids following marriage. Wanapum women who marry into another group usually move to the homeland of their new husband.

The Setting

As indicated by their name the "River People," the Wanapum live a life that is based on unwritten laws and their beliefs. They live along the central portion of the Columbia River, one of the great rivers in North America. Historically, their villages and fishing camps were located from Wenatchee to Wallula Gap. Priest Rapids was an important fishing area, characterized by a series of seven river rapids. The Wanapum regularly traveled east to the Moses Lake area and west to the Natches area for various food and other resources.

Today, most of the Columbia River has been dammed, resulting in a series of lakes. These dams (e.g., Grand Coulee and Bonneville) were built throughout the Columbia River drainage between the 1930s and 1970s for irrigation and electricity. A portion of the river located just downstream from Priest Rapids and part of the Wanapum homeland is the last area of the entire Columbia River that has not been dammed and flooded. This fifty-one-mile-long stretch, known as the Hanford Reach, is included within the 560-square-mile Hanford Nuclear Reservation. The U.S. Government created Hanford in 1943 to build a plutonium production plant for its atomic weapons program. Hanford kept this portion of the river from being dammed up because it needed a fast flowing supply of cool water.

The area where the Wanapum lived and traveled is beautiful. The landscape is generally flat and open, with sand dunes, canyons, hills, and occasional mountains. The soil is sandy, and native vegetation is dominated by sagebrush and native grasses. With only six inches of rainfall a year, the area is desert-like. Summers are hot and winters are relatively mild. High winds are common. Today, most areas of native vegetation have been replaced by Euro-American–related developments such as irrigated orchards, vineyards, cattle operations, wheat farms, and cheat grass.[1]

Traditional Subsistence Strategies

The traditional diet for the Wanapum was, and still is, based on the salmon. Arlene Buck, Wanapum elder, described the traditional seasonal movements as she heard it from her father:

My Father used to mostly talk about the fish. How he remembered when the Salmon used to be in the hundreds and you could look on the River and anytime you wanted it and you could get up and go out there and get some. He talked how easy it was to travel because they were on horseback then and he said how they lived in tule mat lodges.[2] And that it was so easy to store while they traveled. Because they never lived here all year round. They would be here during the winter and then when it became time to gather the food to preserve, they would go out and they would move down to Horn Rapids, down by the Tri-Cities. And they would get fish there and then they would move from there and go get the roots after the First Foods Feast. And then they would move up after the berries. He would take us to Wenatchee and to Stampede and up that way and tell us places where they used to camp. And up there during the berry season or the root season and then he would say "Then after that they'd make it back towards this way for fall to get the fall fish." Then they would smoke the fish they had. You know they had different ways of preserving the different kinds of fish. Some you couldn't dry or you couldn't can or whatever, so they would smoke it and have it that way. Then they would stay all winter again and then they would start all over again.[3]

Today, the people still eat the traditional foods, although these foods are more commonly consumed during the meal following Sunday services and ceremonies.

Medicines extracted from plants were also important to the people. Over seventy-five plant species are known to have a variety of uses for healing and other purposes. As Patrick Wyena, Wanapum, recalls:

I can remember when I was five or six years old, my Mother used to get sick and she'd send me and my brother out to this hillside to pick a certain plant that we would have to bring home. She would boil it up and she would drink it. It was medicine, something that people would call weeds, that would grow along the roadway or whatever and cured common colds or get rid of fevers. There's different things out there. We would get sent out maybe once a week to get medicines during the winter and fall.[4]

Maintaining the use of these medicines is today an important cultural tradition to the Wanapum.

Social and Political Organization

Historically, the Wanapum lived along the river in villages of from twenty to fifty people. Several related families lived together in mat lodges made from tules, a plant from river marshes that hardens into long sticks. These sticks were then sewn together to form long mats. Villages had a longhouse, in which their weekly, three-day-long religious services were held. The longhouse was also used for many different kinds of ceremonies such as the naming of a child, a funeral, or the First Foods Feast. It was also used for social gatherings which brought friends and relatives from villages throughout the region.

Certain people within the village had spiritual gifts they developed over a long period of time. Gifts were related to areas such as religion, healing, hunting, and fishing. When village-level decisions were needed, the group gathered and discussed the issues. In time a consensus emerged and the decision was made.

Elders were knowledgeable and highly respected throughout the community. The elders spent time talking to the children and sharing the stories and teachings. The teachings covered the creation stories, historical events such as floods, and explanations for landforms. Within the teachings were lessons for living life. The teachings, taught as oral traditions, lasted for days, and were repeated often. Child rearing was strict. If one child within the village misbehaved, all the children in the village were punished. Punishment was generally administered by one individual, known as the "whip man." More generally, children were corrected by adults in the village, not just by their parents.

Religion and World View

The Wanapum practice the Dreamer Religion. The Dreamer Religion was rooted in ancient Plateau Indian religion, but recast by the religious prophet Smohalla (pronounced SHMO-hala) in the mid-nineteenth century. Puck Hyah Toot was the leader of the Priest Rapids Longhouse (the traditional religious community) during the middle decades of the twentieth century and led the Wanapum into the modern era. Today, Rex Buck, Jr., is the religious leader. Priest Rapids got its name in 1811 when a fur trader, Alexander Ross, encountered an Indian religious leader, or priest, at the rapids.

The Dreamer Religion, also known as *Waashat* (pronounced WASH-ut), provided an individual with a disciplined way of life that would lead him or her through this world and into the next world upon death. Certain individuals were shown the way to live when they were asleep and given prophesies about the future. Smohalla, for example, saw the coming of the railroad, the dams, and the loss of the salmon based upon dreams he had. For the Wanapum, religion and life are one and the same. They do not divide their life into religious and nonreligious spheres as many Euro-Americans do. Songs, an important element of the Dreamer way of life, serve as a form of prayer. During weekly services the Wanapum gather to sing, pray, and give thanks to the Creator. Seasonal ceremonies, such as Indian New Year (celebrated on winter solstice) and the springtime First Foods Feast, are major events for groups to gather and fulfill their responsibilities to the Creator. Funerals are also important times because the people have responsibilities that must be carried out to assist the deceased person. The sweat lodge purification ceremony cleanses the body and the mind and continues to be important in the lives of the people.

Just as the Wanapum do not divide their life into religious and nonreligious spheres, neither do they divide life into human and nonhuman spheres. All plants, animals, rocks, and land are related and have spirits. As one elder put it, "To an Indian all land is worth something, right to the tiniest animal that was here. He was put here for some reason. We respect the life that it carries."[5] All have a responsibility to one another to care for each other. There is an order to everything. The teachings tell the Wanapum about their responsibilities to the land; to the creatures that live within, on, and above the land; to the ancestors who are buried in the land; and to the ones who have yet to be born. Included in the teachings are prophecies about events that are forthcoming.

The Wanapum consider their presence on earth as part of a longer journey. As Rex Buck, Jr., explains, "When our time came we left willingly, we left ready. We left everything behind and we didn't look back because we weren't leaving, we were only going ahead. Just a little while ahead, and our children would follow us in time."[6] While on earth, the Wanapum are caretakers, responsible for the land and passing on the teachings of the natural world to the next generation. According to Mike Squeochs, a young Wanapum father,

To me a Wanapum is a person who lives for the river, for the fish, for the animals, everything that consists of the land and that's what my Grandmother has taught me and I'm trying to teach that to my children and my wife so she learns what we do here, why we're here and how we live, our ways of life. That's what I try to teach.[7]

THREATS TO SURVIVAL

Historical Threats

Influences from the outside started impacting the Wanapum hundreds of years ago. The arrival of the horse in the mid-1700s changed modes of transportation and quickly became a new symbol of power and authority. In the late 1700s, new Western items from the Pacific fur trade began working their way into the mid-Columbia. New goods were highly desired for making clothing, jewelry, and tools. Native Americans were attracted to such new materials as iron, copper, and glass beads for use as tools, jewelry, and decoration. They obtained these goods from the traders by exchanging beaver, deer, and elk skins. The fur trade brought many changes to the local communities. Successful hunters and traders rose in prominence, changing the traditional system of power and prestige. Game was depleted, which upset the ecological balance that had existed for generations.

Another impact came from the spread of European diseases. Indian people suffered from various epidemics such as smallpox, which reduced the population from around 2,000 in 1780 to about 300 in 1870.[8] Before long, many places were abandoned, and the survivors congregated in villages with other survivors. While smallpox has nearly been eradicated in the United States today, other European diseases such as sugar diabetes and alcoholism continue to threaten Native American lives. These diseases are generally caused by a change in diet and lifestyle, from traditional foods and daily food gathering, to foods high in sugar and fat and requiring little physical effort to obtain. This change came about when the U.S. government gave the Indians white flour and sugar commodities and prohibited them from hunting and gathering traditional foods.

Within decades, fur trade posts were established throughout the region. A Hudson's Bay Company post, Fort Nez Perce, operated at the mouth of the Walla Walla River from 1818 to 1848. The trading post substantially increased the types and quantities of Western goods available to the Indians. It also increased job opportunities for Indians who took on hunting and trapping for the trade market. Further social changes occurred when employees of the post took Indian wives and produced mixed-blood children.

Missionaries began moving into the region during this time. Whitman Mission, located near present-day Walla Walla in Cayuse Indian country to the southeast of the Wanapum, operated from 1836 to 1847. During this time, Marcus Whitman attempted to convert many local Indians to Christianity. Other missions located throughout the region converted large numbers of Indians. The missionaries' challenge to the Wanapum's traditional culture and its *Waashat* religion was to become another of the many cultural disruptions experienced by the Wanapum.

The migration of settlers from the east to the Willamette Valley in western Oregon increased dramatically from the 1830s to the 1850s. Before long, it was clear that the government would have to do something to make room for the thousands of Easterners who were planning on moving west. The government's solution was to force Indian tribes living along the Mid-Columbia River to sign treaties in which the tribes ceded (relinquished ownership of) lands to the U.S. government, although they retained certain rights of access to the resources on these lands. The tribes were then moved to designated reservations. In return, the tribes received various treaty rights, money, supplies, and other promises from the government, many of which were never kept.

The treaties were negotiated by Isaac Stevens, Washington's territorial governor, and Joe Palmer, Oregon's superintendent for Indian affairs, who brought together many tribes at the Walla Walla Council in 1855. Here they managed to get Native American spokesmen to make commitments for their respective tribes. The treaties were phrased as though they were freely negotiated. In reality, the tribes had no choice; the military was resolved to solve the Indian "problem" one way or another. In many instances, three different languages were being spoken and many misunderstandings occurred during the negotiations. The Walla Walla treaties created the Nez Perce Reservation, the Umatilla Reservation, and the Yakama Reservation in areas near the Wanapum.

The Wanapum, however, led by their leader Smohalla, had no interest in making any treaty or moving away from their homeland, and he led them back to Priest Rapids. Because few Euro-Americans were interested in the Priest Rapids area, the government did not press the matter. From here, Smohalla's Dreamer Religion gained support throughout the reservations. Before long many individuals supported Smohalla.[9]

The Wanapum population gradually declined during the late 1800s and early 1900s. During the early nineteenth century, the Wanapum numbered about 2,000. Estimates from the mid-nineteenth century, after Smohalla returned with his followers to Priest Rapids, were around 400. An epidemic in the 1870s caused the death of about seventy people. In the early twentieth century most Wanapums became members of different reservations where they had family ties. Tribal membership gave each of them access to reservation land. Over the years, some Wanapum from Priest Rapids moved to a reservation for marriage, health, or work. By the 1930s, the Priest Rapids village had decreased to thirty to fifty members.[10]

Reservation life was afforded no sanctuary, however. On the contrary, federal policy was to concertedly attack native culture in order to eliminate as quickly as possible Indians as separate peoples.

Up until the early decades of the 20th century, Indian agents, missionaries, and other government officials made various attempts to eliminate the Dreamer Religion on the reservations. Policies were also put in place to eliminate Indian language, foods, dress, songs, prayer, traditions, and beliefs. However, in the 1930s the Bureau of Indian Affairs, under the leadership of a new director, John Collier, reversed its anti-Indian policies. Indians were now free to practice their religion, to speak their native language, and to promote their arts. By the 1930s, however, many on the reservations had abandoned traditional ways. They were unable to practice their traditional religion and self-sufficient way of life, and yet were unable to find work in the non-Indian world. As a result, many Indians living on the reservation became dependent on the government for food, supplies, medical care, housing, and education.[11]

The Wanapum were able to maintain their traditional way of life along the Columbia River into the 1940s, partly because Whites had little desire for the lands on which they lived. In the 1940s, however, the Wanapum began to lose access to their traditional lands. In 1943, for example, the federal government closed off about 600 square miles of the southern part of the Wanapum homeland to build the Hanford plutonium plant as part of the war effort. Camps were abandoned and places where firewood, fish, and medicines were often obtained were fenced off. Important religious areas such as Gable Mountain could no longer be visited.

A few years later, more Wanapum lands were taken by the U.S. Army. They needed several hundred square miles to the west for the Yakima Training Center, a bombing range and military training area. The result was the loss of rangeland for hundreds of horses owned by the Wanapum. The crowning blow came in the early 1950s. The local county government constructed two dams (Priest Rapids Dam and Wanapum Dam) which flooded most of the Wanapum's critically important riverside lands. This effectively ended the old way of living. Up to this time, the Wanapum were still living in multifamily tule mat lodges just as they had in the past, with no modern conveniences. Now changes would have to be made.

Current Events and Conditions

To help compensate for the loss of their homeland, the Grant County Public Utility District (PUD) provided forty acres below Priest Rapids Dam, downstream from the traditional village of P'Na, for a new Priest Rapids village. The PUD built three modern homes and provided a Quonset hut for the village longhouse. This area continues to serve as the central village for the Wanapum today.

Many of the Wanapum today work for the PUD in dam operation and in jobs designed to promote and perpetuate the Wanapum culture. The village has grown to twelve homes and about 100 people. Many of the new generation have grown up, married, and are raising their families in the village. Attendance at Sunday services in the longhouse is on the rise, both from village residents and those with Wanapum ties living outside Priest Rapids. Children go to school in nearby public schools and some go on to college. They are good athletes and participate in area sports. New technology such as satellite television and the Internet are commonplace.

Reservation Realities

Still today, reservation living often inhibits ambition and self-reliance. As one Wanapum man explained;

When you live on a reservation you become dependent on hand outs, welfare, commodities, or whatever. You get a tendency of not wanting to work because you got all these free hand outs and you continue living your wild life and you never actually try to succeed in life because you got all these things and you got a majority of people that want to help you all the time. You never, you never try to do anything on your own, make a living for yourself.[12]

From an environmental perspective, regionwide population increase and land development continue to pressure the Wanapum way of life. In the past, the land was able to take care of itself, but no longer. The dams have disrupted the river ecosystem. Irrigation has led to an explosion in agriculture that has done further damage to the natural ecosystem. The nuclear facilities at Hanford have created one of the nation's most polluted and dangerous nuclear waste sites. The salmon are nearly gone. The traditional foods and medicines are getting harder to find. Meanwhile, farmers and orchardists are putting new ground into production, developers are building more houses, and the demands for natural resources such as water and fertile soil keep growing. "When will it end?" is a question often heard.

Nowhere is conflict over resources better illustrated than the recent fight for the Hanford Reach, the last fifty-one miles of the Columbia River which has not yet been dammed for power production or irrigation. The last salmon spawning beds on the middle Columbia are found here. The last 12,000 years of ancient sites, historic Indian villages and cemeteries, and natural river resources are still found on the Reach. Elsewhere they are under water. Through the Environmental Impact Statement process, the National Park Service determined that the area should be preserved as a wild and scenic river, kept in federal ownership, and managed by the National Park Service. This position had the overwhelming support of the public, the Wanapum, and the other tribes. However, local counties, farmers, developers, and politicians believed that the area would be better protected if transferred out of federal control and managed by the local counties. A major problem with that approach is that, once it is transferred out of federal ownership, many of the laws that protect the resources along these last fifty-one miles would not apply. One needs only look to the surrounding areas saturated by farms and orchards and houses to see what could result.

By the end of 1999, after a long and bitter struggle, opponents and proponents of the Hanford Reach failed to agree after years of trying. In the spring of 2000 President Bill Clinton, using powers granted to the president under the Antiquities Act of 1906, declared the Hanford Reach and surrounding areas the Hanford Reach National Monument. The U.S. Fish and Wildlife Service will manage the monument and work with a committee of local and federal agencies and stakeholders to ensure that the resources are protected and made available to Native Americans and the public.

Desecration of Burial Sites

Another struggle for the Wanapum is the desecration of Indian burials by insensitive and reckless people. In the early 1900s, it became a favorite pastime of some individuals to dig up Indian cemeteries in search of skulls and grave goods. Known as "pot hunting" or "grave robbing," this illegal activity continues to this day and hardly a month goes by without a cemetery being disturbed. Construction projects also lead to the accidental unearthing of human remains, especially when efforts are not made to check for burials before the bulldozers arrive. For example, in 1994, a cemetery was disturbed during construction of a government research laboratory at Hanford, and in 1996 a cemetery was uncovered during the construction of a Tri-Cities golf course. The Wanapum worked with neighboring tribes to repair the cemeteries and return the ancestors to the ground.

Ancestral burials have a much greater significance to the Wanapum and other Indians than for many Euro-Americans. Disturbing the remains of their ancestors is a serious matter. It is the responsibility of the Indians living today to care for the remains of the ancestors, to make sure the burials are not harmed or uncovered. To the Wanapum and other Indians, it is appalling to "see the bones of our ancestors strewn about like garbage," as the late Frank Buck, Wanapum leader, phrased it. Anthropologists and archaeologists have added to the stress created by the burial problem over the years. In 1924, for example, archaeologists from the Smithsonian Institution in Washington, D.C., came to the Mid-Columbia and excavated a Wanapum cemetery at Wahluke. The human remains and associated grave goods continue to be stored in boxes at the Smithsonian, among the remains of tens of thousands of other Indian ancestors excavated from many parts of the United States.

In 1996 a prehistoric human skeleton eroded out of the riverbank in Kennewick, Washington. Soon after the discovery, the acting deputy coroner, who is also an archaeologist, sent one of the bones to a laboratory for destructive radiocarbon dating and DNA analysis. This testing was performed despite the Native American Graves Protection and Repatriation Act (NAGPRA), which required consultation with local tribes before any such testing could occur. When the landowner, the U.S. Army Corps of Engineers, learned that the remains were prehistoric, and thus subject to NAGPRA, they confiscated the remains and initiated efforts to return them to local tribes. A small group of physical anthropologists and archaeologists stopped this effort by suing in federal court because they wanted to conduct their own studies. The case is still in court.[13]

Unrecognized Tribal Status

The Wanapum are an "unrecognized tribe," meaning they have no political relationship with the United States. This fact often prevents federal agencies from involving the Wanapum as they do the approximately 560 federally recognized tribes, villages, and bands. The Wanapum are not unique in this regard. There are about 200 unrecognized tribes throughout the United States facing similar problems. An example of how lack of recognition has hurt the Wanapum is found at Hanford. The Nez Perce, Umatilla, and Yakama Tribes have received millions of dollars in grants over the last several years to assist in the cleanup of nuclear waste; the Wanapum are not eligible for such funds.

Issues also exist with the neighboring federally recognized tribes. Both the Yakama Nation and the Confederated Tribes of the Umatilla Indian Reservation retained rights to lands within the Wanapum homeland when the treaties were signed in 1855. Tribal rights to these lands agreed to in the 1855 treaties have led federal agencies to involve these tribes in agency decisions, sometimes to the exclusion of the Wanapum. When situations such as this arise, intertribal politics can divide the tribes and prevent them from working together for common causes such as salmon restoration and cultural resource protection. However, other situations, such as an inadvertent discovery of unearthed human remains or a report of looting or vandalism of a sacred place, pulls the tribes together and decisions are made as one.

Mainstream Temptations

Retaining the Indian way of life continues to be a struggle. School, sports, Nintendo, and satellite television make it hard for children and adults to devote the time required to learn the language, the songs, and the teachings. In the past, there were fewer diversions, and the Wanapums' strict child-rearing practices ensured time for learning the culture. Today, the temptations are many, and strict child rearing has given way to a permissive approach, just as it has throughout mainstream society. Whereas once the village people all took a role in disciplining children, today this has become the sole responsibility of the immediate family. Teaching the children to be Wanapum is an important issue. Mike Squeochs, the young father, says, "I do worry about them losing it. To me it's something that I have to teach and if we can teach it to them, hopefully it's going to go further and it will continue because that's something that I'd really hate to lose. I'm hoping we can keep it going with them."[14]

RESPONSE: STRUGGLES TO SURVIVE CULTURALLY

The struggles and serious and important issues described here consume Wanapum thoughts on a daily basis. The Wanapum are raised to know what they have to do to survive in this world. The answers are found in the teachings that have come down to them through their elders. They work to protect the land, speak the language, sing the songs, protect the ancestors, gather and prepare traditional foods, attend Sunday services in the longhouse, and participate in the ceremonies.

Into the 1950s, the Wanapum still lived in traditional housing and practiced their religion in the traditional longhouse just as they always had.

Why didn't they go to the reservation? The answer is found in the teachings of the religious leader Smohalla. About the time the treaties were signed, dreams and visions came to Smohalla. He started preaching a return to Indian ways and a rejection of the Euro-American way of life that was destroying the Indian people. Smohalla foretold of a time when all white people would perish from earth and those who had retained the Indian way would return to earth and live again. Rather than go to the reservation, he led his people back to Priest Rapids. The values instilled in the Wanapum over countless generations have shaped the way they respond to the realities of life in the twentieth century.

Teaching the Children the Wanapum Way

The Wanapum work hard to teach their children the Wanapum way. The discipline of the religion remains strong in many of the families. The children are no longer forced to learn the ways, but they are encouraged to do so. The large numbers of young people participating in the longhouse activities show their willingness and their parents' perseverance to remain Wanapum. They are proud to be Wanapum and plan to carry on the traditions when they too have children. They help gather and prepare the traditional foods, they take time to learn the songs, they listen to the stories, and they come to Sunday services. "I think that our kids have the understanding that land is important to them," says Rex Buck, Jr. "But I don't think they have the tie yet. I think that tie will come, I believe it will come. It came to me and I believe it will come to them."[15] Maintaining the traditional ways is the key to survival as explained by Lenora Seelatsee, Wanapum elder:

The world's moving too fast. My father would say the world is moving so fast that the White Man's going to get so far ahead and when his time runs out, he's not going to know how to survive. He said that you, being who you are, you'll remember, because you sing, you pray and as long as you keep doing that, these things will come back to you. The foods, the medicines, the life. Everything's there, it's handed to you, as long as you continue. We'll survive, they'll not know how to survive.[16]

The children are also influenced by the general tribal resurgence going on around the country. Powwows are held in most parts of the United States, especially during the summer months. Almost every weekend young people will attend a powwow to sing, dance, drum, or simply see friends. The growth of Indian-owned casinos and businesses (the Wanapum have neither) is creating unprecedented opportunities for Native Americans. Some Wanapum leave the village to share these opportunities with their relatives and friends, but many eventually return to Priest Rapids.

Education

The Wanapum began sending their children to local county schools in the 1940s, knowing that education would be important to their future. Usually, a Wanapum child would be the only Indian in the class, and sometimes the only one in the school. The following story from Lenora Seelatsee illustrates what it was like in the 1960s:

When I went to high school I wanted to quit because the children there in school started finding out I was an Indian. They pulled my hair, they did war whoops, and so I came home, told my Dad, "I'm quitting, that's it. I don't care what you said about education." And he said "No you're not." I said "we'll see" and went and did my chores. The next morning I got everybody ready to send them off and he says "what are you doing?" And I said "I said I quit." Boy he took his belt off and I was out that door. I got on the bus, I went to school. I told my Mom, "they make fun of me." She said, "well, you will just have to show them you are as good as they are." "But how?" "Well, what do you like in school that you are good at?" I said my shorthand, my typing, the sports. She said, "well, excel in that." So our teacher in shorthand said whoever can do a hundred words in a minute in brief forms at the end of the second week will get an "A" for the rest of the year. So I studied, because we had a two-hour bus ride. I studied up, I studied back, I studied in my break times between laundry and I did it and got it. And I started making friends. And PE and volleyball, made 16 points right off the bat. I started making friends there.[17]

Learning the ways of the education system has helped the Wanapum in their dealings with the Euro-American society. A high school education is valued, college less so.

One area in particular in which Wanapum are acquiring expertise is natural and cultural resource management. By gaining knowledge in ways to protect the environment, the burials, the archaeological sites, and the traditional plants and animals, the Wanapum are able to be more directly involved in decision making and doing the work. It is very important for Native Americans to be part of the consultation process of such federal laws as the National Environmental Policy Act (1969), the American Indian Religious Freedom Act (1970), the Archaeological Resources Protection Act (1978), and the Native American Graves Protection and Repatriation Act (1990). The Wanapum work with the other tribes to gain experience in cultural resource management methods and to provide a united front on common issues.

The Wanapum excel in natural and cultural resource tasks because caring for the land, the spirits of the land, and the ancestors is something they have been taught to do all of their lives. It is a very satisfying job for them. As Jason Buck, a Wanapum cultural resources technician working for Grant County PUD, explained when asked about his interest in cultural resource protection, "This is where my ancestors are. I just try to preserve it for future use and for the younger people, younger than I am. I'm still learning myself and that's why I wanted to do it, to learn more about myself and more about my people."[18]

Working with Agencies

Adherence to their religion has led the Wanapum to work hard to protect the land and all its resources. Their need to take care of the land has led the Wanapum to establish relationships with those all around them: the neighboring tribes, the public, Grant County, the PUD, schools, Washington State, the Army, the Department of Energy, and city and county governments. The Wanapum make an effort to attend meetings and express their views on the proposals being discussed. They try to explain why the land is important, why the plants and animals should be allowed to live in harmony, why the landforms and archaeological sites are important to preserve, and why the cemeteries must be protected. The Wanapum have succeeded by building working relationships that, for the most part, keep them from being overlooked and surprised by decisions affecting them. But their success comes through hard and diligent effort. Those relationships have to be renewed and rebuilt every time agency managers, officials, and other individuals are replaced.

The Wanapum understand that the Euro-American society is here to stay. The coming of the white people and the destruction of the environment were prophesied long ago. Their elders told their children to work with the newcomers so that they would be able to stay and take care of the land and the ancestors. But it is difficult for the Wanapum to say too much because many topics are sacred and should not be discussed with outsiders. Rex Buck, Jr., explains:

My Uncle Frank once told me, "I wonder what is going to happen to me when my time comes because of all the things we have had to go and explain to society. So that they will understand us, so that they will understand who we are, so that they will listen to us a little bit. I wonder what is going to happen to us because some of those words are sacred."[19]

An example of a relationship with an agency is the long-standing one with the U.S. Department of Energy's Hanford Site. When the U.S. Army came in 1943 to build the atomic weapons plant, hundreds of Indian and non-Indian residents from the Hanford area had to move. The Wanapum began a relationship with the U.S. government that continues to this day. The Wanapum agreed to abandon their seasonal camps and restrict their travel through the area, but they asked two things of the government: (1) allow them to stay at Priest Rapids and (2) allow them to protect the graves of their ancestors. Over the years, they have worked with the government to achieve various things such as access to fishing sites, access to areas to collect firewood, the marking or fencing of cemeteries so they would be protected, access to religious areas for ceremonies, and participation in cultural and natural resource work. Because it is the right thing to do, Hanford officials have found ways to work with the Wanapum even though they are officially unrecognized.

In a similar way, the Wanapum have established a relationship with the U.S. Army's Yakima Training Center, which controls the Wanapum lands to the west. These lands are important for hunting, root gathering, and spiritual needs. The following memo, written by a U.S. major in 1975 as guidance to military personnel, illustrates the success the Wanapum have had in working with others:

Military commanders and Department of Army civilian administrators must, in future decisions involving the Wanapum Indian people, demonstrate a degree of cultural empathy and sincerity in dealing with the moral rights of these people. They ask nothing more than their historical right to practice their religion, to gather roots, to hunt and fish in their traditional ways on the lands that their ancestors for generations uncounted, have lived in peace and harmony with nature. After all, one of the good things the white culture brought to this country was respect for individual freedom, respect for other religious beliefs, and the moral rights of people to remain proudly independent. The Wanapum people ask no more than this.[20]

Most important for the Wanapum has been the relationship with the Grant County Public Utility District (PUD). In the early 1950s, the Wanapum were faced with perhaps the greatest impact to their way of life in the modern era. The PUD came to the Wanapum and told them they wanted to build two dams that would flood their homeland and force their removal from their ancient village P'Na at Priest Rapids. The Wanapum would now lose much of their remaining ancestral lands. Having once been free to live anywhere in an area encompassing millions of acres, they would now have to live on a forty-acre parcel set aside for them at the base of the Priest Rapids Dam.

The Wanapum leaders worked with the PUD officials to carve out an agreement that would keep the Wanapum at Priest Rapids and enable them to fulfill their responsibilities to the Creator for as long as possible. To this day, the Wanapum and the PUD have a close working relationship. The PUD provides job opportunities for many Wanapum, underwrites the cultural program, and helps maintain the longhouse and village at Priest Rapids.

Building trust, respect, and mutual understanding is a never-ending process. Many people still do not agree that Native Americans should have any rights beyond those granted to all American citizens. For example, efforts

Puck Hyah Toot with a Grant County PUD official discussing the impacts the dams will have on the Wanapum, ca. 1957. Photo: Grant County PUD.

are under way in Congress, led by politicians from Washington State, to change the Indian treaties and eliminate the concept of tribal sovereignty. A local congressman, Doc Hastings, has proposed amendments to change the Native American Graves Protection and Repatriation Act to restrict the rights Native Americans have to the burials of their prehistoric ancestors. The aboriginal and treaty rights of Indians to fish are also under pressure.[21]

Working with Their Neighbors

The Wanapum follow an approach in working with their neighbors similar to their approach to working with agencies through mutual trust, respect, and understanding. In the early twentieth century, for example, the Wanapum formed friendships with local farmers who lived near their traditional fishing grounds at White Bluffs on the Columbia River and Horn Rapids on the Yakima River. They shared resources and helped each other, and the Wanapums became valued members of the community. As one Wanapum leader explained:

Things were changing at that time. There were settlers coming in, homesteads that were going up, and the Wanapum way of life was beginning to come to an end. But they had a good relationship with the newcomers because the Wanapum had a good heart. They loved the land, they loved their ancestors, and they were always welcoming whoever came to offer them whatever they had, to share with them whatever they needed.[22]

To this day, old-timers talk fondly about the days when the Wanapum would stop by their farms on the way from their fishing camps offering salmon in trade for fruits and other items.

With the support of the Grant County PUD, the Wanapum today have cultural programs to educate the public about their way of life. They do this by going to school classrooms and talking to children about Wanapum culture and by maintaining a visitor center where the public can learn about the Wanapum people through traveling museum exhibits, brochures, and special presentations. Experience shows that once people understand the Wanapum, they are much more open to letting them be Wanapum. This has been especially important in keeping open access to land where traditional food resources are located. This openness has also led to development of friendships over the years with people who have then helped the Wanapum overcome other challenges.

FOOD FOR THOUGHT

The Wanapum have faced struggles in the past and are sure to face more in the years to come. Robert Tomanawash, Wanapum elder, helps guide his people by drawing on traditional Wanapum values, while giving consideration to the realities of the future. The strategy is working, as the Wanapum are on the rise, both in numbers and in regional influence. The Wanapum can serve as a model for other small groups struggling to survive within a receptive, but often apathetic, dominant society.

Questions

1. One of the foundations of American society is the freedom of religion. Over the years, various attempts have been made by the government or Christian organizations to eliminate Native American religions. The strength of the Wanapum clearly emanates from their adherence to their religion. In what ways have other groups described in this volume or elsewhere used religion to maintain their cultural identity and deal with change?

2. As Euro-Americans and other non-Indians continue to purchase land in the Mid-Columbia and transform it from its natural state to farms, orchards, and housing developments, the Wanapum and other native peoples are finding it increasingly difficult to locate their native resources for food, medicines, and other cultural items. This raises questions regarding ownership of land. When someone purchases property, does that give that person the right to everything on that property? Should the Wanapum retain rights to traditional resources on that parcel that are needed for them to retain their cultural identity? What about land

owned by the government, such as national forests and parks? Must the Wanapum lose these rights because someone else holds legal title? What would you do if you were in the Wanapums' situation?

3. The Kennewick Man case is a good example of an intercultural situation that, at first glance, appears unresolvable. The tribes who historically occupied the area where this 9,200-year-old skeleton was found believe he should be put back in the ground in accordance with the principles of their religion. A small group of scientists believe there is important information contained in these human remains that may shed new light on the peopling of North America. When the local federal agency in charge of the case sided with the Indians, the scientists sued. Interestingly, there are dozens of cases in which human remains were discovered in North America where archaeologists and Native Americans were able to come to an agreement. The key appears to be having a prior relationship based on trust, respect, and understanding which enabled the opposing groups to work out an arrangement acceptable to each. Can you think of examples from your own experience where difficult problems were resolved because opposing groups had developed good relationships? Or failed to be resolved because relations were poor?

4. Many cultural groups are finding it hard to get the younger generation to carry on the traditional ways. Just as the nineteenth-century Wanapum were attracted to the new goods brought by the fur traders, so too are today's Wanapum attracted to the new things brought by the dominant society. This phenomenon applies not only to the Wanapum; peoples around the world are being attracted to goods from Western cultures every day. Through their products and advertising, major corporations such as those operating fast food restaurants, selling soft drinks, and operating theme parks are quickly changing the world. What kinds of impacts do you think such forces are having on traditional cultures? What are some ways that you think a tribe's elders could be most effective in encouraging the younger generation to carry on their cultural traditions? What would be the wrong way to approach it?

5. In the early part of the twentieth century, the U.S. Government attempted to end the Native American way of life. They made it difficult for Native Americans to practice their religion and forbade the use of Indian language in schools. Today most Native American groups are in danger of losing their traditional language. Many believe that if their language disappears they will lose a fundamental part of their Indian identity. Do you think Indian languages should be taught in public schools where there are large numbers of Indian students? Why would knowing the Native language have such a big impact on being Indian?

NOTES

1. Cheat grass *(Bromus tectorum)* is an annual grass that was introduced to North America from Eastern Europe in the nineteenth century. An aggressive species, it has spread widely across the intermountain West, squeezing out native species.

2. Tule *(Scirpus acutus)* a reed grass, produces stems as long as eight feet in length. Tules are used by the Wanapum to make matting for housing and other

purposes. See Eugene S. Hunn, *Nich'Wana (Big River): Mid-Columbia Indians and Their Land* (Seattle: University of Washington Press, 1990), 189–196.

3. This and other quotations, unless otherwise noted, were obtained from transcriptions of an interview conducted by Karen Thomas during production of the documentary film *Disturbing the Dreamers* (Wanapum Natitayt, 2000). Transcriptions are on file in the Wanapum archives, Grant County Public Utility District, Ephrata, Washington.

4. Ibid.

5. Ibid.

6. Ibid.

7. Ibid.

8. Robert H. Ruby and John A. Brown, *Dreamer-Prophets of the Columbia Plateau: Smohalla and Skolaskin*, Civilization of the American Indian Series, vol. 191 (Norman: University of Oklahoma Press, 1989), 11. For regional population trends, see Deward E. Walker, "Plateau," in *Handbook of North American Indians*, vol. 12 (Washington, D.C.: Smithsonian Institution, 1998), 467–483.

9. For more information on Smohalla and the Dreamer Religion see Click Relander, *Drummers and Dreamers* 1956; (reprint, Seattle: Pacific Northwest National Parks and Forestry Association, 1986).

10. Based on information provided by elders in the Priest Rapids village.

11. Thomas, transcriptions.

12. Ibid.

13. See Roger Downey, *The Riddle of the Bones: Politics, Science, Race and the Story of Kennewick Man* (New York: Copernicus, 2000); David Hurst Thomas, *Skull Wars: Kennewick Man, Archaeology, and the Battle for Native American Identity* (New York: Basic Books, 2000), and the National Park Service web site (www.cr.nps.gov/aad/kennewick/) for more information on the Kennewick Man case.

14. Thomas, transcriptions.

15. Ibid.

16. Ibid.

17. Ibid.

18. Ibid.

19. Ibid.

20. Ibid.

21. For further reading on these and other issues affecting Native Americans in general, see Alvin M. Josephy, Jr., Joane Nagel, and Troy Johnson, eds., *Red Power: The American Indians' Fight for Freedom* (Lincoln: University of Nebraska Press, 1999).

22. Thomas, transcriptions.

RESOURCE GUIDE

Published Literature

Downey, Roger. *The Riddle of the Bones: Politics, Science, Race and the Story of Kennewick Man*. New York: Copernicus, 2000.

Hunn, Eugene S. *Nich'Wana (Big River): Mid-Columbia Indians and Their Land*. Seattle: University of Washington Press, 1990.

Josephy, Jr., Alvin M., Joane Nagel, and Troy Johnson, eds. *Red Power: The American Indians' Fight for Freedom*. Lincoln: University of Nebraska Press, 1999.

Mooney, James. *The Ghost-Dance Religion and the Sioux Outbreak of 1890*. 1896. Reprint, Lincoln: University of Nebraska Press, 1991.

Relander, Click. *Drummers and Dreamers*. 1956. Reprint, Seattle: Pacific Northwest National Parks and Forestry Association, 1986.

Ruby, Robert H., and John A. Brown. *Dreamer-Prophets of the Columbia Plateau: Smohalla and Skolaskin*. Civilization of the American Indian Series, vol. 191. Norman: University of Oklahoma Press, 1989.

Thomas, David Hurst. *Skull Wars: Kennewick Man, Archaeology, and the Battle for Native American Identity*. New York: Basic Books, 2000.

Walker, Deward E., Jr., ed. "Plateau." In *Handbook of North American Indians*, vol. 12. Washington, D.C.: Smithsonian Institution, 1998.

WWW Sites

Grant County PUD Cultural Resources Program
http://www.gcpud.org/stewardship/culturalheritage.htm

Hanford Site Cultural Resources Program
http://www.hanford.gov/doe/culres/index.htm

Kennewick Man
http://www.Kennewick-man.com and http://www.cr.nps.gov/aad/kennewick/

Save the Hanford Reach
http://www.3-rivers.com/hanford_reach/

Organization

Wanapum Cultural Resources Program
Grant County PUD
P.O. Box 878
Ephrata, WA 98823

PART 2

ETHNIC MINORITIES

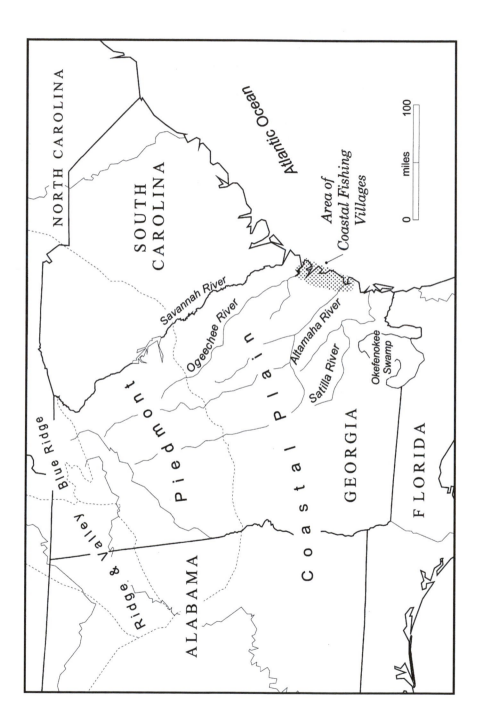

Chapter 9

African-Americans in the Coastal Zone of Georgia

Ben G. Blount

African-Americans in contemporary United States are not in most senses of the term an "endangered" population. They constitute between 10 and 12 percent of the population of the United States, and they are not declining in absolute numbers or percentage of the total population. Even if one were to consider African-Americans to be under duress, as in the rollback of affirmative action, it is very unlikely that they would be thought of as endangered. Certainly their situation is radically different from that of many small-scale, indigenous societies.

Yet if the perspective is shifted from population and ethnicity to ways of life and cultural heritage, then the association of African-Americans and endangerment does not seem as remote and unlikely. Endangerment still may not seem imminent, but African-American culture is undergoing change, especially in rural areas. African-Americans, themselves, are concerned about maintaining their heritage and identity, and they are taking various steps to try to preserve what is distinctive about African-American culture. The focus of attention on African-American leaders and their historic contributions to the United States is one example. The recent trend toward the use of African-like personal names is another example.

The extent to which African-American culture in general is in danger of disappearing may be debatable, but a good case can be made that, in some instances, African-American ways of life have been fundamentally eroded. African-Americans in the coastal zone of Georgia can be seen as an instance of that type. Perhaps it is more accurate to say that the ways of life of African-Americans who live in coastal Georgia have been undergoing change and that the changes are reducing their cultural distinctiveness as African-Americans. What has changed primarily are the ways of making a living, and as those have changed, the ways of living have been transformed along with them. In this chapter, the focus is on the changes in means of livelihood, and thus in the ways of life, among fishing communities along Georgia's Atlantic Coast.

CULTURAL OVERVIEW

The People

According to the Bureau of Census, approximately 167,000 people of African descent lived in the six coastal counties of Georgia in 1996, or 27 percent of the total population. Like other populations of African-Americans in the United States, those individuals have lines of descent that link them to Africans brought to the Americas during the Atlantic slave trade of the seventeenth and eighteenth centuries. Since the plantations of the southeastern United States were one of the destinations of the slave trade—Charleston, South Carolina, was a major port; Savannah, Georgia, a secondary one—the continuity with African ancestry may be very salient. That is particularly the case with the people identified as Gullah in the coastal areas of North and South Carolina. They represent the most distinctive, best-known case of African and African-American linkages. Not only are there genealogical connections, there are cultural retentions that collectively can be referred to as "Africanisms." Those would include, among other features, words from African languages, forms of music and musical style, and material culture, such as basketry. Although strictly speaking there is no Gullah community on the Georgia coast, very similar but much smaller groups, the Geechee, are found on the coast, especially on Sapelo Island.[1] The relevant point, however, is that the Gullah and Geechee are specific cases of a general phenomenon; African-Americans on the South Atlantic coast of the United States have ties to their African ancestry that are more direct and more immediate than they are in other areas of the country.

Culturally, African-Americans on the Georgia coast are shaped by their African ancestry, by their history on southern plantations, by the history of their minority status, and by the Civil Rights struggle, to identify only a few of the major phenomena.[2] Underlying those events are ever-present life-shaping elements, such as the ways of making a living, and living and interacting with each other in communities. Also the majority of the population has been rural and poor, and when all of the factors listed above are put together, the composite picture is a cultural and physical landscape of rural African-American communities that is relatively distinct.[3]

The Setting

Historically, there has been no particular reason why Georgia's coastal area should be well known. It is only 100 miles long, and there are no major tourist areas comparable to Myrtle Beach or Hilton Head, South Carolina, or to the well-known resorts of the Florida coast, such as Daytona or Miami Beach. There are no famous beaches, no places where large numbers of university and high school students go for spring break. There are no major coastal zone industries, as found farther north along the Atlantic Coast, no casinos to attract tourists and provide jobs and employment for local people.

A major factor that transformed the coastal zones of several Atlantic states was the construction of Interstate 95. That interstate highway is the New York–Miami corridor, and it is one of the most heavily traveled interstate systems in the United States. The coastal areas of North Carolina and South Carolina were, like Georgia, relatively remote and isolated until after the construction of I-95. Population was low, and a large proportion could be called indigenous, with families having lived in the area for several generations. Pocket areas of the Carolinas and much of the Georgia coast are still like that. Georgia has been, by far, the least affected by the tourist and population boom experienced by other states. Not coincidentally, the last section of I-95 to be completed was in Georgia.

Even after completion of Interstate 95 in 1974, the coastal zone of Georgia was slow to change. The physical setting itself has played a limiting role. The entire coastal strip of Georgia is lined with barrier islands. There are dozens of small, unnamed islands (some are islands only at low tide), but there are more than a dozen larger, and named, islands. The islands tend to be long and narrow, on a north-south axis. They are relatively recent in geological terms, dating back to approximately 50,000 years ago. Throughout that time, the islands have buffered and protected the mainland from waves, currents, and storms. As a consequence, the inland areas behind the islands consist of wide expanses of salt marsh, interlaced with countless streams, channels, and creeks. Georgia has almost one-half of the remaining salt marsh area on the eastern seaboard of the United States.

Several historical consequences follow from the configuration of the Georgia coast. The highways, including I-95, lie along the inland edges of the salt marshes, and what travelers along them see are huge expanses of "swamp." While salt marshes are highly productive ecological systems, they have little or no "tourist" appeal. Georgia has almost ninety miles of beach, but virtually all of that is on the ocean side of the islands, very difficult to reach, and thus largely invisible. Of the thirteen major islands, only three are connected to the mainland by causeways and are accessible by automobile. The vast majority of travelers on I-95 never even see the islands, much less the beaches. The volume of tourism on the Georgia coast is thus much lower than in any other state. In fact, the coastal zone is still undeveloped to accommodate tourists, although that is now beginning to change. A consequence of the lack of tourism development is that the region is still comparatively poor and rural.

The second major consequence of the configuration of the Georgia coast—the salt marshes, waterways, and barrier islands—is that forms of livelihood have been largely limited to fishing and agriculture. The wetlands and waterways serve as nursery areas for many species of fish and shellfish, making the coastal strip a rich region for fishing.

Traditional Subsistence Strategies

Africans brought to the southeastern United States came primarily from the west coast of Africa. There, they would have lived in societies that relied principally on plant cultivation for food and in which they would have been connected to an elaborate network of markets for trade and barter. Fish from that area of the Atlantic was an important food and an item for trade. Once Africans arrived in Georgia, however, the vast majority of them were field-workers in plantation agriculture. As slaves, they did the hard work of planting, raising, and harvesting crops. In addition to the cash crops, largely rice in the coastal area, there were gardens to produce vegetables for human consumption. Much of the daily food came from the gardens. The early African-Americans who lived on the islands and mainland areas near the shore also engaged in fishing as a way to supplement their food supply. In some cases, plantation owners encouraged the African-Americans to make and use small boats for inshore fishing, within sight of land. Although few records are available, fish were probably an important food source for the first generations of African-Americans in the Georgia coastal zone.

After the Civil War and the abolition of slavery, options for African-Americans were limited. The period of Reconstruction—the economic recovery program for the Southern states—was a time of extreme poverty and hardship for many residents in that part of the country, and especially for African-Americans. Elsewhere in the South, many African-Americans moved to towns and cities. This option was almost nonexistent on the Georgia coast. Savannah was the only city on the coast, and there were only a very few small towns. For most of the African-Americans, the options were limited to continuing to work as field hands, to strike out on their own as household farming units, or to fish for a livelihood. Plantation agriculture, much of it wet-rice cultivation, was widespread after slavery, but by the early twentieth century rice cultivation had disappeared. It was no longer economical when based on hired labor and it was not practical on a small scale. Family farms were based in subsistence and cash crops, but it was a difficult and precarious existence. Today, small-scale farming has largely disappeared.

Fishing, however, has a continuous history on the coast and has been the mainstay of the African-Americans there for more than a century. Newspaper accounts of the 1890s in Savannah (and in Charleston) indicate that fishing, as an enterprise, was in the hands of African-Americans. They caught the fish in small boats close to the shore, undoubtedly as part of their diet, but also as a commercial enterprise. Fish were sold in markets and even peddled in the streets, largely by African-American women.[4]

Again, there are records indicating how many African-Americans moved from the plantations into fishing, especially in the rural areas of the coast, but whatever the numbers it is safe to say that fishing would have been an important subsistence activity. Fishing would have been, in fact, one of the very few livelihood options open to African-Americans. There was little or no competition in fisheries from whites. At that time, whites were mostly interested in agriculture and commercialism, and although a minority in numbers, they controlled the economy through virtual monopoly of those activities. African-Americans, most recently freed slaves, did not have the economic means to compete in agriculture and commercialism, and there were few labor opportunities available other than as laborers on farms. The major option not co-opted by the whites was fishing. By the turn of the nineteenth century, commercial fishing was an African-American industry, though a comparatively small-scale one.

The first two or three generations of post–Civil War African-Americans on the Georgia coast were a majority in numbers but an ethnic minority in a system that was staunchly segregationist. Predominantly rural, poor, and uneducated, they were faced with the difficult task of making a living in a region of the state that also had the same characteristics. They coped however they could, forming and relying on socioeconomic ties within and among families and communities. The sense of community was especially strong, since there were internal pressures for close-knit relations and since there was virtual exclusion of them on the part of the politically and economically stronger whites. Distinctive African-American coastal communities remain to the present day.

The coastal counties of the state still are underpopulated, rural, and poor, compared to other counties in the state of Georgia. Current events, however, indicate that changes are under way. Population growth and tourism are expanding, initiating a transformation of the region and producing further pressures on African-Americans and their ways of life. They were already under pressure from other changes that began approximately two generations ago in the 1930s. Two of those events in particular have had major implications for African-Americans and their means of livelihood.

Social and Political Organization

The setting for much of the social organization is the household and the local community. The rural coastal communities, consisting typically of a number of residences clustered along a street or road, are fairly small and scattered. Some of the houses are brick and reflect some degree of prosperity, but most are comparatively small, wooden structures, many very modest in design and appearance. Some are freshly painted, often in a bright, cheerful color, but others remain unpainted. The houses typically have yards, usually with abundant shade trees and often with a variety of other plants including shrubs, flowers, and potted plants. Commonly, there are chairs, benches, small tables, and perhaps a grill for cooking. If the house has a porch, chairs or swings are likely to be there. Radios and even televisions are also sometimes on the porches. Weather permitting, much of the social life among family and neighbors occurs outdoors, with people sitting under the trees or on the porch, enjoying food, drink, and visiting with family, friends, and neighbors.

Neighbors are likely to be relatives, especially in the male line but sometimes also linked by marriage. Relatives tend to live near one another, for social and economic support. Making a living in rural areas was, and still is, difficult, and a large social support group was advantageous. Insurance against hard times is provided by extended families. If some members of an intergenerational family have serious economic needs, a large family would likely include someone who would be able to help. Reciprocity is not only valued but often a functional necessity. The social gatherings in peoples' yards and at church maintain and intensify social obligations and responsibilities, first along family lines, kinship lines, neighborhood lines, church lines, and then community lines. In the rural communities, everyone knows everyone else, and harmonious relationships are highly valued and promoted.

Public schools serve as focal points for school-age members of the coastal communities. Most of the children in rural areas ride buses to and from school, and again, extended family, kinship, and neighborhood are reinforced through those shared experiences. The schools and extracurricular activities expand the social networks and interactions, linking students across communities and providing them with common background and opportunity for meaningful social experiences.

Political structures characteristic of counties in the United States exist in the coastal region of Georgia, and local African-Americans are subject to the power and authority of local officials. During the decades of segregation, local African-Americans were undoubtedly subjected to racial discrimination, overt and covert. Nowadays, discrimination is less direct and obvious, but racial tensions and injustices continue. De facto segregation is still very much a fact of life, and African-Americans are keenly aware of the political realities above the level of the communities, even though they may have members of their communities serving as officials, even as sheriff.

At the community level, political organization is much more informal and tends to be based principally on age and respect. Community elders lead by example, and members of the communities generally try to emulate and follow them. The church is an especially important arena for the formation and validation of local political authority. Respected elders in a community are likely to serve as deacons in a local church, which lends them religious authority to underscore their political standing.

Religion and World View

Religion plays a central role in family and community life. Churches of various denominations, but especially Baptist, are found throughout the countryside, and local communities may have more than one church. Church services tend to be well attended, and on Sundays, the services often last for several hours. On many occasions, food is served, extending both the length and the social intensity of the gatherings. The churches, a focal point for community interaction, draw families and neighborhoods from an area together into a larger social group. While religious issues predominate in church functions, topics of broader community interest can be raised and discussed, either in sermons or among clusters of individuals before and after the formal services. In that sense, churches constitute social and political forums for the discussion of issues that affect neighborhood groups and the broader community of African-Americans.

As noted, local leadership is usually tied to churches, and ministers and deacons enjoy status and respect. Also as noted, age is a critically important feature of the system of respect. Older men and women tend to be viewed and accorded respect, a characteristic that is distinctively African in origin. A cultural premium is also placed on being a good speaker; a person who can address audiences effectively and who can entertain others in informal, friendly conversation. Despite the apparent modest economic circumstances found in the communities, there is a vibrancy and enjoyment of life, expressed through socializing within the neighborhood and the church.

The commitment to Christianity varies, of course, across individuals in local African-American communities. In general, however, the commitment appears to be very strong and taken very seriously. Christianity is at the core of the world view of the people, and it provides them with spiritual support and sustenance. Their faith also undoubtedly is valued as a support to see them through difficult and trying times. Nowadays, more and more of the youth in the rural coastal communities appear to place less value on local traditions and institutions, including the role of the church, but the church still remains the central foundation of meaning in life.

THREATS TO SURVIVAL

The threat to the survival of the way of life of African-American fishing communities on the Georgia coast is not as immediate or dramatic as it is in some small-scale societies, for example, those in the path of deforestation by giant timber companies. The consequences, however, are much the same on a long-term basis. Threats to the daily patterns of life associated with fishing have occurred in two waves. The first began several generations ago, when Italian immigrants arrived on the coast and began to take control of the oyster fishery. Soon afterward Portuguese immigrants arrived and began to take control of the shrimp fishery. These events wrested control of the fisheries from African-Americans and started their downward spiral in commercial marine fishing. The second wave, from the "discovery" of the Georgia coast as a tourist destination, is currently under way. African-Americans are being pushed even farther from their lives based on marine fishing.

Loss of Control of the Fisheries and Wage Labor

At the beginning of the twentieth century, oysters were plentiful along the Georgia coastline in the mouths of streams, creeks, and rivers. African-Americans had harvested them for food and to sell for several generations. The abundance of the oysters caught the attention of new residents of the Georgia coast, some recently arrived from New York and Baltimore and some from southern Europe. In both cases, they came from regions where commercial fishing occurred on a much larger scale; they were attuned to fisheries in a way that the Georgia coastal populations were not. They were also familiar with the modern technology of the time, which would allow them to increase the volume of fish caught, processed, and sold. They were able to see the possibilities of larger enterprises, to commercialize the fisheries on a much larger scale. The oysters were the first fisheries to undergo that process. At the turn of the century, responding to demands from other areas of the United States, oysters were the most valuable seafood product in Georgia. In order to help meet the demand, a process of canning the oysters, originally developed on the northeastern seaboard of the United States, was put in place. Canneries were built on the Georgia coast, beginning just before and after the turn of the twentieth century. By 1902, six canneries were operating along the Georgia coast, and by the 1920s, the Maggioni family owned most of the canneries in Georgia.[5]

Gathering oysters was enormously difficult work. Oyster fishers stood in small boats and dipped a pair of long-handled tongs into the water. The tongs were inserted into the bottom mud, closed, and hauled, hand over hand, to the surface, hopefully full of oysters. "Tonging" required strength and stamina, limiting the activity to strong, able-bodied men. Oyster fishing also tended to be a family activity, within and across generations. The increased demand for oysters led to more work for African-Americans, but the extent to which it led to increased economic opportunity can be questioned. Once commercialization was under way, the oyster fishers were no longer in control of the fishery, no longer independent fishermen. They simply caught and sold oysters to the canneries. The owners of the canneries made most of the profits. African-Americans, in effect, became laborers in their service.

Shrimp trawler, Darien, Georgia, May 1996. The boat is decorated for participation in the annual Blessing of the Fleet, a ceremony to bless the fishermen and the boat for the upcoming shrimp season. Photo: Ben G. Blount.

The commercialization of the oyster fishery contributed in a second way to the transformation of African-American fishing families into wage laborers. Cannery work required large amounts of labor. The oysters had to be sorted, shucked, and processed for canning, which also was difficult, laborious, tedious work. Virtually all of the cannery workers were women, and the majority of them were African-Americans. The wages were low and the benefits nonexistent, but the cannery jobs further pulled African-American fishing communities into the wage labor economy.

The oyster canneries lasted only about two decades, from approximately 1910 to 1930. They went out of business for a number of related reasons. By the end of the first quarter of the century, roads and railroads had been expanded throughout the mid- and south Atlantic region, linking the major cities and providing easier, more rapid transport of commercial goods. Since the shipment of fresh oysters was more feasible, the need for canneries was reduced. In addition, the abundance of oysters also declined, as a result of overfishing and increased pollution. Oysters were being harvested at a rate that precluded sufficient time for their full maturation, and the number and size of oysters was in significant decline by 1940. Pollution of the coastal waters was vastly increased by a new industry that began on the coast in the 1920s and 1930s: the pulp timber industry.

The pulp timber industry was a transplant from the northeastern region of the United States. Having depleted many forested regions of that area, a number of paper and timber companies relocated to the southeastern coast. Labor was plentiful and cheap, and land for growing the pine trees necessary for the industry was also available and exceptionally cheap. The coastal strip of Georgia was an underpopulated and economically depressed area. The agricultural base of the area had been in decline for some time, and for poor families, simply making a living was a daily challenge. Any industry that provided jobs was welcomed. Pine tree plantations replaced agriculture as the major economic activity of the region, a pattern that continued for the last three-quarters of the twentieth century. The place of African-Americans in this industry was as wage laborers. The lowest paid, they did the hardest work, planting and harvesting the trees and tapping the trees for turpentine, a major ingredient in the nationally growing paint and chemical industry. However exploitative the work in the pulp timber industry, African-Americans entered into that economy in large numbers. The industry provided badly needed jobs for individuals who left or were forced out of the fisheries.

For those who stayed in fishing, perhaps the major factor that altered their lives was the emergence of the modern shrimp fishery. African-Americans had fished for shrimp throughout the history of their fishing on the coast, fishing near the shore from small boats and with hand-thrown nets. Shrimp have always been plentiful along the coast. The configuration of the coastline, with large areas of protected waters behind the barrier islands and in the estuaries where streams, creeks, and rivers drain into the sounds, favors the growth of shrimp. Despite the abundance of shrimp, they were not a species especially targeted by fishermen until the first few decades of the twentieth century. Shrimp is the favorite seafood in the United States today, but that was certainly not the case at the turn of the century. Prior to that time, shrimp were used primarily as snacks served with drinks in bars. They were served salted or in brine. The salt made drinkers thirsty, much as salted peanuts or popcorn in bars do today.

Like the oyster fishery, the modern shrimp fishery began when outsiders moved to the Georgia coast. At first, the shrimp fishermen came from the northeastern coast of the United States, especially from Baltimore and New York. They set in motion for the shrimp fishery the same process that had led to the dramatic increase in demand for oysters. Shrimp were also caught for and processed in canneries, and in some cases, canneries processed both oysters and shrimp. They soon were shipped across the United States, including California. The same factors that led to the decline in the oyster fishery also occurred in the shrimp industry, but whereas the oyster fishery never recovered, the reverse was the case for shrimp. The fishery expanded and grew at a remarkable rate as a result of new technological developments that made large-scale commercial harvesting of shrimp possible. In addition, a new group of immigrants from southern Europe, in this case, the Portuguese, brought with them an awareness of the potential of shrimp as a major seafood commodity and the ability to harness the new technology toward that end.

Three technological developments occurred in the early part of the twentieth century that changed the shrimp fishery forever and altered the position of African-Americans in that fishery. The first of those innovations was the internal combustion engine. Gasoline-powered engines were available by the turn of the century, but they were little used for fishing boats for another decade. Their use had to await the capacity for the construction of boats that were sturdy enough to accommodate engines. By the early 1920s, power-driven boats had become common, and they were, of course, larger, faster, more durable, and more efficient than the smaller, open wooden boats, for any fishery. The small wooden boats of African-American fishermen became outmoded and inefficient. The boats alone gave an advantage to the Portuguese-American fishermen, but that was only a part of the story. Shrimp still had to be caught in nets, and that is where the third technological innovation became relevant.

The new, far more powerful boats had the power to pull nets through the water, and a new type of net system was developed precisely for that purpose. The new device was called an otter trawl, apparently because its movement through the water as it was towed resembled the swimming of an otter. The otter trawl consists of a long net open at the front and tied to two boards, called otter doors. The doors, in turn, are attached to the boat by long, steel cables. As the cable is extended and the net is lowered into the water, the boards are forced open by the pressure of the water, opening wide the entrance to the net. As the net is pulled through the water, it sinks to the bottom but remains open from the pressure on the boards. The net, then, acts as a giant scoop, catching shrimp and any other fish that happen to be in the path of the net. The entire process is referred to as trawling, and the boats are classified as trawlers. By the 1920s, the power-driven otter trawl was in common use in the coastal waters of Georgia. Also by that time diesel engines had replaced gasoline ones, since they were more efficient and safer. The transformation of the fishery was well under way.

Trawlers are capable of catching large quantities of shrimp. In comparison to the hand-thrown cast nets the amount of shrimp caught was many times greater. What, however, was to be done with this large quantity of shrimp, if there was only a limited market for shrimp? The answer was the creation of a market for shrimp as a seafood, rather than just snacks to consume with beer. An advertising campaign was developed for shrimp, not just on the Georgia coast, but also along the mid- and southern Atlantic and the Gulf coasts of the United States. The newly improved transportation system of roads and railroads made the shipment of shrimp to markets feasible, and in a very short period of time, a demand for shrimp developed among the American public. It became a major seafood item, and the shrimp fishery on a large scale was born. The shrimp fishery replaced and then far surpassed all other fisheries. On the Georgia coast, 95 percent of the commercial fishing is currently for shrimp.

The capital necessary to acquire a boat, diesel engine, and otter trawl was beyond the means of the vast majority of African-Americans. Not only were they unlikely to have sufficient funds, they also were unlikely to have the collateral to obtain the funds through loans. In addition, the weight of racial discrimination was undoubtedly a factor, placing them at a major disadvantage in accessing the capital needed to invest in the new, technological shrimp fishery.

The birth of the new shrimp fishery eclipsed the old, cast-net shrimp fishery, thereby eliminating that way of fishing and the livelihood associated with it. African-Americans in that fishery had to turn elsewhere. A few of them were able to buy boats and enter into the trawl fishery, a situation that remains to the present day. Some of them were able to work as "strikers," or laborers, on the shrimp trawlers, to sort the shrimp from other fish when the nets were periodically raised and their catch was dumped on the deck of the boat. Most of the displaced African-American shrimpers, however, had to enter the economy in any arena they could manage, typically as wage laborers.

At the beginning of the twentieth century, then, African-Americans had controlled the fisheries on the Georgia coast. One generation later, they were almost completely replaced, remaining primarily as wage laborers in the two major fisheries, oysters and shrimp. They had been economically marginalized, pushed from a self-sufficient to a peripheral and dependent position. The process of marginalization is virtually identical to what occurred in the areas of the world that are referred to as "developing." New people arrive, usually of European origin, and their understanding of large-scale economic operations in the modern world is beyond what the local populations have experienced. They also have greater financial means, which allow them to exploit the natural resources and to assume a stronger economic position in the broader community. The marginalization, and consequent changes in livelihood and ways of life that occurred in the Georgia coastal zone, could have occurred on the coasts of Nicaragua, Senegal, India, or anywhere else in the developing world.

Tourism and Development

This new wave of changes has resulted from the discovery of the Georgia coast by tourists and by individuals, especially retirees, as a place to live. As noted above, the Georgia coast had been largely invisible to travelers unless they had a reason to leave the main transportation routes. During the late 1990s more and more individuals learned that the relative isolation of the Georgia coast, its low population, and lack of development make it a desirable place for vacations and residence. The environment is comparatively pristine, certainly in comparison with the mid-Atlantic coasts to the north and the Florida coasts to the south. The Georgia coastal zone, however, is on the cusp of major change. Tourists are beginning to go to the Georgia coast in increasing numbers, both for the historical aspects of the Savannah area and for the natural beauty of the wetlands and islands of the coastal strip. Service industries are appearing, and condominiums and new houses are springing up. The cost of land and of homes is increasing rapidly, although it is still considerably lower than in other, neighboring states.

Economic Changes

As tourism and residential development progress, as more people are drawn to the Georgia coast, the economy changes. The pulp timber industry, dominant for half a century, is beginning to yield to a service-based industry, operating and supporting hotels, restaurants, and recreational businesses for tourism and for the construction of new homes, subdivisions, and the businesses needed to service them. For African-American communities along the coast, these developments bring a rising cost of living, in all its aspects. Coastal tourism economies tend to be expensive, placing hardship on local populations. The price of land begins to soar, which is just now under way in the coastal strip. The increase in land value means that taxes also increase, which places special burdens on low-income families. The net effect, long term, is that poor, local residents cannot afford to remain in their native area. They sell their property, and they move away. African-Americans make up a disproportionately large number of those individuals, and as a group, they are the most affected. Their ways of life are the most threatened.

The threat to the economic stability of the African-Americans on the Georgia coast extends, of course, to the remaining fishing families and their place in local communities. Other factors are a threat to them. The fishing industry is undergoing changes from a number of sources, but there are two principal ones. The first source of change is within the industry itself, and it can be summed up by the term "capitalization": increasingly, individuals must have available capital to upgrade and modernize their fishing operations. The cost of operating shrimp boats increases year by year, but the number of shrimp does not increase. The margin of profit requires efficiency and an increase in scale. The cost of catching the shrimp has to decrease as operating costs rise, and since the margin per yield of shrimp tends to decrease, the number caught must increase. The individuals in the fishery who can afford to modernize their boats (e.g., by upgrading electronic devices such as computers) and to have more boats on the water are in general more likely to survive economically in an ever more competitive industry. The few African-American boat owners and operators in the industry are being squeezed out. They find the competition and the ability to survive more and more difficult. Their way of life, seriously altered two to three generations ago, continues to slide away.

RESPONSE: STRUGGLES TO SURVIVE CULTURALLY

African-American marine fishermen have been able to take only limited action to resist the changes that have overtaken them in the past 100 years. They have always been a distinctive minority with limited political and economic clout, and the magnitude of the changes overtaking them would have made any resistance difficult under the best of circumstances. The transformation of the Georgia coast from plantation agriculture, to the pulp timber industry, and now to tourism and land development, all are part of broad sweeps of changes that have significantly altered rural life throughout the United States. Small-scale family-based ways of making a living have given way to wage labor in corporate enterprises, and those changes have been coupled with movement away from the land and sea to urban areas where jobs are more readily available. The premium has always been on economic growth and development. African-Americans have tended to do what other portions of the population have done—seek gainful employment as a way of making a living, even at the cost of loss of traditional way of life. To do otherwise was to move against the grain of changes brought about by the urban, industrialized world.

Despite the enormity of the pressures for change, some responses by African-American communities to protect their way of life can be discerned. The principal one is the Civil Rights movement, a major advance, despite its limitations, toward greater political, legal, and economic rights and justice. The Civil Rights movement in the coastal counties of Georgia began very late in relation to the United States in general. Dramatic confrontations occurred in some areas of the coast, especially among the last areas to change. The confrontations sometimes involved courthouse "stand-offs," with virtually everyone present armed with concealed weapons. Once the local African-American communities became aware of the possibilities that the Civil Rights movement afforded them, they were not to be denied, even if armed struggle was necessary. They prevailed.

The Civil Rights movement provided the legal framework within which African-Americans could press for rights and opportunities on a variety of issues. Some of the demands they have made are specific, such as attention to roads and parks in their communities, but in general they are for rights to self-determination. Perhaps the hope for the preservation of ways of life begins there, with an insistence that quality of life is itself important and the source of efforts toward equality and justice.

Commercial fishing is beset with problems, but African-Americans are among the "players," and they can persist and push for their rights to maintain their livelihood without the weight of racial discrimination hanging over them as heavily as it once did. After several generations of erosion of their ways of life, they can insist on the right to compete equally.

Fishing as a way of life is under duress for all commercial fishermen on the Georgia coast, and long term survival will be difficult for all of them. The Georgia Shrimpers Association has hired a public relations specialist to present the case to the public and policy makers that Georgia's coastal fishermen make an important economic contribution to the coastal economy. This initiative may help everyone, but the forces of economic development, gentrification, and tourism will likely overwhelm all efforts at sustaining the traditional African-American fishermen's way of life. There appears to be a sense of resignation that once the current generation retires, their way of life will have come to an end.

Although no numbers are available, it is nonetheless clear that contemporary people fish for recreation and to supplement their food supply and diet. The seafood industry also provides employment, as workers on shrimp boats, in seafood houses, and in the wholesale and retail fish business. A few African-Americans also own and operate their own boats, both in the blue crab fishery and in the shrimp fishery. What remains is a much smaller proportion of the population than in the days of their great-grandparents.

FOOD FOR THOUGHT

The threat to the continuance of fishing families and communities among African-Americans in coastal Georgia is not unique. The actual historical circumstances may be unique to that part of the world, but populations throughout the world have been, and continue to be, affected by the same set of forces. Those forces are the ever-increasing scale and scope of economic growth and development. Economic growth depends ultimately on the exploitation of natural resources, soil in the case of farming, trees, and water in the pulp timber industry, and life in the sea in fisheries.

The issue that confronts African-Americans on the Georgia coast, and millions of other people throughout the world, is not how to exploit natural resources to make a living. Rather, the issue is whether the economic dimensions of making a living off of these fisheries is to be the sole standard by which to judge and measure progress. What remains unquestioned is whether the most economically profitable way is the right way, even in the face of massive depletion of resources and clear evidence that resources cannot be sustained. Standards for traditional ways of life receive low priority, if any attention at all. Accordingly, traditional ways of making a living are sacrificed, as are all other aspects of the quality of life, including maintenance of communities, kin groups, and even family, if they are in the path of large-scale economic growth and development. The issue becomes clearer that some greater balance is needed. Such changes do not require extraordinary events and resources. They require the will of individuals in communities to reorder priorities and put them into effect. It is within grasp, not something in the distant future that may or may not be attainable.

Questions

1. Goals of conservation and preservation in the contemporary United States typically focus on wilderness, nature, green areas, historic areas, and historic buildings and structures, but ways of life are almost never included. Why do we tend to exclude ways of life, such as African-American fishing societies, as worthy of conservation? Why do "tradition" and "way of life" tend to be undervalued?

2. Why is it that in the contemporary world economic development and growth take precedence over all other kinds of development, especially cultural development?

3. Why do natural resources, such as fish, tend to be viewed in the modern world primarily, or even solely, for exploitation? Why do we not give primary consideration to sustainability, to preservation of the resources?

4. Why are all stakeholders, including the African-American fishing communities, not given a voice and role in the planning and decision processes?

5. Is sustainability likely to occur in local communities that do not share in the vision and decisions about planning and local resources?

6. What innovative steps could be taken to try to reverse some of the unidirectional development and loss of quality of life seen among African-Americans on the Georgia coast? Could, for example, a local property tax policy be implemented to keep traditional land values low and affordable for rural communities and thus help stem the dislocation and marginalization seen in recent decades?

NOTES

1. The differences between Gullah and Geechee are relative and matters of degree. The principal differences appear to be related to views about origins. Descendants of African slaves in Georgia consider themselves to have different origins in Africa from those in the Carolinas. They also want to distinguish themselves from the Carolinians. The two categories are, however, highly similar, since Africa is the origin of each group. In addition, each group had to accommodate and adapt to similar constraints on ways of life in plantation life.

2. The coastal counties of Georgia, it might be noted, were among the last in the United States to be integrated. For an account of the civil rights struggle in the last coastal county to be integrated, McIntosh County, see Melissa Faye Green, *Praying for Sheetrock: A Work of Nonfiction* (Reading, Mass.: Addison-Wesley, 1991).

3. An excellent account of the forging of African-American cultural history in

Georgia can be found in Mart A. Stewart, *"What Nature Suffers to Groe": Life Labor, and Landscape on the Georgia Coast, 1680–1920* (Athens: University of Georgia Press, 1996).

4. A brief account of the role of African-American men and women in Savannah during the last decade of the nineteenth century can be found in Robert E. Perdue, *The Negro in Savannah, 1865–1900* (Jericho, N.Y.: Exposition Press, 1973).

5. A historical account of the commercial development of the oyster and the shrimp fisheries can be found in William C. Fleetwood, Jr., *Tidecraft: The Boats of South Carolina, Georgia, and Northeastern Florida, 1550–1950* (Tybee Island, Ga.: WBG Marine Press, 1995).

RESOURCE GUIDE

Published Literature

Fleetwood, William C., Jr. *Tidecraft: The Boats of South Carolina, Georgia, and Northeastern Florida, 1550–1950.* Tybee Island, Ga.: WBG Marine Press, 1995.

Green, Melissa Faye. *Praying for Sheetrock: A Work of Nonfiction.* Reading, Mass.: Addison-Wesley, 1991.

McFeely, William S. *Sapelo's People: A Long Walk into Freedom.* New York: W.W. Norton, 1994.

Perdue, Robert E. *The Negro in Savannah, 1865–1900.* Jericho, N.Y.: Exposition Press, 1973.

Savannah Unit Georgia Writers' Project. *Drums and Shadows: Survival Studies Among the Georgia Coastal Negroes.* Athens, Ga.: Brown Thrasher Books, 1940.

Stewart, Mart A. *"What Nature Suffers to Groe": Life, Labor, and Landscape on the Georgia Coast, 1680–1920.* Athens: University of Georgia Press, 1996.

Sullivan, Buddy. *Early Days on the Georgia Tidewater: The Story of McIntosh County & Sapelo.* Darien, Ga.: McIntosh County Board of Commissioners, 1995.

WWW Sites

Coastal Georgia Business, Cultural, and Travel organization
http://www.coastalgeorgia.com

Organization

Georgia Shrimpers Association
Darien, GA 31305

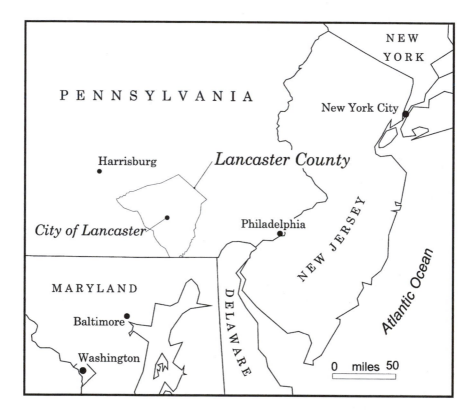

Chapter 10

The Amish of Lancaster County, Pennsylvania

Tom Greaves

To most Americans visiting the Lancaster area of southeastern Pennsylvania, the Old Order Amish are a picturesque oddity—a small, mostly farming group easily identified by their unusual clothing and the fact that they rely on horse-drawn buggies for transportation. Probably most Americans today regard the Old Order Amish as somewhat odd, perhaps antiquated, but they also accord them respect and admiration. Here is a group that is bucking the tide, insisting on its lifeway and religious beliefs, refusing to be seduced by the noisy calls of commerce and career that dominate so much of contemporary American life.

Against this backdrop, imagine the broad attention the following news story captured when it broke on July 20, 1998. Following an intensive undercover investigation, three young Lancaster Amish men, together with eight members of the Pagan motorcycle gang, were arrested and charged with conspiracy to distribute illegal drugs. One of the three Amish was a juvenile; the other two were in their mid-twenties. They were charged with buying quantities of cocaine from members of the Pagan gang and then reselling it to other Amish youths. The two adult Amish men admitted their guilt, expressed deep remorse, and in June 1999, were sentenced to a year each in prison.[1]

When the arrests were announced, media coverage was intense, not only in the United States, but also in other countries. The arrests appeared sharply at odds with the plain and pious lives of the Amish. Does it mean that the Amish are finally caving in to the temptations and dangers of modern society? That is the fundamental question around which this chapter is built. The Amish are an "enclave" society, a small community harboring its own lifeway, surrounded by an enormous, different society. The surrounding society controls law, politics, wealth, the economy, new technology, and most of the means of communication. And it is not just that the Amish are surrounded. The dominant surrounding society penetrates inside the society. Tourism intrudes. Land prices rise. Regulations affecting fundamental Amish beliefs and customs are applied. Vandalism and crime victimize them. Throughout their history, being Amish has always been difficult, but certainly today the difficulties are immense. Do the Amish have a future?

CULTURAL OVERVIEW

The People

Most Americans probably know something about the Amish. They are the people who use horses and buggies, who plow with horses, who wear quaint clothes—all mandated by their religious beliefs. They speak a dialect of German as well as English. All of this is true, but much that Americans commonly believe about the Amish is not true. So who are the Amish and what are they really like?

To understand the Amish one must understand their history. The Amish have their roots in the radical wing of the Protestant movement that broke with the Roman Catholic Church in the early 1500s. Out of this ferment of zealous argument and great personal risk arose a cluster of sects, known as the anabaptists, which asserted that one's religious commitment was a personal decision, and that a community of believers should develop through the inspiration of its members rather than through the exercise of governmental authority. They believed that scriptures should be read literally, the church should be separated from secular government, and military service should be rejected. They concluded that baptism should occur not in infancy, but, rather, as an adult when the individual could accept the baptismal vows freely and knowledgeably. The anabaptist movement spread quickly, particularly in Switzerland, Germany, and the Netherlands, but encountered vigorous repression from state authorities, whether Catholic or Protestant. Anabaptists endured ferocious persecution and thousands were slaughtered, imprisoned, drowned, burned at the stake, or beheaded. Yet, anabaptist groups endured and grew.

In the 1690s a division among the Swiss anabaptists emerged. Jakob Amman, of the city of Bern, concluded that his anabaptist contemporaries had by then become too worldly. He vowed to establish a stricter code of behavior and taught that persons who did not conform should be excommunicated from the fold and shunned—neither spoken to nor acknowledged thereafter. Among his many stipulations were that married men should wear untrimmed beards and that both sexes adopt conservative dress. In 1696 Amman moved to the French Alsace region where followers of a Dutch anabaptist leader, Menno Simons (they became known as Mennonites), were established. Amman's teachings were sufficiently different from those of the Mennonites, however, that although the two groups had much in common they did not merge. From the followers of Menno Simon and Jakob Amman came America's Mennonites and Amish.[2]

William Penn, founder of the Pennsylvania colony, encouraged the anabaptist groups to migrate to Pennsylvania, promising a climate of religious tolerance. Many Mennonites and Amish accepted and began to establish themselves in Penn's colony in the early 1700s, first in the Philadelphia area and then to the west near Lancaster. Theological arguments within the Amish and Mennonite communities led to further divisions and factions. Today there are several varieties of Amish and Mennonites. The most conservative communities have come to be called Old Order Mennonites and Old Order Amish. Old Order Mennonite and Old Order Amish communities recognize their many similarities and cooperate together, especially in maintaining their schools.

The Amish are the best known of a distinctive segment of the Pennsylvania population often called the Pennsylvania Dutch. ("Dutch" is a misnomer. The word derives from "Deutch," meaning "German.") Pennsylvania Dutch people sustain a strong tradition of family farms and local businesses, continue to speak a locally distinctive dialect of German in addition to English, and are most associated with the rural areas of central and southern Pennsylvania. A large portion of the Pennsylvania Dutch belong to one of three religious faiths: the Mennonites, the Amish, and the Brethren. The Old Order Mennonite, the Old Order Amish, and the more conservative of their neighbors make up Pennsylvania's "plain people," so called because they wear distinctive, old-fashioned clothing and maintain a religiously centered lifestyle that rejects the fashion and consumerism of our contemporary society. Although this chapter centers on the Old Order Amish (who will hereafter be called "Amish" for simplicity's sake), it is important to recognize that not all Amish are of the Old Order variety— indeed, there are at least four varieties of Amish in the Lancaster area.[3] Tourists often wrongly assume that all the "plain people" they see are Amish.

The Setting

There are no longer Amish communities in Europe, but in North America the Amish have flourished. Amish communities are found especially in Pennsylvania, Indiana, Iowa, Michigan, Ohio, and Wisconsin, but communities are also located in Delaware, Florida, Illinois, Kansas, Kentucky, Maryland, Minnesota, Missouri, Montana, New York, North Carolina, Oklahoma, Tennessee, Texas, Virginia, and West Virginia.[4] Amish settlements are also found in Ontario, Canada.[5] In 1990 there were about

135,000 Old Order Amish in North America, grouped into about 900 worshiping congregations, called "districts." Their current population is estimated at more than 150,000; their numbers double about every twenty years.[6] As will be discussed later in this chapter, their expanding population has brought both strength and difficulties to the Amish.

This chapter focuses on the Old Order Amish in one place, the Lancaster area of southeastern Pennsylvania. There are two reasons for this. First, Pennsylvania's Lancaster County is the historical anchor for Amish in America. Amish communities in many other states were often founded by Amish from the Lancaster area.[7] But there is a second reason to focus on the Lancaster Amish: there has been more scholarship written about the Lancaster County Amish over a longer period of time than about Amish anywhere else, and the reader seeking further information will find much more material to work with here.

Lancaster County has an irregular shape, roughly forty-six miles from east to west and forty-three miles from north to south at its widest points. Along the western border of the county flows the Susquehanna, one of the Middle Atlantic's largest rivers. The city of Lancaster, located toward the center of the county, serves as the county seat. It lies less than seventy miles from Philadelphia and Baltimore, both huge population centers. The city of Lancaster is itself a bustling, growing city with a current population of about 55,000. Yet most of Lancaster County is rural and scenic, with gently rolling farmlands separated here and there by higher, forested ridges. The valley lands, cross-cut by streams and creeks, are principally devoted to agricultural and dairy farms, with neat farm buildings, tall silos, and carefully bounded fields very much the rule.

Historically, the city of Lancaster has maintained a mixed economy built on agriculture, grain milling, lumbering, and various industries. After World War II tourism was added to this mix when people became attracted by the plain people and the scenic agricultural setting. Tourism is now a central element in the area's economy. Finally, for the past two decades, Lancaster has become widely known for a large outlet mall, one of the earliest of this genre, bringing throngs of shoppers from long distances and spawning many additional malls and retail establishments. Because tourists arrive by car and bus, highways have become heavily trafficked and large-scale road improvements are a perennial fact of life in and around the city of Lancaster.

Not surprisingly, growth has been a prominent feature of the area. Lancaster County has the second-fastest rate of growth among all of Pennsylvania's counties. Lancaster County's population grew by more than 10 percent over the past decade, and the number of licensed businesses grew by 7.5 percent between 1990 and 1998.[8] Fortunately for the Amish, the city of Lancaster has absorbed much of the county's explosive growth, though the rest of the county has felt growth's reverberations in tourist

Baling winter forage, Lancaster County, Pennsylvania, October 2000. Five-mule team drawing an iron-wheeled sulky, in turn hauling a motorized baler with iron-wheeled wagon. Photo: Tom Greaves.

pressure and rising land values. These and other factors pose serious challenges to the Amish's cultural future.

Traditional Subsistence Strategies

While there is nothing in the Amish religion that mandates that the Amish be farmers, farming is the principal and traditional economic pursuit of the Amish. Amish farms are family-sized enterprises, and most of the labor is supplied by the family members themselves. The reliance on family labor, draft animals (mainly horses and mules), and limited types of farm machinery means that farms of large acreage are not feasible. Labor needs that exceed what the family can supply, notably for barn raisings, are handled by community efforts. When large cash expenditures are required, as in the case of serious medical costs or purchasing land, relatives of the family contribute. When this does not suffice, the need may be met from the community at large. But these are unusual needs; in routine circumstances, an Amish farm and the family that works it are self-sufficient.

The cash needs of Amish farms are not trivial. The purchase of seed, pesticides, fertilizers and the need to acquire and replace farm machinery and traction animals mean that each farm is a complex financial operation. Those with dairy herds have different, but very substantial, cash requirements as well. Compared with non-Amish farms, however, operating costs are lower, and Amish farms are often quite prosperous.

In Lancaster County good farmland is limited and expensive. Meanwhile, the Amish population is expanding. Increasingly, Amish go into small businesses, including carpentry, masonry, furniture making, harness making, quilt making, retail shops, and roadside vegetable stands.[9] At the same time, the size of these businesses is limited by the Amish reticence to hire paid employees (and assume the role of boss and manager) and their reluctance to borrow money from banks.[10]

Social and Political Organization

As previously noted, Amish families belong to worship groups, usually composed of from twenty-five to thirty-five families, called districts. A district is served by two ministers and a deacon, chosen by the district's members. The highest religious authority is an Amish bishop, who presides over a group of affiliated districts. There is no national office or church authority above the bishops and no seminaries or formal theological training for Amish clergy. The Amish do not build churches. Worship services in most districts are held every other Sunday at members' homes. Districts subdivide when their membership becomes too large to worship in a home or farm setting.

The Amish do not live in villages or occupy zones where only other Amish live. While they may in places be in the majority, they always have non-Amish neighbors. Many will be other plain people, especially Brethren and Mennonites, but there will also be neighbors running farms or local businesses who do not practice a "plain" lifestyle at all (to whom the Amish refer to as "English"). Amish families deal with all of these people as neighbors, friends, and the suppliers of goods and services on which they depend. Thus, an Amish community, or, more precisely, an Amish district, is a religious congregation, not a village or town. Beyond the household there is no geographic unit within which people are Amish and beyond which they are not. So, while the religious congregation is centrally important to an Amish family, it is not the only community within which an Amish family lives. Perhaps this constant interaction and interdependence with neighbors who believe and act differently increase the resilience of Amish people in maintaining their own beliefs and ways.

Growing up within an Amish family differs sharply from many mainstream patterns. Children are often born in hospitals, though birthing at home under the care of Amish midwives appears to be somewhat more common. Because the Amish eschew insurance plans and policies, hospital bills are paid by the family, perhaps assisted by the community. Amish tend to have large families. Six or seven children is typical. Children usually attend school in one-room schools, taught by an Amish teacher selected by the community and supervised by a board from the community. Both men and women are teachers, but most teachers are young, unmarried Amish women who themselves have been good students of the same or a nearby school and are seen to have promise as teachers. Formal schooling ends at the eighth grade; the remainder of life preparation is learned on the farm, the craft shop, or the job.[11]

After schooling is finished Amish girls and boys intensify their work on the family farm or enterprise. By their mid-teens both boys and girls begin a unique period of their lives, *rumspringa*, during which they have much independence. They have yet to undergo adult baptism with its vows and commitments, and they are not yet officially members of the Amish faith. *Rumspringa* lasts just a few years for girls, who are usually baptized during their mid to late teens, but for boys it may last a decade or more. Most appear to link themselves to informal youth "gangs" or "crowds" with such names as the Rockies, the Pilgrims, or the Orioles. There are about two dozen in Lancaster County, commonly with from 100 to 200 members each.[12] While most engage in such activities as sings and sports activities, a few are "fast," holding dances known as "hoedowns" at which drinking, the latest music, and general mischief occur. Members of these groups may decide to wear clothing styles which are "cool" at the moment, may drive cars, may date non-Amish friends, may follow popular music trends, and, in other ways, behave much as mainstream American youth do. The drug selling incident described at the beginning of this chapter reflected the *rumspringa* period and these fast gangs.

So long as *rumspringa* stays within reasonable bounds, Amish communities can see some value in it. It satisfies the curiosity of youth about the outer world, and it makes their vows of baptism, which end *rumspringa*, more genuine because the individual understands what is being permanently rejected. In Lancaster County at least four of every five Amish youth choose Amish baptism and the life that follows, which illustrates how effective this traditional lifeway is in recruiting its next generation.[13] *Rumspringa*, however, is also a worrisome aspect of Amish life, and the episodes of serious and extreme behavior may be increasing.

Religion and World View

Religion lies at the heart of being Amish. Religion founded the Amish, sustained them during the times of persecution, and lies at the center of their existence today. So what do the Amish believe? There are strongly debated differences from district to district, but the following basic explanation of beliefs and practices is likely to be true of any Old Order Amish district.[14]

First, the Amish believe that humility and yielding to the dictates of God are fundamental. A proper Amish person will banish all inclinations of self-pride, arrogance, aggressiveness, and drawing attention to oneself. For this reason Amish are reticent to pose for cameras, to be quoted in newspapers, or to appear to speak for others. Baptism is understood to be a personal *yielding* to God's expectations, rejecting for life all individual ambitions to set oneself apart through personal achievement. Humility is reflected in their rejection of stylish clothes and the neat but unadorned functionality of their tools, buggies, farm buildings, schools, and houses. While mainstream Americans take pride in acquiring the things that make them the envy of others; the Amish completely reject such behavior: what is good and desirable is God and His works. To take pride in one's own possessions and accomplishments is to distance oneself from God.

A second central belief is that the human community is God's instrument. All people must devote their effort and concern to the good of the community. This principle is reflected in the photogenic barn raisings that frequently appear in the mainstream media. When misfortune strikes an Amish person, it is the community that responds. Amish do not purchase health or fire insurance or collect social security because it would enmesh them in external businesses and bureaucracies. Rather, it is the family and the community that covers those needs. Amish attend closely to their good standing within the community and participate in its social life. Individuals whose behavior or attitude provokes the disapproval of their neighbors must seek strenuously to apologize and win back community approval. Those who refuse may suffer the community's strongest punishment, permanent shunning.

A third key belief is that the Amish's upright, Godly life cannot be protected without staying quite separate (i.e., keeping a distance) from the surrounding mainstream society. This belief is reflected in their preference for living in communities, close to other Amish families, rather than migrating into cities family by family. Separation underlies their well-known rejection of electricity from regional power grids. To become a customer of the power company would draw the family home into the larger world. This is also why Old Order Amish reject radio, television, and residential telephones.

At bottom this is also why the Amish insist that their children's formal education last only through the eighth grade, and, if possible, be taught by Amish teachers under the Amish community's close supervision, in a one-room school house. Classroom education beyond the eighth grade is, the Amish believe, unnecessary to supply the needs of a God-fearing Amish community and would threaten its separation, and its ability to act in Godly ways.[15]

Separation does not mean that the Amish refuse to deal with the county, state, and federal governments. The Amish usually vote, and they cooperate with legal requirements so long as they do not entail compromise with their religious mandates. Thus, the Amish observe traffic laws when using public highways. The Amish pay taxes without complaint (including social security taxes, even though they refuse to collect the benefits). They pay the local school district's property tax even though their children go to their own schools, which they also support financially, thus paying for two educational systems while using only one. While the Amish will not run for public office (something that focuses attention on the individual), the Amish will meet collectively with political leaders to discuss issues. The Amish recognize the authority and legitimacy of external government, but they do not seek to lead it or become part of it. The Amish refusal to engage in military service is consistent with the commitment to living apart from the larger society, but it also reflects the commitment to nonviolence that comes down from their earliest Protestant teachings, nearly 500 years ago. Nevertheless, staying separate does not mean that the Amish ignore their non-Amish neighbors. In 1973 the author's own town of Lewisburg in central Pennsylvania experienced a devastating flood. As the water began to recede, Amish and Mennonites arrived unasked to dry out cellars, move furniture back, make repairs, and bring water and food to families and businesses.[16] Being Godly entails a concern for people in general, not just family and congregation.

Fourth, the Amish believe that keeping to the holy path takes constant vigilance. The acceptance of any change, however small, could be a step away from upright life. So, under the guidance of the bishop, the Amish examine and evaluate each new possibility for its potential impact. Will it weaken or strengthen the community? Will it move the community deeper into dependency on the outside world? Will it erode the ethic of humility? Will it lead children astray?

Telephones are an example. Home telephones are useful if there is a medical emergency. Phones are important for running a business. Telephones also interrupt family life, draw its members into social relationships with others, funnel commercial selling into the family precinct, and, through the wires leading from the house, physically link each household to an outside corporation. Telephones have been debated district by district, and in each case the verdict has been that telephones must not be installed in the home.[17] Amish are not prohibited from using public pay telephones, however, and in some districts clusters of Amish businesses or farms have found it acceptable to have the local telephone company install a pay phone in a booth nearby. Cell phones, which have no wire connections, are the subject of current discussion.[18] Does the absence of a connecting wire make cell phones acceptable, or are new rules about wireless connections needed?

Many decisions of the Amish seem curious: Farmers may not use tractors to plow, but they can, in some districts, use internal combustion engines to power farm machinery hauled by animals. Mobile farm machinery may have metal wheels, but not rubber tires. Amish may ride in cars but not drive them. Farms and craft shops can use electric machines if powered by a generator, but not if they draw power from a power company. Amish businesses may, in some districts, install computers if non-Amish employees operate them. Some Amish districts allow dashboards in buggies, others do not. To mainstream Americans these distinctions may seem pointless, but each has been evaluated against its potential to harm fundamental Amish values and community life. Old Order Amish believe that every small change, over time, will have lasting effects. And they are right.

As the above decisions indicate, the Amish believe that remaining true to their religious obligations compels them to make very careful judgments about each new change. Each district has a religiously sanctioned bill of particulars known as the *Ordnung*. The *Ordnung* is a lengthy set of dos and don'ts that specifies how the Amish should live life in accord with Biblical teachings. The *Ordnung* is normally unwritten, but is so frequently quoted in daily life that its content is completely known by the community. Among districts in the same affiliation group the dictates of the *Ordnung* are essentially identical. Between different affiliation groups there are likely to be small but vigorously disputed differences in what is allowed or proscribed.

In the preceding sections we have not only described the Amish, but at various points we have also mentioned stresses that now confront the Amish and threaten their future as a distinct cultural and social group. The next section focuses on these threats.

THREATS TO SURVIVAL

Threats from the Larger Society

The Amish have been identified as an enclave society. The Amish are surrounded by an incomparably larger, more powerful society, differing dramatically in lifestyle and values. The surrounding dominant society runs the major political, economic, technological, and ideological context with which the Amish must cope. Further, the surrounding society is not only all around the Amish community, but also within it. Tourists, journalists, photographers, and researchers follow the Amish about and intrude on their privacy. Salespeople seek them out to sell them the many products they need, such as agricultural seed, farming implements, cloth, tools, and so on. Many of their immediate neighbors are not Amish. Along the road, billboards huckster all manner of attractive products, services, and experiences. Store shelves are loaded with enticing products the Amish should not buy. The fundamental problem the Amish face is that they are confronted every day by a powerful surrounding society that doesn't let them alone.[19]

Increased Population

The second problem is increasing population. As mentioned earlier, the Amish population is doubling about every twenty years. The number of Lancaster County Amish religious districts has gone from 5 in 1900 to 113 in 1996 serving some 17,000 people.[20] The aspiration of Amish parents is to provide each grown and married son with a working farm. An expanding farm population requires more farmland in each generation, but farmland in Lancaster County is not expanding.

A third problem is that the Lancaster area is experiencing a booming influx of businesses and non-Amish population growth. The highways are clogged with cars. Quiet country roads are now laden with speeding automobiles, making travel by buggy distinctly dangerous. Because Lancaster is an easy drive from Philadelphia via the Pennsylvania Turnpike and just a short trip from Baltimore and Washington, D.C., vast shopping complexes have been built in Lancaster. Its outlet mall, particularly, is a regional magnet for shoppers. As a result, good farmland is being built over, and the prices of what remains are out of reach. The Amish would have a serious land problem even if their population were unchanging, but because they are growing rapidly, the problem is acute.

Tourism

A fourth problem is tourism. The Lancaster area tourism industry, much of it focused on the Amish, has intensified. The main highways are lined with restaurants hawking Amish-inspired food, especially shoo-fly pie, a molasses-based dessert. In the tourist areas a welter of souvenir shops sell an astonishing array of "Amish" items that ridiculously caricature them. While tour buses make an effort to remain at a discrete distance, the tourism pressure is intense. The Lancaster Amish find themselves struggling to preserve the privacy of their own social space.

Other Concerns

Four more examples of threats are the following: (1) Various recent cases of serious misdeeds, including drug use, among some of the youth crowds are worrisome. Thus far the Amish appear to have few ways to stop this. (2) Government regulation of agriculture is increasing, particularly of pesticide use, environmental rules, and programs to reduce the cultivation of an important Amish crop, tobacco. Given Amish insistence about not joining government programs or taking direct government payments, difficulties are on the rise. (3) In the wake of public concern about the employment of children, the federal government has issued new regulations concerning the sorts of work in which youths below the ages of eighteen and sixteen can engage. These rules run afoul of the Amish tradition of learning a trade immediately after the eighth grade. (4) The Amish will not buy insurance or hire lawyers. The increasing frequency and cost of liability lawsuits against agricultural, construction, and service providers pose an increasing danger to the Amish. Each of these four are, in fact, specific forms of the first problem, being an enclave community. The outside, dominant society introduces changes that the Amish cannot ignore and which, if left without solution, undermine and threaten their religion and their lifeway.

RESPONSE: STRUGGLES TO SURVIVE CULTURALLY

As we have seen, growing numbers and diminishing agricultural land are powerful forces the Lancaster Amish cannot avoid. Their main responses have been of two types, to move away from Lancaster County or to enter nonfarming occupations. The pattern of moving away from Lancaster County is well under way, accounting for the wide distribution of Amish in other parts of Pennsylvania, in other states, and in Canada. Migration to escape problems building up in the home locality is as old as the Amish themselves, and it continues to be an available solution today. One can assume that the Amish populations will continue to grow in other American states where good agricultural land is still affordable and Amish communities are welcome.

Migration to new jurisdictions can mean that a number of old struggles must be repeated in the new setting. For example, the Amish communities have been in Ontario, Canada, since 1923. Here, as in the United States, they encountered agricultural bureaucracies that had little experience with nonparticipating groups of farmers. In the 1960s and 1970s, the Ontario Amish had to insist on being exempted from being enrolled in Canada's national old-age pension system, from making payments for Amish employees into the national pension plan, from the requirement that every citizen have a social insurance number, and from participation in the national health system. Some solution to each of those problems was eventually found. More troublesome has been Ontario's regulation of milk and dairy producers, a core part of the Ontario Amish economy. Ontario's government sought to make uniform the way in which milk is handled, accumulated, and brought to market. The Amish refused to take part in the dairy farmers' regional management system, and they had objections to mandated electrical refrigeration of the milk and Sunday pickups by milk tanker trucks. Solutions to those matters were also eventually found, but a new issue, expensive licenses to share in the dwindling market for cream, is now threatening Amish dairymen. Newspaper reports predict that many of Ontario's 4,000 Amish will leave Canada because of these problems.[21] If that happens it will illustrate once again the Amish preference to move elsewhere when difficulties become intractable. We should remember too, of course, that migration is not an easy option. Uprooting and going to a new, unknown setting is difficult and stressful, especially for a people whose family, community, and ties to the land are so important.

Among the Lancaster Old Order Amish, a second response to growing population and diminishing land is to earn a living at something other than farming. This trend has been carefully studied and analyzed in Lancaster County and in Indiana County, located in western Pennsylvania near Pittsburgh, and in Ontario and elsewhere.[22] What is clear is that, when farming becomes out of reach, many Amish stay on, but earn a living in a nonfarm occupation. We saw an instance of this in the drug episode. One of the two Amish adults had started a roofing business. One of his employees was the other arrested Amish man.

The data do not show that large numbers of Amish men and women are working for *non-Amish* companies. Rather, the pattern is for Amish entrepreneurs to establish a small enterprise, gradually build it up, employ first family members who are often unpaid, and then gradually hire paid employees, both Amish and non-Amish. The growth rate of these small enterprises in the Lancaster area has been phenomenal, with over a thousand Amish-owned enterprises established in the period from 1970 to the mid-1990s, almost one third of them in the most recent five years. Most of them are small—83 percent of one sample had fewer than four full-time employees, owner included—but in the aggregate the sample suggests that Amish-owned enterprises in 1992 in Lancaster County employed nearly 1,700 full-time and 1,200 part-time Amish and another 420 non-Amish.[23]

Amish enterprises include woodworking shops which produce furniture, cabinets, picnic tables, storage sheds, lawn furniture, and a vast array of other wood-crafted products. Others participate in the building industry, engaged in painting, roofing, masonry, and general contracting. Still others own retail stores selling hardware, dry goods, and groceries, in many combinations. Some businesses—for example, blacksmithing, buggy repair, and harness making—serve primarily Amish customers; others sell items attractive to tourists, including traditional Amish crafts such as quilts and foods. Some businesses are owned and operated by Amish women.

Amish-owned businesses pose fewer incompatibilities with Amish ways than might be thought.[24] Amish clothing is worn on the job, neighbors and family members may be employees, and the business can close when barn raisings or family events require. The German dialect may be used within the business and with local customers. Further, Amish business can draw on a number of Amish traits that help it succeed. Amish families will assemble start-up capital from among themselves. And Amish workers are productive—one's personal standing is tied to it. A lazy employee working in a local, Amish-owned business will soon find that his family and neighbors know about his sloth and will think less of him. Finally, Amish businesses do not pay social security and unemployment insurance for Amish employees, which lowers labor costs.

Although Amish businesses have advantages, they also operate with limitations their non-Amish counterparts do not have. In some districts the bishops allow telephones and electric machinery inside the shop, but in others they do not. Amish businesses do very little advertising because advertising is inconsistent with the humility ethic. Some have no identifying exterior signs at all. Amish enterprises must remain small. Having many employees and major physical assets leads to unavoidable involvement in the bureaucracies that administer those programs. Finally, small-town America is experiencing a vigorous displacement of small, local businesses by large, outside corporate chains. A chain motel opens and the local motel dies. A chain restaurant opens and patrons of the local cafe diminish. Drawing on greater capital, on the equipment of modern business communications, and on advertising campaigns, chains exert great pressure on family-run local businesses. Amish businesses will be somewhat protected when they rely mostly on Amish and other local customers, and their reputation for high quality and sound value is a major asset, but their ability to compete with the larger business world for regional and larger markets is in doubt.

Through much of the above discussion, we have noted the dilemmas posed by new technology. Automobiles and trucks, electric power from public utilities, telephones, and even zippers on clothing have been rejected as posing too great a risk to the Amish lifeway. But, in rejecting new technology, the Amish are not unmindful of what is being forfeited. We see in Lancaster County repeated readiness to seek ways to acquire some of the benefits of new technologies so long as the Amish lifeway is not jeopardized. The benefits of telephones, and their wires, can be obtained, and the cultural costs minimized, if pay phones are installed out on the road, or in the shop, but not in the home. Allowing electric wires from the power company into an Amish home invites radio, television, and the Internet. That they oppose. But a dairy farmer cannot keep summer milk cool without refrigeration. The solution: use a diesel-powered electricity generator in the barn to power the refrigeration unit. The solutions the Amish devise seem odd and contradictory to the mainstream outsider, but what they show is that the Amish are continuously engaged in a search for ways to accept change selectively where the benefits are apparent and the risk of being Amish is low.

FOOD FOR THOUGHT

The Amish of Lancaster County show us that it is possible to survive, and even to flourish as a distinctly different culture enclaved within America's mainstream society. To do so is not easy, and every year brings difficult new dilemmas. The future of the Amish is not unclouded, but across the past two and a half centuries Lancaster's Old Order Amish have remained strong despite the dramatic transformation of the surrounding dominant society.

Questions

1. Religion lies at the heart of being Amish. How does this differ for typical members of mainstream society?

2. Imagine that you are an Amish person who decides to start a business. What type of business would allow you to operate without having to contradict key Amish beliefs and behavioral requirements? What types of businesses would necessarily result in being required to contradict those requirements?

3. Despite the freedom allowed by *rumspringa*, an estimated 80 percent of Old Order Amish youth choose to be baptized and follow the traditional Amish faith and lifeway. What are some factors that are probably important in leading to this result?

4. The Amish have been in Lancaster County about 200 years—about ten generations. Imagine that you were hired by a reservation-based American Indian tribe to advise them on what they should do to assure that ten generations (about 200 years) from now their descendants will have retained their cultural core as successfully as the Amish. What would you advise? If the tribe does all you propose, will it be enough?

5. What main forces are confronting the Amish now and how might those forces change in future years—200 years from now? Will the Amish be able to devise successful solutions to those forces and still remain Amish?

NOTES

Professor Lois M. Huffines read an early version of this chapter and advised me on a number of important points. Her assistance is greatly appreciated. All errors that remain, of course, are entirely mine. I am also much indebted to Librarian Dot Thompson of Bucknell University's Bertrand Library for her assistance in locating elusive published sources.

1. There was much news coverage of this case. One useful article is David Remnick, "Letter from Lancaster County; Bad Seeds," *The New Yorker*, July 20, 1998, 28–33.

2. For a well written history of the Amish see Steven M. Nolt, *A History of the Amish* (Intercourse, Penn: Good Books, 1992).

3. For a detailed comparison of the four varieties, see Donald B. Kraybill and Marc A. Olshan, eds., *The Amish Struggle with Modernity* (Hanover, N.H.: University Press of New England, 1994), 54–74.

4. *New American Almanac*, 30th ed. (Baltic, Ohio, 1999), 68, 74.

5. T.D. Regehr, "Relations Between the Old Order Amish and the State in Canada." *Mennonite Quarterly Review* 69, 2 (1995): 151–77.

6. Kraybill and Olshan, *The Amish Struggle*, 9.

7. See David Luthy, "Amish Settlements Across America," *Family Life* (April 1991), 20.

8. Web site, Lancaster County Chamber of Commerce: http://www.lancaster-chamber.com/econdev/business growth.htm. See also Donald B. Kraybill and Steven M. Nolt, *Amish Enterprise: From Plows to Profits* (Baltimore: Johns Hopkins University Press, 1995), 26–29.

9. See Kraybill and Nolt, *Amish Enterprise*, 46–50.

10. Kraybill and Nolt, *Amish Enterprise*, report that Amish business entrepreneurs judiciously contract loans from banks, but prefer to develop the business gradually, minimizing debt obligations. See especially pp. 56–57.

11. In 1972 the U.S. Supreme Court, in *Wisconsin v. Yoder*, ruled that Amish religious freedom entitled them to be exempted from compulsory school attendance after the eighth grade.

12. Remnick, "Letter from Lancaster County," 29.

13. Donald B. Kraybill, *The Riddle of Amish Culture* (Baltimore: Johns Hopkins University Press, 1989), 140. See also Kraybill and Olshan, *The Amish Struggle*, 10.

14. Summaries of core Amish beliefs are found in many sources. One useful rendition is Kraybill, *The Riddle of Amish Culture*, Chapters 2 and 3.

15. Education does not end at the eighth grade, however. The Amish believe that subsequent education should be conducted under the guidance of Amish parents and other adults who teach domestic and occupational skills in real-life settings, as well as social and religious expectations for an Amish life.

16. In addition to being part of Lewisburg's oral tradition, the assistance of Amish and Mennonites during the flood is reported in "Diary of a Flood," *Union County Journal*, July 6, 1972, 1, 6.

17. See Dianne Zimmerman Umble, *Holding the Line: The Telephone in Old Order Mennonite and Amish Life* (Baltimore: Johns Hopkins University Press, 1996).

18. See Howard Rheingold, "Look Who's Talking," *Wired*, January 1999, 128–31, 160–63.

19. A useful account of these change pressures in Lancaster County can be found in Randy-Michael Testa, *After the Fire: The Destruction of the Lancaster County Amish* (Hanover, N.H.: University Press of New England, 1992).

20. Carleen Hawn, "A Second Parting of the Red Sea," *Forbes*, March 9, 1998, 140; Conrad L. Kanagy and Donald B. Kraybill, "The Rise of Entrepreneurship in Two Old Order Amish Communities," *Mennonite Quarterly Review* 70, no. 3 (1996): 266–67.

21. Regehr, "Relations between the Old Order Amish and the State in Canada," 151–77; Bob Harvey, "Ontario's Amish Exodus: New Dairy Laws Send Whole Communities Packing Up for the U.S.," *The Ottawa Citizen*, April 25, 1999, A1.

22. See Donald B. Kraybill and Steven M. Nolt, *Amish Enterprise: From Plows to Profits* (Baltimore: Johns Hopkins University Press, 1995); and Conrad L. Kanagy and Donald B. Kraybill, "The Rise of Entrepreneurship in Two Old Order Amish Communities," *Mennonite Quarterly Review* 70, no. 3 (1996): 263–79.

23. Kraybill and Nolt, *Amish Enterprise*, 43–44; Kanagy and Kraybill, "Rise of Entrepreneurship."

24. Kraybill and Nolt, *Amish Enterprise*, Chapter 12.

RESOURCE GUIDE

Published Literature

Hostetler, John A. *Amish Society*. 4th ed. Baltimore: Johns Hopkins University Press, 1993.

Hostetler, John A., and Gertrude E. Huntington. *Amish Children*. Fort Worth, Texas: Harcourt Brace Jovanovich, 1989.

Kanagy, Conrad L., and Donald B. Kraybill. "The Rise of Entrepreneurship in Two Old Order Amish Communities." *Mennonite Quarterly Review* 70, no. 3 (1996): 263–79.

Kraybill, Donald B. *The Riddle of Amish Culture*. Baltimore: Johns Hopkins University Press, 1989.

Kraybill, Donald B., and Steven M. Nolt. *Amish Enterprise: From Plows to Profits*. Baltimore: Johns Hopkins University Press, 1995.

Kraybill, Donald B., and Marc A. Olshan, eds. *The Amish Struggle with Modernity*. Hanover, N.H.: University Press of New England, 1994.

Niemeyer, Lucian, and Donald B. Kraybill. *Old Order Amish, Their Enduring Way of Life*. Photographs by Lucian Niemeyer, text by Donald B. Kraybill. Baltimore: Johns Hopkins University Press, 1993.

Nolt, Steven M. *A History of the Amish*. Intercourse, Penn.: Good Books, 1992.

Testa, Randy-Michael. *After the Fire: The Destruction of the Lancaster County Amish*. Hanover, N.H.: University Press of New England, 1992.

Umble, Dianne Zimmerman. *Holding the Line: The Telephone in Old Order Mennonite and Amish Life*. Baltimore: Johns Hopkins University Press, 1996.

Videos

The Amish: A People of Preservation. John L. Ruth, producer, Worcester, PA: Gateway Films/Vision Video, 2000.

An Amish Portrait. University Park: Pennsylvania State University, 1989.

WWW Site

Resource website maintained by the publisher of an area information publication
http://www.amishnews.com/

Chapter 11

The Hmong in Wisconsin

Jo Ann Koltyk

Hmong families began leaving refugee camps in Thailand and arriving in Wausau, Wisconsin, and other cities in the United States in spring 1976. Most of them came with very few belongings, leaving behind their lives in Laos as self-sufficient farmers. The mountainous terrain and hot, humid climates of Laos were now replaced by cold weather, snow, and the relatively flat land of Wisconsin. Their new physical landscape pales in comparison to the new cultural landscape that now surrounds them. Of their rapid transplantation from a Third World country to a postindustrial setting, some Hmong have said that it was akin to taking a quantum leap of 200 years into the future.[1] Wausau, a small city in the central part of the state, has a population of approximately 32,000 residents. The Hmong population in 1998 represented about 11 percent of the city's population. This chapter explores the most commonly asked questions regarding the Hmong: Who are they? Why did they come to America? What problems have they faced here? How are they faring? How have they rebuilt their Hmong culture? What changes have they made to their lives and their traditions over the last twenty-four years? And what is their future as Hmong Americans?[2]

CULTURAL OVERVIEW

The People

The precise origins of the Hmong remain obscure. Hmong folk legends speak of their ancestors as having come from an icy land of long winters and long dark nights. Some theorists conclude that the Hmong migrated into China from the high steppes of Tibet, Siberia, and Mongolia. The Hmong are first noted in early Chinese writings dating from about 2700 B.C. in which they are settled along the banks of the Yellow River. In these writings they are called the "San Miao" (or Three Miao) and are referred to as troublemakers for attacking the Chinese settlements encroaching on their lands. The word "Miao" in Chinese is considered derogatory; some linguists have translated the written Chinese characters for Hmong to mean "wild uncultivated tribes." Others have suggested that the character of the "grass" or "vegetation" radical above a "field" on the Chinese character may suggest that the Hmong are "sons of the soil," or the original people of China.[3]

Hmong people today state that they prefer to call themselves Hmong. Some Hmong leaders have suggested that the word Hmong means "free," thus symbolizing the characteristics of the Hmong to remain free and independent of outside rule. The Hmong have a history of being on the move, either migrating to new places to find fertile fields or else escaping repressive governments or economic situations. Throughout these migrations the Hmong have placed value on family and kinship connections, and on their independence as a people. Each move has required them to be persistent and yet flexible and creative in how they adapt to new places.

The Setting

The Hmong began emigrating from China into regions of Vietnam, Laos, and Thailand in the early nineteenth century to escape Chinese imposed rule and taxation. Most of the Hmong people living in the United States have come from Laos. Laos is a mountainous country with tropical jungles, isolated villages, and very few large cities. The climate is tropical with a dry season from December to May and a rainy season from June to November.

More than sixty minority groups including the Hmong live in Laos. As horticultural farmers, the Hmong settled in the mountainous lands above 3,000 feet, where they practiced slash-and-burn agriculture to clear fields for planting. The Hmong grew rice, corn, and an assortment of vegetables, and they cultivated the opium poppy as a cash crop. They supplemented their diets by hunting and gathering and raising pigs, chickens, goats, and cows. When soil fertility became exhausted, the whole village moved to new land.

Traditional Subsistence Strategies

Subsistence strategies were divided by gender. Men cut down trees, burned the fields, and cared for the horses and cows. Women carried away brush, helped plant the crops, and weeded the fields. Harvesting was carried out by the whole family. Women gathered firewood and water, processed and cooked the food, took care of the children, and made all their family's clothing. Women's geometric embroidered and appliqué needlework decorated the clothing of both men and women and served as markers of identity for the various Hmong groups throughout Laos, Vietnam, Thailand, and China. The Hmong were relatively self-sufficient in their mountain villages. Cash from their opium crop was used to buy what they could not grow or make.

Moving into Laos did not free them from political and economic turmoil. When the French colonial government in Laos attempted to impose taxes on the Hmong, further rebellions occurred as the Hmong struggled to maintain their independence. Civil war in Laos continued during World War II and again from 1949 to 1975. The Hmong were recruited in the 1960s by the U.S. Central Intelligence Agency to serve as a secret guerrilla fighting force during the Vietnam War. They were supplied with arms, ammunition, and food in return for their allied services to the United States.

Hmong traditional subsistence economy and life in general was severely disrupted during the period from 1955 until 1975. As Hmong men and boys were called into military action, villages experienced a shortage of male labor needed in planting season. Women's roles in household economy were changing as they were pressed into doing the work left vacant by the males. Many Hmong villages became dependent on airdrops of rice and other goods. As the warfare and bombing escalated, Hmong villagers fled into resettlement zones within Laos. The Hmong were introduced to wages from military payrolls at these large centers and had opportunities to start up small businesses or engage in trade to supplement or replace their lives as self-sufficient farmers.

In April 1975, when Saigon fell into the hands of the Communist government, U.S. troops were pulled out of Vietnam. Support to the Hmong and their secret army was terminated. Shortly thereafter the Hmong fell victim to persecution and genocidal attacks by the new Communist government in Laos, the Lao People's Democratic Republic, for their support and involvement with the U.S. government. Hmong soldiers and their families fled across the Mekong River into Thailand for safety. Many casualties occurred during their attempt to escape.

When surviving Hmong reached Thailand, they were placed in refugee camps. Further changes in traditional life took place in the camps. The camps were crowded, noisy, dirty, and lacking in economic or educational opportunities. Except for small vegetable gardens, the Hmong were completely dependent upon international aid for their livelihood while in the camps. Entrepreneurial activities such as the selling of their embroidered needlework generated some money. The most famous, newly created needlework called *paj ntaub* or story cloth was pictorial rather than geometric in design and told the story of the Hmong and their escape from Laos. These story cloths were marketed throughout the West. Relatives already resettled in the United States helped market the embroidery pieces and sent money back to aid their relatives in the refugee camps. People languished in these camps, some for as many as twenty years before they could be resettled in the West.

Social and Political Organization

The unifying force in Hmong culture is the patrilineal clan and kinship system. There are about twenty clans in Hmong culture. Clans divide into smaller kinship units of lineages, sublineages, and households which control all aspects of Hmong social, economic, and political life. Within the clan and lineage system, members have various rights and obligations to their relatives and clan group. In Laos, lineage members lived in the same village and shared in farming activities and ritual practices. The household is the most important group in Hmong culture for the operation of daily social and economic needs. Households consist of an extended family, usually a man and his wife, his sons and their wives, and their children. It is in the household that one learns his or her roles and responsibilities as a Hmong person toward others in one's kinship unit. Primary values taught in the Hmong family are those of respect for one's parents and elders, putting group needs before one's own individual needs, and avoiding any conflict and actions that will bring shame to the family. A person's identity is never derived solely from being an individual but rather from his or her identification and role within the group. Wealth, in many ways, is measured by the strength of one's family and clan ties.

Religion and World View

Hmong culture is traditionally an oral based culture. Only after the 1950s was an alphabet developed by missionaries to give the Hmong people a written language. Within this rich oral tradition lie Hmong songs, stories, proverbs, folktales, myths, and many folk beliefs and rituals. Hmong cosmology speaks of a world of spirits existing in both the natural and supernatural world. Supernatural beings, nature spirits, and ancestral spirits or the souls of the dead continue to interact with the living. Human beings, in their interactions with the natural world, can upset the balance of the spirit world through inappropriate or careless behavior and cause illness to fall upon themselves or others. Humans can protect themselves from spirit harm and illness by maintaining and propitiating the spirits through performing rituals, maintaining taboos, and seeking the aid of a shaman who can negotiate with the spirit world to try to correct the imbalance and restore harmony to the individual and the community.

Hmong cosmology is intricately woven into daily life in terms of food practices, ethnomedical beliefs regarding illnesses and accidents, and life cycle events such as pregnancy, birth, marriage, and death. Most of these events call for special ritual offerings. Animal sacrifices are made in order to placate or appease spirits or to gain their help in worldly matters. Agricultural cycles, such as the harvest and the new year, are also tied to ritual ceremonies in order to bring future health and prosperity to family and village.

THREATS TO SURVIVAL

Demographic Trends

Of the nearly 7 million Hmong in the world, most still reside in their homeland of China. The principal countries of resettlement for the Hmong refugees from Laos have been the United States and Canada, along with Australia, France, and French Guiana. As of July 2000, about 250,000 Hmong reside in the United States. The largest Hmong populations are in California, Wisconsin, and Minnesota. Wisconsin currently has about 50,000 Hmong. Other states with significant Hmong populations include Michigan, Illinois, Colorado, Oregon, Massachusetts, North Carolina, and Washington. The Hmong face many problems in the United States. The main problems are employment and economic self-sufficiency, adjustment and adaptation, family and intergenerational conflict, legal and medical issues, education and training including learning the English language, and discrimination.[4]

The Hmong immigrated to the United States as families rather than as individuals. Families typically are large. The Hmong are a pronatal culture with high birthrates. Nationally, about 50 percent of the immigrant population is under the age of fourteen; 25 percent is under the age of five. In Wausau about two-thirds of the present population of 6,000 are children. Individuals age sixty or older represent about 5 percent of the population. A large proportion of young married couples between the ages of twenty and thirty-nine significantly define the population as well. In 1985 about eighty-five percent of the Hmong population were unemployed for various reasons. Many people forty-five and older either had health problems or were unable to learn English sufficiently for employment. Individuals between the age of sixteen and thirty-four were also unemployed because they were attending school or vocational training programs. In 1991 about 60 percent of the 508 Hmong families were receiving public assistance. The majority of them were attending language classes and job training programs, or they were enrolled in public schools.[5]

Conditions over the Last Twenty Years

Unemployment

One of the biggest concerns facing the Hmong has been that of employment and obtaining economic self-sufficiency. A very high proportion of the Hmong population came to the United States with little or no formal education and were unfamiliar with literacy. Their occupational experience as self-sufficient farmers or military soldiers did not translate into employment opportunities in the United States because most jobs in the economy needed skilled laborers. Without education or job training many Hmong found themselves on the social welfare rolls, dependent on cash benefits, low-income housing, and food stamps for their livelihood. Seasonal farm work or menial jobs were the only ones available to the majority of Hmong families. Minimum wage jobs, however, were not enough to support their large families, and until they were proficient in English even the minimum wage jobs were out of their reach. Job training programs and English language learning became top priorities for this group. The greatest public fear at this time was that the Hmong would become entrapped in a cycle of poverty and remain on the welfare rolls indefinitely.

First Wave of Hmong

Initial resettlement experiences in Wausau as well as elsewhere in the United States were similar for many Hmong families. Because the Hmong had no prior immigration to the United States, there were no established Hmong ethnic communities to help and guide families in their adjustment to new cultural surroundings. Individuals had to rethink many of their normal daily habits and routines from simple acts of getting food and communicating to a total rethinking of their spiritual beliefs, concepts, and values.

Language Barriers

Unable to speak English at the time, most families felt isolated and frustrated by not being able to communicate their needs to their sponsors. Basic food needs such as their preference for a bag of rice over such foreign foods as cans of spaghetti, white bread, or instant rice only added to the Hmong's sense of isolation. Answering the telephone or a knock at the door brought confusion and, for some, terror at not being able to know what was being said or asked of them. Going to the grocery store confounded their situation when most of the product packaging required reading English. Even the act of paying for the groceries became an embarrassment. Many families just held out the money and trusted that the cashier took the right amount.

The printed word surrounded the Hmong—bus schedules, washing machines at the laundromat, junk mail, rental agreements, health clinic forms, and paperwork for school attendance. All these things required assistance. A tremendous amount of pressure was therefore put on the few Hmong individuals who were bilingual and who could act as cultural brokers, interpreting and bridging the Hmong world to the non-Hmong world they lived in. Many times, children themselves were engaged in the brokering process for their parents. As the children began to work their way through the educational system, their English language skills became crucial to their non-English speaking parents and relatives. Children were relied on by Hmong and non-Hmong people to translate complex medical procedures, interpret legal documents, make appointments, and even be mediators in their own parent-teacher conferences. All this caused a great deal of conflict within the Hmong family because it reversed traditional parent/child roles. The elders were now dependent on the young. Their leadership roles were diminished by the fact that they did not understand the new cultural rules. Those individuals who did understand the new culture assumed positions of authority for the family.

Cultural Crisis

Hmong attempts to control their lives through practicing their traditional cultural and religious beliefs proved to be difficult. The landscape of the American home and neighborhood made some rituals meaningless or came under intense scrutiny from non-Hmong neighbors. Neighbors complained to police when noise from shamanic rituals went on for hours. The sacrifice of a chicken or pig was difficult in homes that were carpeted or did not have a backyard or basement. Furthermore, their American neighbors, who regarded animal sacrifice not as ancient rituals that worked for the Hmong but rather as cruelty to animals, created a stigma and stereotype of the Hmong as "primitive," "barbaric," and "backward." The Hmong wondered, too, if their rituals had any power in a world lit up by electric lights day and night or if their rituals, shortened and adapted to fit the weekend, could still be effective. Would their ancestors be able to find them in this strange new world? Would the deceased be able to find their way back to their birthplace (the place where their placenta was buried)?

Hmong customs such as polygyny (multiple wives), early teen marriages, and bride capture challenged the legal system in Wausau and elsewhere. Families who had expected to resolve their personal and family problems within their own lineage and clan systems were surprised when the American legal system overruled their own traditional customs.

Medical misunderstanding over illness interpretation and treatment was as troubling for the medical profession as it was for the Hmong. Many Hmong had a fear of hospitals and doctors. Illness in Hmong culture is attributed to both natural and supernatural causes, an idea not easily understood by Western medical doctors who put their faith in scientific instruments and tests. High blood pressure, viruses, and vaccinations were foreign concepts to most Hmong. Drawing blood was felt to weaken the body. Cutting open the body in surgery risked the chance of releasing one's soul, causing further possibilities of illness and even death.[6] American doctors did not consider the Hmong belief in soul loss to be a valid cause of illness nor did they trust some of the ancient remedies that the Hmong used to cure illness such as herbs, massage, or the power of the traditional shaman.

Women were especially vulnerable to cultural misunderstanding with doctors and hospitals during their pregnancy and childbirth experience. Hmong women practice various taboos that guard the safety of the mother and the baby. A woman is prohibited from eating various foods and is limited in her various activities from work, cooking, visiting, and touching or eating items considered to be cold. The birth of a baby traditionally took place at home with the help of the woman's husband and mother-in-law. Gynecology and prenatal care was regarded as invasive and embarrassing, especially having a male doctor perform pelvic exams. The birth process in the hospital was seen as noisy, uncomfortable, unnatural and hindering the birth process. The practice of episiotomy (surgical widening of the birth canal during delivery) was unheard of and abhorred, and for some, not being able to receive the baby's placenta after birth was culturally shocking. Many Hmong women wait until the last minute to enter the hospital to have their babies because they do not want to be bothered by all of these medical interventions in what is supposed to be a normal human process.[7]

Death rituals came under attack as well. Death in every culture is handled by its own set of cultural rules. Traditionally, Hmong families kept the deceased in their house, where they washed and handled the body, and held a wake around the deceased until all the appropriate relatives arrived. Special burial rituals were necessary to show the deceased the way to the afterworld. These rituals were accompanied by a large drum and the playing of a reed instrument called a *qeej* (pronounced "keng"). An appropriate number of cows were killed in order to feed the funeral guests and to symbolize the status and importance of the deceased person. Burial customs utilized geomancy, a practice in which one is buried at a particular and auspicious location according to landscape and other factors. A proper burial place ensured good fortune to the relatives of the deceased. Death in the United States, however, is controlled by state regulations and funeral home rules, specifying who can handle a corpse, where a person can legally be buried, and what the visiting hours will be. Many of the traditional Hmong customs had to be relinquished to the funeral home, which brought about a crisis in their ritual obligations to the dead.

A great deal of psychological stress was placed on families as they made adjustments to their new social, cultural, and economic lives. The toll on family relationships and gender roles was greater in some families than others. The husband was traditionally considered the head of the household, yet he was now unable to continue his traditional roles and work in America. With only a welfare check to support their families, men felt a loss of self-worth. Men regarded low-income jobs as demeaning and lowering their status. Women's traditional duties of child care, housework, and gardening were continued despite immigration, and because many low-income jobs, such as seasonal farm work, was traditionally regarded as women's work, women did not hesitate to take these jobs. For women, then, the daily round of work had more continuity than it did for men. The elders, however, became dependent on their sons and daughters for everything; some were even afraid to leave the house lest they get lost and unable to communicate their needs to the non-Hmong community. Parents felt frustration over their children as well. Peer pressure from school caused many youths to rebel against the old-fashioned ways of their parents. Parents no longer seemed to know their children because they did not understand the values their children were acquiring. Parents felt a loss of control over their children and yet were unable to discipline them under American law.

The education of their children was valued, yet families could see that their own Hmong culture was being lost as their children learned more and more about American culture and language. Children were becoming less adept at speaking Hmong and, in many families, they were unable to converse with their grandparents. For the youth, watching television and becoming involved in school events took precedence over traditional Hmong arts like needlework, storytelling, and singing. The workweek also became an overarching structure in people's lives. Few people had time to carry on traditional activities other than the elderly and the unemployed. These activities no longer made sense to many young adults in an urban environment.

As more children learn American ways their belief in the Hmong spirit world are challenged by scientific knowledge. Christian Hmong families also challenged non-Christian Hmong about the need for "pagan" rituals such as shamanism, ancestor worship, and animal sacrifice. Conversion to Christianity is perhaps one of the greatest dangers to traditional Hmong religious beliefs. Although the majority of Hmong throughout the world continue to practice animistic beliefs and ancestor worship, about one-half of the Hmong living in the United States have converted to Christianity and have discontinued these practices. They actively proselytize their religion. This has created much tension and animosity between Christian Hmong and non-Christian Hmong over religious beliefs and practices. However, Christian Hmong, like non-Christian Hmong, still emphasize kinship connections in church membership, and kin ties remain strong within the church.

Hmong migration to communities like Wausau also affected every aspect of the city's infrastructure and social environment. Schools, hospitals, and law enforcement agencies all had to make adjustments and increase their facilities to handle a new group whose culture and beliefs differed radically from local norms. Public schools in Wausau were not initially set up to handle bilingual learning or the influx of so many young Hmong children within the school system. High welfare use, unemployment, increases in local taxes for schools, and cross-cultural misunderstanding fueled prejudice and anger among the non-Hmong population regarding their new Hmong neighbors in Wausau.

RESPONSE: STRUGGLES TO SURVIVE CULTURALLY

All humans have the capacity to be resilient and creative in solving problems despite disruption and change to their lives. The image of the Hmong as helpless or entrapped in a cycle of poverty denies agency and creativity to them. It also blinds us from seeing the Hmong as active participants in their own process of building new economic and social lives in America. The use of traditional cultural strategies, coupled with the use of modern technology, has created a vibrant Hmong culture in America.

Kinship Connections

Hmong families began rebuilding their communities almost immediately after they arrived in the United States by activating their kinship connections. Unaware of the operational importance of kinship and clan affiliation, initial resettlement policy had dispersed Hmong families throughout the United States. Hmong families, however, began secondary migrations to areas in the United States where they could reunite with lineage and clan members. Leaders at all levels of the kinship system worked to provide economic and social aid to their relatives and to ease many problems of adjustment and adaptation to a foreign culture. Hmong Mutual Aid Associations were set up all across the country to help families find housing, employment, and job training and to facilitate their adaptation to their new communities.

Use of Technology

The Hmong quickly adopted all aspects of communication technology to sustain and facilitate their social networks and to maintain their cultural traditions and practices. Telephones, tape recorders, VCRs, camcorders, and computers have provided relatives with avenues for dispersing advice and information to family members as near as next door or as far away as Thailand. Cassette tapes became important for disseminating family and local news and for preserving traditional songs, stories, and herbal remedies. The camcorder was quickly perceived as one way to preserve a cultural heritage that was rapidly disappearing with their children's generation. Families started documenting family gatherings, weddings, funerals, shamanic rituals and church events, new year celebrations, Hmong soccer matches, school events, and Hmong beauty pageants. Tapes and

Hmong women and a day of picture-taking in the park. Photo: Jo Ann Koltyk.

videos circulated widely throughout the Hmong diaspora communities in America and abroad. Videos became such a popular form of ethnic entertainment that Hmong entrepreneurs began making and marketing videos commercially.[8] Videos made by Hmong returning to the homeland as tourists document Hmong village life and customs. The videos are then sold through the kinship channels to Hmong communities all over the United States. Hmong videos serve as entertainment and also create a heightened sense of group identity and ethnic solidarity with Hmong all around the world regardless of locality. The videos also become a vehicle through which Hmong can compare their past and present lives and identities and give expression to what it means to be Hmong in America.

The computer is also becoming a household item in more Hmong homes as the younger generation move into high school and college. As of 1998, there were more than 4,000 Hmong websites on the Internet, including personal web pages, chat rooms, and information links about Hmong culture, history, and traditions.[9]

The automobile is central to Hmong collective identity, continuity, and belonging in America. Hmong people travel frequently throughout Wisconsin and the Midwest to visit relatives, attend celebrations, and to fulfill ritual and social clan obligations. Wausau's central location within the state allows for easy access to all the other cities in Wisconsin with Hmong populations. Chicago, Illinois, and Saint Paul, Minnesota, two cities with large Hmong populations, are a four-hour drive from Wausau. Hmong people do not hesitate to use airlines to travel nationally to visit relatives in California or elsewhere or to attend Hmong new year celebrations, Hmong national conferences, or church events. Nationally known Hmong healers have also been flown into communities like Wausau to treat illnesses.

Continuation of Traditional Subsistence Activities and Entrepreneurship

Traditional subsistence activities have also contributed to the maintenance of Hmong culture and identity in America. Almost as soon as the Hmong arrived in Wausau, they obtained garden plots either through city gardening programs or from local farmers. Families felt that the garden was one way to cut expenses and supplement their public assistance payments. Women requested seeds from relatives in the homeland and started growing an abundance of foods familiar to their taste. Some families grew enough food to sell at the local farmer's market. The majority of families, however, planted gardens for their own consumption. Hmong women were also involved with seasonal agricultural work such as ginseng and cash cropping of cucumbers and saw this work as natural extensions of their gardening skills while earning extra cash to supplement their family income. Families also gathered wild foods like watercress, fiddlesticks, various edible flowers, nuts, berries, and fruits. Traditional medicinal herbs and plants were grown in pots or in flowerbeds outside their apartments. Men were active in hunting and fishing, taking advantage of deer, squirrel, and game birds as well as fishing in the Wisconsin River. A few families, seeing the demand for live animals for religious rituals, started raising chickens and selling them to the Hmong community.

Preservation of foodstuffs by freezing, drying, and pickling are common economical practices in most Hmong households for stretching limited incomes and for feeding large families cheaply. When Hmong families do buy food they prefer to buy in bulk or wholesale. A whole pig or cow, for instance, is purchased more cheaply than prepared cuts in the grocery store and can be easily divided among relatives.

Practicing traditional subsistence strategies in the United States serves a number of important functions for the Hmong. It is not only economical and practical, but it creates a semblance of the homeland, eases loneliness and homesickness for many elderly and unemployed Hmong involved in these practices, preserves traditional culture, and promotes a sense of well-being and economic self-sufficiency.

Hmong who are not very proficient in English have been able to participate in income-producing activities or provide services to the "traditional" needs of the ethnic community. Women sell and barter a variety of goods including traditional needlework items, embroidery thread, cloth, herbs and medicines, jewelry, and clothing. Many of the goods are either made by the women themselves or obtained from relatives in the home country. Women rely on kinship connections to obtain goods as well as to market them. Individuals also make a livelihood from such services as herbalism, massage, fortune telling, and shamanism. Some Hmong women with good English language skills have become involved in selling established products such as Amway and Mary Kay. Several Hmong college students bought shirts on discount, decorated them with Hmong embroidered designs, and marketed the shirts as ethnic clothing to their relatives all across the Midwest. Another woman made a photographic calendar of herself wearing various traditional Hmong clothing and Western clothing in order to raise money for her tuition at medical school. There seems to be no limit to the type of small-scale entrepreneurial activities taking place in the community.

Frugality is the rule in many Hmong households, and saving is extremely important as an adaptive strategy for families on fixed incomes. Hmong families save money to buy cars, houses, and pay for college education for their children. In fact, education is regarded by the Hmong as the only way to succeed economically in the United States. Currently over 50 percent of Hmong students continue their education beyond high school, either going to college or technical schools. This trend is not just in Wausau but is reflected nationally as well. In fact, approximately 103 Hmong throughout the United States have completed terminal degrees since 1997 in fields ranging from medicine, law, pharmacy, dentistry, education, business, science, theology, and others. In Wausau, graduates have returned to the community as teachers, nurses, social workers, counselors, police officers, and computer specialists.[10]

Building a Community

The Hmong community in Wausau is prospering. Since welfare reform in 1996, the majority of Hmong are now off welfare and working. Only about 6 percent of the Hmong population in Wisconsin are still dependent upon public assistance. It is too soon to tell the effect of welfare reform on Hmong families, but most feel confident and hold the attitude that they are a people with a history of being able to take care of themselves.

Home ownership is also on the increase. Of the 650 Hmong families living in Wausau, about 250 families now own their own homes.[11] Some families own several homes and rent them out to their relatives. There are four Hmong food stores, a restaurant, and several Hmong-owned businesses in the area including a shoe factory, computer consulting business, and home contractors. The community also has a quarterly Hmong newspaper and a weekly radio broadcast in the Hmong language. Hmong language and culture classes have been initiated to encourage the reading and speaking of Hmong. The Hmong community is also active in sponsoring social and cultural events, the most popular being that of the Hmong new year celebration. This is a time when the community comes together to celebrate their cultural heritage and identity as Hmong. The Hmong church (which is modeled after other American churches) has become very active in the area and has grown so large that they are now planning to build a second church to handle all the new members. Membership in the church may be one way in which Hmong ethnicity and identity are maintained in the future. Various informational and support groups have formed within the Hmong community to provide families with counseling, education on legal issues of marriage, child disciplining, women's rights, and others. Community-sponsored soccer teams travel throughout the Midwest to play other Hmong teams. The Hmong are also beginning to take an active part in the non-Hmong community by becoming involved in local government. Hmong individuals now serve as elected officials on city council and school boards in Saint Paul, Minnesota, and in LaCrosse, Wausau, Eau Claire, and Appleton, Wisconsin.

FOOD FOR THOUGHT

Large extended families that rely on kinship connections and traditional strategies of adaptation may seem anachronistic in postindustrial America. For the Hmong, however, these are an asset in today's America, especially when families pool their resources and share. Hmong use of new technology to facilitate adaptation, disseminate information and resources, and maintain traditions and customs provide us with a clear example of how adopting technological change can help maintain tradition and identity.

Questions

1. Is change always a travesty to traditional ways or can it be an opportunity to reformulate what is important to the Hmong as a people?
2. As much of traditional Hmong culture is dependent on the language for enacting many of its rituals, can they retain their cultural traditions without the fluency of the traditional language?
3. Many Hmong are abandoning their ancient beliefs and rituals and turning to Christianity. The Hmong Christian church offers community and group identity to its members. What are the essential elements for one's cultural identity? Can new symbols be just as effective for group cohesion and identity?
4. Kinship still figures prominently in the lives of the Hmong in America. As Hmong youth move through the American educational system, however, they learn to place value on individual autonomy and freedom rather than on the extended family and clan. Jobs and friends may become more important than relatives. What are the advantages and disadvantages of individualism or kin-

related groups? What effect might an emphasis on individualism have on a culture and kinship system such as the Hmong?

5. The homeland has always been important in the lives of many new immigrants socially, economically, and politically. With today's computer and information technology groups are drawn closer together electronically. How does technology transform a group's sense of place and identity both locally and nationally as well as transnationally? What impacts can new technology have on a group's politics, ethnic solidarity, and nation building?

NOTES

Funding for fieldwork conducted in Wausau from June 1991 to June 1992 was provided by a grant from the Wenner Gren Foundation for Anthropological Research.

1. Author's interviews, 1991–1992.

2. The pronunciation of the word "Hmong" rhymes with the word "song." The "H" is sounded by blowing air out of the nose. There are two major dialects of Hmong in the United States: White Hmong and Blue/Green Hmong. The White Hmong use the "H" sound in their dialect; the Blue Hmong pronounce their name as "Mong."

3. For early historical sources, see F.M. Savina, *Histoire de miao* (Hong Kong: Société des Missions Etrangères de Paris, 1930); William R. Geddes, *Migrants of the Mountains: The Cultural Ecology of the Blue Miao of Thailand* (Oxford: Clarendon Press, 1976); Jean Mottin, *The History of the Hmong* (Bangkok, Thailand: Odeon Store, 1980); Keith Quincy, *Hmong: History of a People* (Cheney: Eastern Washington University Press, 1988).

4. The exact population figure for the Hmong is difficult to estimate. China's 1990 census showed a figure of 7.4 million, but this figure most likely includes not only the Hmong but other cognate groups. Sucheng Chan, in the book *Hmong Means Free: Life in Laos and America* (Philadelphia: Temple University Press, 1994), notes that there may be between 2.8 and 5 million Hmong in China. There has never been an accurate count of the Hmong in Southeast Asia. For further discussion of this issue see Louisa Schein, "The Miao in Contemporary China: A Preliminary Overview," in *The Hmong in Transition*, ed. Glenn L. Hendricks, Bruce T. Downing, and Amos S. Deinard, (New York): Center for Migration Studies of New York, and the Southeast Asian Refugee Studies of the University of Minnesota, 1986, 73–85. The Hmong population figures given here are averages based on estimated counts made by Hmong Mutual Associations throughout the United States and tallied by Hmong National Development in Washington, D.C., and by the Office of Refugee Services in Madison, Wisconsin.

5. Statistics given here are from Tim Pfaff, *Hmong in America: Journey from a Secret War* (Eau Claire, Wisc.: Chippewa Valley Museum, 1995); Wausau Hmong-American News, Wausau Area Hmong Mutual Association Newsletter; and personal interviews with the Hmong Mutual Association staff during fieldwork in the 1990s.

6. For a discussion of the concept of soul loss, see Xoua Thao, "Hmong Per-

ception of Illness and Traditional Ways of Healing," in *The Hmong in Transition* ed. Glenn Hendricks, Bruce T. Downing, and Amos S. Deinard (New York: Center for Migration and Southeast Asian Studies, 1986), 365–78.

7. Author's fieldnotes, 1991–1992.

8. Most of the Hmong commercially made videos are self-produced and marketed by Hmong individuals with the help of their kinship networks, thus bypassing more formal and costly middleman distributors. Videos are distributed to local Hmong food stores for sale or rent, and they are sold at ethnic fairs and festivals and by peddlers in Hmong communities all over the United States.

9. In a speech given at the Hmong New Year's Celebration in Madison, Wisconsin, in December 1998, Fungchatou T. Lo, a Hmong professor at the University of Wisconsin-Oshkosh, addressed the audience about Hmong economic and educational successes in America over the last twenty years.

10. For a further discussion of Hmong educational success, see Ray Hutchinson, "The Educational Performance of Hmong Students in Wisconsin," *Wisconsin Policy Research Institute Report* (December 1997), vol. 10, no. 8. See also Jo Ann Koltyk, *New Pioneers in the Heartland: Hmong Life in Wisconsin* (Boston: Allyn and Bacon, 1998), 81–103, 133.

11. Statistics on Hmong home ownership in Wausau were provided by Peter K. Yang, "The Hmong: 20 years in Wausau," *Wausau Hmong-American News*, vol. 9, no. 1 (April 1996), 7.

RESOURCE GUIDE

Published Literature

Chan, Sucheng, ed. *Hmong Means Free: Life in Laos and America*. Philadelphia: Temple University Press, 1994.

Hendricks, Glenn, Bruce T. Downing, and Amos S. Deinard, eds. *The Hmong in Transition*. New York: Center for Migration Studies of New York, and Southeast Asian Refugee Studies at the University of Minnesota, 1986.

Koltyk, Jo Ann. *New Pioneers in the Heartland: Hmong Life in Wisconsin*. Boston: Allyn and Bacon, 1998.

Pfaff, Tim. *Hmong in America: Journey from a Secret War*. Eau Claire, Wisc.: Chippewa Valley Museum, 1995.

Smith, J. Christina. "The Hmong: An Annotated Bibliography, 1983–1987." Southeast Asian Refugee Studies Occasional Papers. Minneapolis: University of Minnesota, Refugee Studies Center, 1988.

———. "The Hmong: 1987–1995, a Selected and Annotated Bibliography." Southeast Asian Refugee Studies Occasional Papers. Minneapolis: University of Minnesota, Refugee Studies Center, 1996.

Films and Videos

Becoming American. Iris Film and Video, 1982. Documents a Hmong family's journey from a refugee camp in Thailand to Seattle, Washington.

Between Two Worlds: The Hmong Shaman in America. Taggart Siegel and Dwight Conquergood, 1985. Documents a Hmong shaman in Illinois.

Great Branches—New Roots: The Hmong Family. Rita LaDoux, Kathleen Laughlin, and Nancy Haley, 1983. Illustrates Hmong family structure in urban America.

Peace Has Not Been Made: A Case History of a Hmong Family's Encounter with a Hospital. John Finck and Doua Yang, 1983. Discusses concepts of illness and cross-cultural misunderstanding.

WWW Sites

The WWW Hmong Homepage includes Hmong history, culture, current news, education, research and bibliographies of sources about the Hmong.
http://www.hmongnet.org

This site offers resources about the Hmong for educators, especially K-12 teachers.
http://www.uwsuper.edu/library/hmong.html

Lao Family Community of Minnesota provides information about Hmong culture, the Hmong in Minnesota and the Midwest, and links to other important Hmong resources.
http://www.laofamily.org

Organization

The Wausau Area Hmong Mutual Association, Inc.
(Publisher of the Wausau Hmong American News)
1109 North 6th St.
Wausau, WI 54403–4732

Chapter 12

The Maya in Florida

Allan Burns

CULTURAL OVERVIEW

The People

This chapter is about Mayan people who left Guatemala and have come to Florida and other parts of the United States. This first section provides a brief background on the culture of the Maya of Guatemala so that the threats to their survival in the United States can be better understood.

The Maya of Guatemala make up almost half of the population of the 11 million people in that country,[1] and they speak Maya as their primary language. They are heirs to over three thousand years of Mayan culture, including such archaeological sites as Chichen Itza and Palenque, and a thriving contemporary population of people who still speak Maya and practice the cultural lifeways of this ancient civilization. Approximately 8 million Maya live in Mexico, Guatemala, Belize, and nearby countries as well as in the United States. Many Maya are bilingual, speaking Spanish as well as their own language. There are twenty-three recognized Mayan languages in Guatemala; among the more common ones are K'iche, Mopan, and Kakchikel. Often writers who describe Mayan languages and ethnic groups use traditional names as they were first written in Spanish. Indigenous educational groups in Mexico and Guatemala have changed many of these spellings to reflect the way the languages are indeed spoken; therefore, the same people might be referred to as "Quiche" or "K'iche," "Q'anjobal" or "Kanjobal." Mayan people in Guatemala are distinguished from non-Mayan people by their heritage, language, way of life, and self-identity. Although many Maya look like their ancestors whose pictures

213

appear on the ancient temples and pyramids of Mexico and Central America, to be a Maya is an identity based more on culture than on biological characteristics.

During the last thirty years, and especially during the 1980s and 1990s, a bloody civil war left the countryside of Guatemala in a state of shock and terror. Millions of rural Guatemalan people, Maya and non-Maya alike, fled small villages and towns for larger cities, the capital of Guatemala City, Mexico, and the United States. In 2000 there were an estimated 1.5 million Guatemalans in the United States, probably more than two-thirds of them were Maya.[2]

One of the more isolated and traditional groups of the highlands, the Q'anjobal (pronounced kan-o-BAL) Maya, were among the first to flee the violence that overran their homelands in the early 1980s. There were about 60,000 Q'anjobal Maya living in the highlands when the war began. As violence gripped the highlands, several hundred pioneers fled via Mexico to the United States. There they quickly established a community in exile in the state of Florida. Their culture became transformed as it became part of the immigrant world of South Florida in the 1980s and 1990s.

The Setting

The area of Guatemala most affected by civil war violence and out-migration has been the northwestern highlands which border on the southern Mexican state of Chiapas. The area is known for its beauty. Volcanic lakes, stark mountains, and settlements above the cloud line have made the highlands the subject of postcards and poetic descriptions. The region is divided into areas of high mountains and valleys, and often towns are very isolated. Because of this, each town has a somewhat distinctive local culture; differences in language, dress, custom, and kinship make the highlands a land of cultural distinctiveness. The highlands have traditionally been a place of the Maya. In the larger towns and villages, non-Mayan people, known in Guatemala as *ladinos* or *mestizos*, own stores, contract young Mayan men to work on large cotton or coffee plantations in other parts of the country, or represent the federal government through schools, police, and the military. But the rural population has always been dominant in the highlands. Four to five times as many people live in the rural areas of the *departamentos* (similar to states in the United States) as in urban areas. Many of the Maya who have come to the United States are from small villages and hamlets, many of which are a four- or five-hour walk from a town center. One of the town centers from which Mayan immigrants to Florida came is San Miguel Acatán, a town of a few thousand people. The capital of the Department of Huehuetenango, the city of Huehuetenango, has a population of 40,000 mostly Latino people; the department as a whole has a population of almost 700,000, mostly Maya.

The isolation of the highlands has led to a lack of communication between the highlands and the rest of Guatemala. A tendency toward self-sufficiency and a traditional lack of a strong central government presence in the area made the highlands an area socially and politically distinct from the modern social world of the center of Guatemala. The civil war in Guatemala lessened the isolation of the highlands. Government forces sought out guerrilla groups who were based in this remote area, and as a result, the isolation that had characterized the area became a thing of the past. Army bases, new roads, communication with people who had fled to Mexico or the United States all combined to dissipate much of the isolation of the highlands.

Traditional Subsistence Strategies

The northwestern highlands traditionally was an area devoted to small-scale agriculture and animal husbandry: slash-and-burn agriculture, known in Mexico and Central America as *milpa* agriculture, provided the Maya with corn, beans, squash, and other vegetables. Some coffee production in the lower elevations provided added income. Subsistence in the area was also based on sheep and goat herding. Cash income came from selling hand-woven jackets, ponchos, and skirts made from wool for local consumption, or selling woven cotton shirts, shawls, and other colorful clothing for local as well as tourist markets.

The Guatemalan refugees who came to the United States from Mayan communities were often from mountainous villages with few inhabitants. Many of the Maya said that they were from places like "San Miguel Acatán," but in fact they were from small settlements of one or two families in the vicinity of the town of San Miguel. They survived through corn agriculture on the steep slopes of the mountains, through raising sheep and goats, and through migrating to the rich southern plantations in Guatemala each year to work in cotton picking or the export vegetable industry.

Social and Political Organization

In the years before the civil war in Guatemala, political and religious offices in communities were often combined into one system called the "civil-religious hierarchy" by anthropologists. Within this traditional social and political system, families gain prestige as well as political office by sponsoring different saints' festivals (honoring various Catholic saints) throughout the year. Families would start by helping with a minor festival, and as a result one of the men of the family could be chosen to be a clerk or minor functionary in the town government and have the responsibility for cleaning the church. As a family sponsored more festivals, the political office and religious responsibility would also increase until a man reached the level of mayor or *alcalde* of a town. Finally, when a man had passed through many of the civil and religious offices of the community, he would become part of an elder group of advisors, known as the *principales* of a town.

The civil-religious hierarchy system became less coherent as Guatemala changed throughout the last half of the twentieth century. New political movements arose, and young people fought for the right to run for office unencumbered by duty to a religious system. By the 1980s and 1990s, the system was hardly functioning, but still it held some moral weight in towns and villages. While it was not necessary to pass through the lower ranks of religious and civil responsibility to attain higher offices, there was an expectation that successful officeholders would be involved in the different festivals that characterize communities throughout the year.

Religion and World View

Traditional Mayan religion in the highlands of Guatemala has been mixed with Catholicism for over 400 years. As a result, religious belief combined elements of both traditions in many aspects. For example, the agricultural system depended on rainfall, and so gods of rain were an important part of the Mayan pantheon. Because of the weight of conversion, the rain gods became known by a Christian saint's name, San Miguel (Saint Michael the Archangel). Traditional Mayan religion was focused on agriculture, especially the need to know when rain might fall for planting or harvesting, how to avoid animal plagues, and how to ensure healthy crops. A second area of Mayan religion had to do with reproduction: how to take care of pregnancies, deliver children, and ensure the health of women. A third area of Mayan religion in the highlands concerned the spirits of sacred places and sacred times. Religious specialists prayed and carried out rituals to ensure that wells functioned, roads remained passable, and communities were not destroyed by natural disasters. A fourth area of Mayan religion centered on interpersonal relations: individual and family health—both physical and mental—community accord, and conflict resolution.

These beliefs and associated practices have changed dramatically during the last several decades in Guatemala. Protestant and evangelical mission activities weakened the importance of indigenous specialists in *costumbre* (traditional ways), because the new religions brought in by North American missionaries regarded traditional practices as pagan. Likewise the Catholic Church worked energetically to move from spiritual (and often Mayan) concerns to social concerns during the 1960s and 1970s. One example of this was the push made by many Catholic missionaries, both priests and lay workers, to bring the "theology of liberation" to Guatemala. This movement focused on improving the material conditions of poverty throughout Latin America, especially Guatemala, as a religious goal. Many craft and agricultural cooperatives were formed among Mayan people based on this religious movement. During the worst violence of the early 1980s, these cooperatives and other organizations were particularly targeted by the repressive military government as examples of communism.

THREATS TO SURVIVAL

The Immigrant Maya in the United States

The civil strife that began in the 1980s in Guatemala and continued through the 1990s wreaked havoc on traditional Q'anjobal Mayan communities. Like the conquest some 500 years earlier, the effects of guerrilla warfare, government reprisals, the reorganization of Mayan communities under military control, and the return of refugees from Mexico all contributed to a radically disrupted life in Guatemala. The army admitted to burning over 300 villages. The violence and collapse of the peasant economy of Guatemala pushed millions of Maya out of their traditional homelands into nearby Mexico, to the United States and across the Western Hemisphere.

The diaspora is now transnational: Mayan refugees travel between the United States, Canada, Mexico, and even Guatemala as they create a new culture away from their traditional homes. The exact number of Guatemalans who began a diaspora of individuals, families, and communities to the United States is hard to calculate. An estimate of the number of Guatemalan Maya in Florida in 2000 is about 60,000. Major Guatemalan Mayan communities also exist in Los Angeles, Phoenix, Houston, New York City, and various cities in Florida. It is difficult to ascertain just how many Maya have come to the United States because the Mayan flight from the terror of Guatemala induced many to come here illegally. Also, travel to and from Guatemala was often accompanied by changes of name and stated country of origin (as will be discussed below).

Legal Status

One of the threats to the survival of Mayan culture in the United States comes from the institutional culture shock of immigration and political asylum. The United States has had such a strict political asylum policy that, despite the rampant killings in their homeland, only a handful have received any kind of legal status. Mayan peasants, without the skills and experience of immigration that characterizes Mexican farmworkers, often came to the United States with only the clothes on their back and a vague notion that here there would be safety. When they applied for political asylum, they found that they did not have even the basic political resources of birth certificates, documentation of torture or repression, or often even personal names that made sense to U.S. immigration officials.

217

Fluid Identities

Very rural Q'anjobal Maya use Mayan family names (patronyms) in their private lives, but use Spanish first names as their official names. A Q'anjobal Mayan woman escaping the horrors of the Guatemalan "hidden war" of the 1980s might be named Antonia Julia, be married to Pedro Francisco, and have a child named Andres Andres. Added to this cultural practice of using first names and not surnames, many of the Maya who escaped adopted false names as they moved through Mexico, using a name like Antonia Sanchez in order to blend more easily into Mexican society. When Antonia Sanchez came across the U.S. border in southern Arizona, she might even give another name, "Maria Perez," to the border official when she was asked for identification. Finally, perhaps she was stopped on her way to Florida on I-10 in Texas. Her fellow travelers in the van might warn her to give a false name so, if they are caught again, her name will not show up on the electronic database of "*la migra*," the U.S. Immigration and Naturalization Service (INS).

The adoption of false names (pseudonyms) on top of a cultural preference for using only first names in Spanish makes it difficult to discern the numbers of Maya who have entered the United States as refugees or economic migrants. It also is a subtle but important way by which Maya slip in and out of different identities in the diaspora. The result is a culture in the United States that is in jeopardy of disappearing through a process of acculturation into the underclass of farmworkers, construction workers, and service employees.

The facility of changing identities is illustrated by the following incident. It is a late Friday evening in the house of Pablo Francisco (not his real name) where some young men who have recently crossed the border between Mexico and California before coming to Florida sit around the table and talk. "Would you like to be a Mexican?" one asks me, laughing. "Perhaps," I reply. "Well, for sixty-dollars I'll give you this Mexican birth certificate I have," he says. "I used it to cross the border, but now that I'm here I really don't need it." We all laugh at the incongruity of me, a North American university professor and anthropologist, adopting the identity of a Mexican farmworker. My American sensibilities were shocked at the cavalier attitude of the young men around the table trading stories of changing official identities at the drop of a hat, but then I remembered that the importance of such documents as birth certificates, visas, and identity cards is something outside of the history of rural Maya from Guatemala who rely on their strong family ties, their personal identities as community members, and their roles as farmers, teachers, religious specialists, or shop owners. More important, the idea of putting one's name on a list reminds the Maya of the past. The "death lists" of the 1980s were tools of terror that led to disappearance, extrajudicial killing, and torture—a fate that befell tens of thousands of Guatemalan Maya and other Guatemalan citizens during that time. It is no wonder that these young men gave little importance to the official nature of names and identity.

Waves of Mayan Immigration to Florida

The Mayan immigrant community in Florida can be divided into two waves of transnationalism: the first wave of "pioneer" Mayan families who arrived through the 1980s and the second wave of "adventurers," mostly young single men, who make up the bulk of immigration between the late 1980s and through the 1990s.

First Wave

The 60,000 Mayan Indians from Guatemala who now call Florida home began arriving in 1982 to work as migrant farmworkers. The first town they came to was the agricultural community of Indiantown, a town named after an old Seminole camp on the eastern shore of Lake Okeechobee. While the Maya did not choose Indiantown for any symbolic connection to American Indian life, the name of the town seemed to them appropriate as a destination point. In spoken Spanish, it was *el pueblo de los Indios*. This was an ironic name to the new immigrants, as the term *indio* still carries a derogatory meaning in Guatemala. Indiantown thus was easy to remember and had a self-deprecating, humorous ring to it. The name of the town they now call home threatens their survival as Mayan people: the name of the town implies that they are now more North American Indians than Maya.

Indiantown is located inland in the rich citrus and winter vegetable zone of South Florida on the shores of Lake Okeechobee. The town experiences waves of other agricultural workers during the different booms of lemons, oranges, winter vegetables, cattle, and landscape sod. The town had a permanent population of 3,000 people in the early 1980s when the Guatemalans began to arrive, but the influx of farmworkers during the peak harvest seasons (October through March) doubles the population to over 6,000 inhabitants. Other farmworkers the Guatemalan Maya met were African-Americans, Puerto Ricans, Mexicans, and a few Haitians. Each group had found an economic niche in the different labor opportunities of Indiantown: African-Americans worked in the sod industry, Mexicans in the orange groves, Puerto Ricans in vegetables, and Haitians in service. The Guatemalan Maya were not easily integrated into any of these occupational niches. They quickly learned that they could not compete with skilled Mexicans in the citrus groves, but they could work quickly in the stoop labor of tomato and other vegetable picking.

The work they found was in the fields: men and women picked vegetables, citrus, and planted crops and endured low pay, constant fear of deportation, and exposure to pesticides and other farmwork–related illnesses. Women who were not working in the fields cooked food, watched children, took in laundry, and got other service jobs in the community. A few got jobs at the local Catholic service center or worked as aides in the elementary school. For the most part, though, the economic struggle to pay rent, feed families, and send a few dollars back to Guatemala meant that women and men both worked sixteen- to eighteen-hour days whenever they could. They learned to adapt to new economic opportunities. When work was scarce, they moved to cities and towns like West Palm Beach, Jupiter, and Lake Worth. They also migrated to Georgia and the Carolinas for work in the poultry industry. Those Maya who could not move up the migrant stream to other agricultural areas waited out the season, growing thinner as their incomes dwindled. By the end of the 1980s, the Maya began to find a specialty: golf course construction and tending greenhouses of large nurseries in South Florida.

But the Maya had been cut off from their land and their settlements, where they and their families had lived for generations, and from their own identity as a people. In Guatemala, being Maya was not unusual. The traditions of different towns, each with its own economic specialties, distinctive clothing, and oral literatures, gave Maya an identity that was not so much talked about as lived through interactions with other people, both Maya and non-Maya. The Maya who made up the first wave of immigrants to Indiantown were strangers to the other farmworkers who lived in Indiantown. Many spoke only Q'anjobal, and their command of Spanish was rudimentary. Children of other ethnic groups called them "watermelons" because the word "Guatemalan" sounded like the word "watermelon." Mayan families grouped together, living two or three to a household not just to save enough money to survive but also to hold together in a strange and often hostile community. "They should all be shot," said an elderly resident when asked his opinion of the new Maya immigrants. "They leave garbage all over the place," he said, "when they wash their clothes, they just leave them on the ground to dry. They don't even know enough to use a clothesline."[3] This kind of insensitivity to the plight of the Mayan immigrants led to a siege mentality among those who understood how inhospitable small towns can be to newcomers.

Second Wave

During the past ten years, a search for economic survival has brought a second wave of immigration from Guatemala. Guatemalan families now regularly send at least one son or daughter to the United States, hoping that the remittances they send back will allow them to endure the economic crisis that has characterized Guatemala for the past two decades. Here in the United States similar decisions are made: breadwinners in families, both women and men, look for work that has less risk of discovery and deportation. This is in sharp contrast to the traditional pattern of decision making in Guatemalan Mayan families. In Guatemala, Mayan families look for ways in which to build up cultural capital, prestige, and social wealth through participation in community service and civil offices.

Environmental Crises

People in cultures around the world face environmental degradation and the loss of land, resources, and the interconnection of plants, animals, and people that characterizes a healthy environmental world. The Maya have faced a double environmental crisis: the first was the crisis of the scorched-earth policy of the Guatemalan government in the 1980s. Villages and fields were burned and lands were appropriated, and the concentration of land in the hands of the upper elite increased. One young boy, twelve years old said, "We had corn, we had wheat, we had everything." Then the Guatemalan army burned the lands surrounding his village.[4] The policy at the time was to break the support of "Communist" guerrillas by making it impossible for them to live off the subsistence crops of the Mayan peasants. Crops were destroyed and the Mayan regions were put under military command, leaving little recourse other than migrating for wage labor to the southern cotton plantations of Guatemala or to the countries to the north: Mexico and the United States.

The second environmental crisis faced by the Maya was the conditions they found in the United States. The multicrop subsistence agriculture, which formed the basis of Maya life in Guatemala, was unknown in the United States. Instead, monocrop agriculture, based on a factory model, was the norm. Their traditional knowledge of the interconnections between legumes and other vegetables, the mixing of corn with squash and other crops, was unknown in the factory farms of South Florida. Thousands of acres were given over to winter vegetables, other thousands of acres to different kinds of citrus, and still other thousands to cattle production. The Mayan immigrants, used to working to ensure environmental sustainability through multicropping, had little recourse but to work in the Florida fields as wage workers. Their skills in horticulture and agronomy were lost in Florida. Golf course landscapers were the first to discover the special skills of the Maya. Soon the Maya of South Florida found work where their skills were needed and valued. The Maya of Indiantown and surrounding communities became among the most-sought-after golf course construction workers.

Young Guatemalan Mayan people learn about their past at the yearly festival of Saint Michael. Photo: Allan Burns.

RESPONSE: STRUGGLES TO SURVIVE CULTURALLY

Festivals

Responses of the first wave of immigrants to Florida in 1982 included attempts to reconstruct some of the anchors of their normal life. One of these was the annual festival of San Miguel, the patron saint of their town, which was celebrated within a year of the first Mayas' arrival. San Miguel is an important saint in Mayan life: he is generally associated with the Mayan deity in charge of rain, Chac, and so has tremendous importance to the agricultural cycle. The feast day of San Miguel is in late September, and organizing the festival of San Miguel became a rallying point for the first wave of immigrants to South Florida. Festival organizers had to negotiate with the local Catholic Church for the grounds to hold the festival, find refugees who knew how to play the marimba[5] (the traditional musical instrument of Mayan communities in Guatemala), and prepare for a celebration of different "queens" of the festival.

The festival was an important event in the survival of the Mayan community in exile. It gave indigenous leaders the opportunity to exercise their skills. Soccer matches were organized, schoolchildren were encouraged to learn dances from Guatemala as well as from other parts of Latin America, and scores of women participated by preparing booths that sold food, hand-woven Mayan fabrics, and artifacts from Guatemala. The festival was used by the first wave of Maya to mark their presence in the community. Other immigrant groups who worked in the citrus and vegetable fields of South Florida were invited to attend. One of the first festivals included dance demonstrations from Puerto Rico, Mexico, and Colombia, as well as a jitterbug demonstration by a local North American barber and his wife.

The election of different queens for the festival was another important element of survival for the immigrant Maya. Competition for queens of festivals has been an element of Guatemalan town festivals for the past decade, and the election of the queen of the workers, the queen of the soccer teams, and the queen of the festival was a way in which to call attention to the advances Mayan women were making in the United States. During the 1986 festival, the queen of the festival presented to the audience a heart-felt message:

Good evening ladies and gentlemen. We, the Q'anjobal people from San Miguel Acatán, Guatemala country, welcome you to this San Miguel Festival.

We appreciate that you are here in this special moment for us. As you know, we have arrived in the United States a long time ago. This is the third time that we celebrate this festival. We haven't done this before because of "special circum-stances"; but now we have help from a lot of people from San Miguel. They have been doing this festival. This is hard work for us. We really love to see each one of the people from San Miguel in this town.

We feel proud because of our heritage. But [it] is hard for each one of us to show who we are and where we come from. We feel that each of you think we don't have anything to do with Nature, but we do in this country.

We want to show each one of you who are not Spanish speakers that we love each other. We want to be friends with you here.

We want you to believe that we are in the United States. We want to show you our tradition, our custom. We love you here and we know that you love us here too. You are welcome in this San Miguel Festival. We hope that you enjoy it and we hope that you have a good time here.[6]

The "special circumstances" that the queen mentioned were those of the civil war in Guatemala. The festival was a chance for the first wave of Maya immigrants to proclaim their presence and to celebrate their own survival after the deaths of so many of their families and neighbors in the highlands.

The Catholic Church in Indiantown worked to give the Mayan immi-grants a future. A referral service that began as a farmworker assistance office began to focus on the Guatemalan Maya. A Mayan paralegal assis-tant was hired in 1983, and soon the center began helping with immigra-tion papers, political asylum applications, and emergency help.

Change from the Second Wave of Mayan Immigrants

Throughout the 1980s it seemed as if the war in Guatemala was interminable. Each month more massacres, more atrocities, and more emigration from the country occurred. But as the decade ended, there was a shift in the composition of Guatemalan Maya who came to Florida. The immigrant Maya who began to arrive in increasing numbers were younger, male, and without family ties. They were "adventurers," single men who migrated directly to the United States with only short stays in Mexico, sometimes working a few months in Cancún or Mexico City, but with the ultimate goal of working in the United States. They came from areas less affected by military brutality, and when they arrived in the United States, they were less attached to centers such as Indiantown. They dispersed throughout the state into cities and rural areas to find work. By the mid-1990s this second wave of immigrants had far outnumbered the first wave of "pioneer" Maya, and the effects on the social institutions of the Maya in exile were striking.

The festival of San Miguel, for example, was dramatically transformed. Instead of Guatemalan Mayan marimba music, the festival began to feature Mexican popular dance bands. The festival mirrored the acculturation that was happening to the young Mayan immigrants as they moved more toward a Mexican farmworker identity. These young men found that they could compete successfully with Mexican orange pickers, much more so than the older first-wave immigrants who had neither the skill nor the stamina to maintain the pace of citrus picking.

The second wave of Maya immigrants to Florida had little interest in community development or Mayan solidarity. Clubs that flourished among the first wave of immigrants began to lose followers and lost much of their previous strength in the community. While political asylum was still an important part of the Mayan experience in the United States, it was less important for these younger men who regarded it as only one of several strategies to use for staying and working in the United States.

Schisms began to develop in the Mayan communities of South Florida. Young men came to the meetings of the Mayan clubs, such as the Q'anjobal Association or Corn Maya, and showed how a clear organizational chart would make the organization more efficient. These organizational charts, drawn with careful lines designating authority and decision making, contrasted with the organizational structure of the fiestas mentioned earlier. There extended families and personal relationships between leaders and followers dictated how the festival was organized. The new immigrant young men had a more "objective" and businesslike way of organizing the refugee community. Anthropologists who have worked in refugee camps in Mexico talk about the importance some refugees place on the idea of "organization." For many refugees, especially those who had worked in cooperative movements, organization is a word of strong association with attempts to wrestle some of the power in Guatemala away from the government and the tiny oligarchy that controls land and resources in that country. Refugees who were drawn to the term "organization," had been trained in the idea of non–kinship based work groups. For them, the neutral lines of the organization chart seemed more modern and efficient than kinship and personal prestige.

As the second wave of Guatemalan Maya immigrants arrived in south Florida, another influence from the non-Mayan world was making itself felt. Protestant and Catholic churches both vied for the souls of the immigrants. Protestant missions set up English classes in trailer camps where new immigrants congregated. The Catholic Church, after refusing to sponsor the festival of San Miguel for several years, invited the community back to hold the festival on church grounds. New clubs sprang up and started holding festivals that were not related to the patron saint of San Miguel. Some of the Maya regarded the sponsorship as a transparent attempt to win profits from the congregation of Mayan people; others considered the new festivals as a sign of the strength of the Maya community.

Other Cultural Responses

The Maya in the Florida diaspora find their distinctive culture and identity unraveling. Their responses are sometimes conscious and planned and at other times simply created out of other strategies for living. These unplanned responses sometimes function to preserve and adapt the Mayan culture even though, if the Mayan people were asked about them, they probably would not connect what they do to the question of cultural survival.

Soccer

One good example of an activity that has a strong functional influence on the survival of the Mayan community is soccer. The soccer matches that have been organized over the years in the community help maintain cohesion in the face of influences that weaken community ties. Each weekend thousands of Maya and other immigrant groups in South Florida play soccer. Soccer maintains and even strengthens Mayan social organization in south Florida in many ways. Organizing the teams, raising the money to buy uniforms, and approaching local authorities to secure a playing field, as well as the logistics of hiring a referee, keeping track of the game, and planning for other games and tournaments are all ways that foster Mayan culture. Through soccer, skills in leadership and organization are maintained and further developed in South Florida. This activity is not thought of as "cultural" in the same way that the Fiesta of San Miguel is "cultural." No one thinks of the way in which the soccer ball is hit or the way in which teams develop strategy as something "Maya," even though close observation shows that indeed these games are closely tied with Maya identity.

When soccer clubs first started organizing soon after the arrival of the first Mayan pioneers to the area, teams were created based on the towns or neighborhoods where people settled. There were Indiantown teams, Stuart teams, and West Palm Beach teams. Within two years, however, the teams began to be organized according to the Guatemalan community of the majority of the players. There were teams of members who had come from Jacaltenango, from Totonicapan, and from small villages like San Miguel. Since players often spoke one of the twenty-six varieties of Maya that was unique to their area in Guatemala, organizing the teams this way made it possible for different Mayan languages to continue to be used in the Florida diaspora community.

The teams did another thing that helped with the threats to survival to Mayan culture in South Florida. Their very existence made the Mayan community more visible. Throughout Mayan migration to the United States many felt they were invisible as a distinct people. They were lumped together with other farmworkers in an undifferentiated mass of migrant workers who came and went through the citrus and vegetable fields of South Florida. The soccer clubs and subsequent tournaments gave them a visual presence among other immigrant groups. The unusual sounding names of their hometowns, the use of Maya when they were talking and shouting at each other on the playing field, and their shorter stature, as compared with Mexicans and other Hispanic groups, were all more notable when there were teams of Maya playing soccer. When individuals worked in the fields, they experienced a loss of identity and often were separated from one another. Even the clothing worn by field-workers blurred the lines of identity. Mayan women comment that they dress just like men do when the men do farmwork.

The soccer clubs also encouraged leadership. Playing fields even for weekend matches had to be reserved through county parks and recreation departments. Statements about insurance liability had to be signed, and cooperation between different teams had to be maintained. Lists of players had to be kept, transportation had to be organized, and during tournaments, trophies and other prizes had to be bought. All of these activities demanded skills in organization and leadership. Often local leaders who did this organizing announced the game as it was played on portable loudspeakers.

One Saturday afternoon, a group of students from the University of Florida and I were in South Florida and happened upon a match between a team of Guatemalan Mayan and Mexican migrant workers. The county park where the match was played was far from the neighborhoods where either group lived. Vans lined the outside streets around the park, and several vans were turned into makeshift food concessions. Corn on the cob, tacos, rice and beans, and fruit were all sold to onlookers and team members alike throughout the afternoon. When the announcer for the match saw us, he welcomed us over the loudspeaker, "Representatives from the University of Florida Anthropology Department are here this afternoon to enjoy the match." The announcer was Maya, and even though he spoke in Spanish so that the Mexican as well as the Guatemalan people could understand him, he used our presence to raise the prestige of this local event, pointing out those of us who had driven four hours to see it.

Immigrant soccer is not often recognized as a way in which people create strategies to survive in their new lives. Nevertheless, every Saturday and Sunday thousands of immigrants come together and play, all the while strengthening bonds that are in danger of disappearing. As a point of reference, in the 1990s the annual championship soccer match for immigrant teams in Miami regularly drew over 60,000 spectators. No Guatemalan Mayan teams have yet made it to this prestigious event, but it is an obvious example of the seriousness of sport among immigrants.

Clubs

Other activities of resistance and response to the immigrant Mayan life in South Florida include radio programs, community events, and clubs. Clubs were first organized in South Florida among Mayan immigrants for the express purpose of educating and preserving Mayan culture in the face of the strong forces toward acculturation found in the United States. Those forces are severe: the need quickly to learn English, the need to regularize immigration papers through INS programs of farmworker amnesty or through political asylum applications, and the need to work alongside non-Mayan people. These forces all hasten the abandonment of Mayan language, beliefs, social structure, and economic strategies. Guatemalan professionals who, in their homeland, were teachers, health workers, and small business people all became field-workers when they arrived in South Florida. English and Spanish were necessary in the workplace, as well as in schools and other institutions.

One of the first clubs to be established was the Corn Maya. Corn Maya was established in South Florida at the same time a similar club, Ixiim (the Maya word for corn), was organized in Los Angeles. The two clubs, both made up of Maya as well as anthropologists and other sympathetic non-Mayan people, were in contact with each other. The clubs, incorporated as nonprofit institutions, combined a number of activities: immigration referral and assistance through the voluntary efforts of immigration lawyers, the sponsorship of cultural events such as the festival of San Miguel, job referral, and emergency assistance. Disagreements over the management of Corn Maya soon led to the formation of several other organizations: the Kanjobal Association, Maya Quetzal, and later the Guatemalan Center, sponsored by the Catholic Church. These other clubs added to the general strength of the Mayan community because each gave opportunities for leadership and organization to members. Other organizations were created in response to particular events. When it appeared that Guatemalans were to be deported in 1997, several thousand Maya marched in Miami as well as in Washington, D.C., to express their opposition to the proposed deportations.

Family Tradition

Family tradition has served as a response to the threats to the continuation of Mayan culture in Florida in the form of birthday parties, baptisms, and other life events that occur in the private settings of homes. Here Mayan culture has been reinforced at a family level. These life events involve cooking enormous portions of traditional foods, hiring a marimba band, and staying up until the wee hours of the dawn, dancing, talking, sometimes drinking beer, and in general celebrating extended groups of family and friends. Marimba players formed clubs to practice and carry on the tradition of playing. Weddings and birthday parties were not considered complete without marimba music, and players received anywhere from a few dollars to a few hundred dollars for playing at these events. At one baptism party, the godfather of the baby girl gave a short speech near the end of the party. It was 3:00 A.M. and a few people were asleep on the sofa in the living room of the small house where the party was held. Some men were outside talking and three or four women stood in the kitchen doorway watching the few couples who were still dancing. When the music stopped the godfather of the baby girl spoke first in Maya, then in Spanish, and finally in English:

It is important that our goddaughter Carmen remember this night. Because I know that she is going to be a leader of her people. Her people have suffered much. She should remember her people, her language, and her customs. I just hope she is able to keep her customs and remain strong, not like other groups that have come here. Because the discrimination here is the worst I have ever seen. To overcome this she will have to have a strong family and culture. Her home in Guatemala is no longer a place for her.[7]

These life events give the Guatemalan Maya ways to express their feelings about preserving their language and values in South Florida. Even the act of finding a spouse and getting married serves as a means of cultural preservation. One young couple said that the reason they had gotten married was because both spoke the same dialect of Maya. This commonality served not only as a point of attraction between them, but also allowed them to share hopes of returning home to Guatemala one day with enough money to buy land. It also allowed them to speak quietly of the horrors of watching their parents being killed before their eyes when they were five years old.[8]

Responses Bring New Problems

Not all of the responses to the new life in South Florida have had such positive effects. Some responses have had the effect of splitting up the community, dividing it, and making communication and community a fragile part of the Mayan culture in exile. Earlier the division of different clubs was mentioned. While the proliferation of clubs has the effect of giving more people chances to fulfill leadership positions, the factions that led to the creation of competing clubs also divided the community into visible camps. Club membership began to be reorganized along extended kinship lines, and old divisions and conflicts that went back several generations in Guatemala were brought to the fore in the refugee world of South Florida. Factionalism caused many people to drop out of clubs. Clubs began to be symbols of difference rather than points of congregation.

Another set of activities lessened the chances for Mayan culture to survive in Indiantown and the surrounding areas. As more and more young men began to arrive in the second wave of immigration, many of the pioneer families moved out of the community to find better work and better housing. The Mayan community in the first several years of the arrival of Maya to South Florida was centered in Indiantown. Indiantown was the recognized new home of the Maya. But factions and new work opportunities led to a dispersal away from Indiantown. Indiantown became something akin to the Mayan ceremonial cities of prehistory. The Maya would come back to the town once or twice a year for events like the festival of San Miguel, but they began assimilating into farmworker communities throughout the United States. This dispersal was not done in terms of large groups of people moving together; instead, individuals or small families left to live in the hinterlands of Florida and other states where they quietly worked the fields and had little contact with other Mayan people.

Once in a while some of the "adventurous" Maya of the second wave of immigration stop in Gainesville. Recently a young Mayan couple arrived when their broken-down car gave out on the interstate. Isadora and her husband Miguel, in their early twenties, were on their way north to look for work. Isadora gave birth in an emergency room at a local hospital. Since they both spoke only Q'anjobal, a translator was called. When asked if they had been to Indiantown or knew other Mayan people, they replied they had never heard of this center of Mayan people in South Florida and were surprised when they were told how many Mayan people were living in Florida. Isadora and Miguel represent an extreme of the second wave of immigrants. An entrepreneurial couple, they work where they can, live from harvest to harvest, and keep to themselves.

FOOD FOR THOUGHT

The Maya of Florida have adapted to two dramatic misfortunes in their lives and culture. The civil war in Guatemala and the campaigns against Mayan villagers throughout the 1980s and 1990s were traumatic to the extent of practically destroying the outward expression of Mayan identity. Subsequent to the violence in the highlands of Guatemala, the government brought people together from scattered hamlets into villages that were called "poles of development." Like the conquest some 500 years earlier, this reduction (residential concentration) of the Mayan population and their forced resettlement weakened the foundation of Maya family and community life.

The second adversity in the lives of the Maya people was their migration to the United States, and the reduction of their many skills and experiences to the work of farm laborers moving up and down different migrant streams.

Mayan women in the United States often travel with their husbands or partners in search of work in the migrant streams. This mobility and the women's need to do farm labor means that they have less time to devote to their families and communities. Cultural practices, including home medical cures, spiritual knowledge, and histories of the Maya people are being lost.

The split between the first and second wave of immigrants is another force that threatens the Maya of Florida. New immigrants, younger and without the first-hand experience of the violence of the last two decades, now speak with pride about Mayan culture. Mayan culture for many of these immigrants is based on folklore and popular mythology. Mayan culture is, for many of these young people, the ancient Mayan ruins, the old Mayan calendar, and the essential Mayan personality they see in folklore performances and read about in popular and tourist literature. The more profound features of being Maya, the deep meanings of the language, the knowledge of the environment, and the delicate organization of village life are of little value in the United States.

The extreme physical stress of farmwork and the uncertainty of farmwork wages, as well as the minority status afforded to Guatemalan Maya in farmwork communities, lead many young Maya to abandon their language and the few family traditions that remain in their lives. Instead they look to fit in with the working-class culture of other farmworkers and are becoming acculturated to a U.S. Latino lifestyle or a generalized American lifestyle when they learn colloquial English.

Questions

1. How can a people survive under conditions such as the Mayas have experienced?
2. How can Mayan culture regain a place of importance in peoples' lives in the

context of farmwork with the mobility, poverty, and uncertainty experienced by farmworker?

3. Will Mayan culture in the United States be reduced to a few folklore performances and some trivial symbols?

4. Will the Mayas' acculturation help them in the long run as young people seek to fit in to the culture of their mainstream friends? Will the Maya of Florida remain a culturally viable community, or will they blend in and quickly lose the memories of these past two decades of civil war and migration?

5. How can Mayan women regain their important cultural role in their communities under conditions of farm labor and farm labor mobility?

NOTES

1. Guatemalan *Instituto Nacional Estadistica* figures.

2. The number of Guatemalans in the United States is difficult to estimate. Many Central Americans are in the country without legal papers. The number cited here is taken from the Guatemalan newspaper *Prensa Libre*, October 1, 2000.

3. Author's field interviews, 1987.

4. Author's field interviews, 1985.

5. The marimba is a wooden xylophone that is central to Mayan ceremonies in Guatemala and in the United States.

6. Allan F. Burns, *Maya in Exile: Guatemalans in Florida* (Philadelphia: Temple University Press 1993), 59–60. This speech was given in English. The speaker was one of the first Mayan women to learn English and to go to college.

7. Burns, *Maya in Exile*, 51.

8. Author's field interviews, 1989.

RESOURCE GUIDE

Published Literature

Burns, Allan F. *Maya in Exile: Guatemalans in Florida*. Philadelphia: Temple University Press, 1993.

Fischer, Edward, and R. McKenna Brown. *Maya Cultural Activism in Guatemala*. Austin: University of Texas Press, 1996.

Manz, Beatrice. *Refugees of a Hidden War: The Aftermath of Counterinsurgency in Guatemala*. Albany: State University of New York Press, 1988.

Montejo, Victor. *The Bird Who Cleans the World and Other Mayan Fables*. Willimantic, Conn.: Curbstone Press, 1991.

Taylor, Clark. *Return of Guatemala's Refugees: Reweaving the Torn*. Philadelphia: Temple University Press, 1998.

Films and Videos

El Norte. Gregorio Nava and Anna Thomas, directors. Trimark Films, 1983.

Mayan Voices: American Lives. Olivia Carrescia. First Run/Icarus Films, 1994.

Popol Vuh. Patricia Amlin, director. Educational Media, University of California, Extensión Media, 1992.

Maya in Exile. Allan Burns and Alan Saperstein, producers. Gainesville, Florida, Ojo Video, 1985.

WWW Sites

Comprehensive Mayan site with thousands of links
http://mars.cropsoil.uga.edu/trop-ag/the-maya.htm

Contemporary Guatemala Mayan art and pictures
http://www.artemaya.com/index.html

MayaQuest
www.classroom.com/mayaquest

Santiago Atitlan, Guatemala—a Human Rights Victory by Stephen Blythe (photoessay)
http://www.travelhealth.com/hmnrts.htm

Organization

Guatemalan Maya Center
110 North F Street
Lake Worth, FL 33460

Chapter 13

The Sicilian Fishing Families of Gloucester, Massachusetts

Christopher Dyer

CULTURAL OVERVIEW

The People

Gloucester, Massachusetts, is one of the historical cores of the American fishing industry. Located northeast of Boston on Cape Ann, a rocky peninsula jutting out into the Atlantic Ocean, Gloucester is famous for its ground fishing.

Many of the residents of Gloucester are descendants from people who settled in Nova Scotia and came to Cape Ann in the nineteenth century. The traditional fishing peoples have included Canadian, Scottish, Yankee, and Portuguese, but today most Gloucester fishermen are of Italian descent and their families make up almost 40 percent of the 27,000 residents of Gloucester.[1] Many have come from fishing ports in Sicily—a part of Italy with a distinctive dialect, tradition, and identity. Today, Sicilian fishermen represent the dominant fishing culture and population of Gloucester. Their culture and history shape the recent past of the historical port of Gloucester, and it is their struggle to survive as a cultural community that is documented here.

The Sicilians came to Gloucester in two waves. The first, in the 1920s, consisted of 343 Italian fishermen, most of whom came without their families. When the fishing grounds played out in the Mediterranean, with many fishermen competing for smaller catches, some young men left Sicily seeking opportunity in the vibrant groundfish fishery—cod, haddock, and halibut, as well as redfish, herring, and mackerel—of New England. As they worked

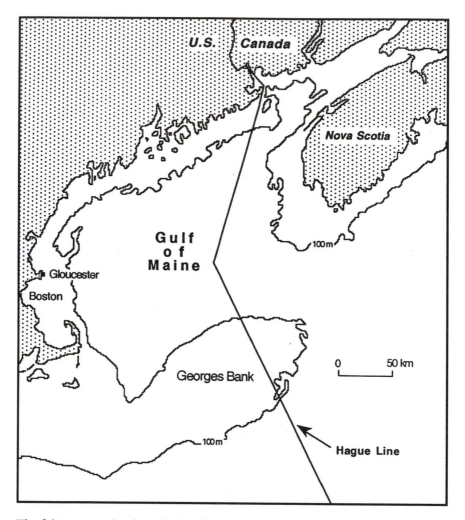

The fishing grounds of the Sicilian fleet of Gloucester. Note the Hague Line, which cut off the fleet from the most productive area of the Georges Bank. Map: Dr. Gerald Krausse.

their way into the labor force, close family and friends followed to establish a Sicilian community within Gloucester.

Migration was based on social networks and kinship. Once a family was established with one or two individuals, others would be urged to join them. After World War II, a second wave of Sicilian immigrants arrived, mainly from Terrasini, Sicily. Day laborers, fishermen, carpenters, bricklayers, and mechanics swelled the ranks of the fishery at a time when the fishing economy was growing.

The traditional fishing family structure consisted of extended kinship networks of fathers, brothers, and cousins who worked together on draggers. Men were responsible for fishing and earning money, and women took care of the household, onshore finances, and child care. The greatest burden of fishing families came from dealing with the uncertainty of a lifestyle wrought from the sea. Wives and families of fishermen depended on the vagaries of the fish catch. Fishing "brokers" (a trip with no fish) were not uncommon. When times were tight, fishing households relied on their extended families and networks to see them through until the fishing improved.

The fishing lifestyle took fishermen away from friends and family. Little time was spent with children between fishing trips, and the wives thus served as both mother and father. Fishermen were, in effect, married to their boats. Fishing trips lasted between seven and ten days, and between trips the fishermen spent much of their three-day shore time repairing and preparing the boat for the next trip. While wives were managing the home and waiting for their husbands' return, they often worried about the dangers of fishing at sea. The waters off New England are treacherous, particularly near Georges and the Grand Banks, where storms can come up suddenly and swamp a boat. These storms can be fatal to fishermen, and waiting for the return of those at sea is an anxious time for fishing households.

The Setting

Dedication to the craft of fishing is reflected in the famous fisherman's statue that looks out to sea to bring the seamen and their boats home safely. The historical plaque hanging in city hall lists the names of the many thousands of Gloucestermen who have lost their lives at sea. The picturesque seawall and the fisherman's statue along the southern end of the harbor contrasts with the middle and northern harbor mélange of wharves, restaurants, seafood processing plants, diesel fuel stations, fishing boats, the famous Cape Ann Ice Company, and numerous clusters of working trucks and semis servicing the fishing industry. At the mouth of the harbor, a seawall capped with a lighthouse provides protection from the fierce winter storms that barrel out of the Gulf of Maine. Dockside streets are packed with restaurants, bars, and small businesses, and the surrounding steep hills are festooned with hundreds of historical homes replete with widow's walks and seaward bay windows.

The Dorchester Company first settled Cape Ann and established the Massachusetts Bay Colony in 1623. Prior to that time, vessels came to Cape Ann to fish in the summer months and returned to England with their salted cod before winter. Early settlers on Cape Ann found that the poor soil made farming difficult, and fishing became the dominant way of life. Fishing for export to Europe and the Caribbean soon became a lucrative business which lasted for centuries.

Traditional Subsistence Strategies

Today, gill nets, longlines, and dragging gear are used to fish for cod, flounder, and other groundfish. Gill nets are squared nets that are suspended in the water to catch fish as they try to swim through them and are caught by their gills in the net mesh. Longlines are series of baited hooks set out offshore by fishing boats. The lines have thousands of hooks, which, after being set for six or eight hours, are pulled in with the caught fish removed by hand from the hooks. Dragging gear are purse-shaped nets that are pulled just above the bottom behind a boat. When the net is full of fish, a winch pulls it up, and the fish are dumped on deck and then sorted and stored in the hold of the boat. Inshore lobstering using lobster pots (traps) is of lesser importance, but the lobsters caught in drag nets are a secondary product that has increased among the dragging fleet.

The Crew

A typical eight-man Sicilian groundfishing boat includes a captain, first mate, cook, engineer, and crew. The captain is in charge of the fishing operations at sea and onshore. His word is law at sea, and he is ultimately responsible for everything that happens on the vessel—both good and bad. A "good" captain is one who can navigate and choose the best fishing grounds and catch a good haul of fish, but has the sense to quit fishing when severe weather threatens or the catch is sufficient and the market is most favorable. The recent film *The Perfect Storm* depicts a not uncommon Gloucester tragedy when the necessity to land a prize haul of fish collides with severe weather.

The first mate is in charge of making sure the vessel's fishing gear is maintained and in good condition. He has the authority to order new fishing gear, ranging from spare net parts to mending twine for net repair and new doors (devices used to keep the mouth of the net open on a fishing tow).

The cook works on deck but also is in charge of the fo'c'sle—the covered area on deck where the crew take their meals. The cook must stock the shelves of the fo'c'sle with food when in port, track the food budget, and prepare meals whatever the seas and the weather. In the early 1970s, most Gloucester boat cooks shopped for wares at small markets, such as the Friend Street Market or Railroad Avenue Market. Later, supermarkets took over most of the business. In good times vessels received credit for food, with the promise that they would pay back what was owed when the catch was sold.

The engineer, like the mate and cook, also works on deck helping "haul in" when a net is landed with fish. His main job is to care for all mechanical equipment including the main engine below deck and the machinery on the deck, making on-the-spot repairs when something breaks down at sea. A stalled engine is dangerous in rough seas, and many vessels have swamped and sunk in stormy weather after the engine stalled. When in dock, the engineer must change the main engine's oil, averaging about 110 gallons every 1,000 hours of travel time, and replace fuel and oil filters.

The remaining crew, the deckhands, are primarily responsible for setting out and hauling in the net and dressing and storing the catch. All crew take turns at watch—usually two or three hours. A key to a successful crew is the ability to get along and work well together. A good crew is expected to be loyal to their boat, but vessel switching is not uncommon when disputes or conflicts arise. Crew might also seek to work their way from one vessel to another as a means of landing a spot on a "highliner" vessel. A highliner has a captain who is consistently successful at filling the hold with fish, thus ensuring good profits for the crew. Once a trip is over and the catch landed in Gloucester, the profits are usually divided up using the "Italian Lay" system. Under this system, the trip's expenses for fuel, ice, and gear are taken off the top, 60 percent goes to the crew, who have to pay for food separately, and the remaining 40 percent goes to the boat and captain. Often the captain also gets 10 percent of the crew's split.

Social and Political Organization

The Sicilian community came to dominate the groundfish fishery of Gloucester. Groundfishing is a year-round activity, although fishing families trap lobster and set gill nets as part of a flexible mixed-fishing cycle. At the turn of the century, fishing was dominated by large fishing schooners that captured many tons of cod and other groundfish. These large-scale operators went out of business in the late 1920s with the influx of fish caught by boats from foreign countries. (This is a pattern that is now recurring, threatening the Sicilians who replaced the schooner-style fishing of the early part of the century.) Individual family-owned family-operated mid-sized vessels (45–75 feet in length) then dominated the fishery, and were at the center of Gloucester's fishing economy and society for decades.

The traditional fishing fleet of Sicilian Gloucester is composed of draggers, using stern or, rarely, side trawling techniques. Most of the fleet bring their fish to Gloucester, although larger vessels may land squid and other species in Portland, Maine, or various landing points in Rhode Island. Gloucester's groundfishing fleet can be divided into three principal groups. First are vessels over seventy feet in length that fish from seven to ten days at a time. These vessels fish from the Gulf of Maine southward in deeper waters primarily with bottom trawls and occasionally offshore gill nets. Recent economic hardships have reduced the traditional crews from ten to twelve to just four or five individuals, with some as low as two, in an attempt to make income exceed operating costs.

Second are the mid-sized fishing vessels ranging from fifty to sixty-nine feet with a crew of two or three. Most vessels work with at least two crew—still down from better days when three to five relatives and working partners fished with dragging gear from three to five days at a time in near-shore waters.

The most viable of the fleet are fishing vessels of a third size: forty-nine feet and less. These vessels, considered day boats, fish with gill nets, long-lines, or otter trawls. Small vessels struggle with depleted near-shore fish stocks, the crowding of waters by larger vessels moving inshore, and re-strictions on fishing areas resulting from marine mammal and groundfish spawning area closures. Yet, economically, they still have the best chance for profits. As of 1996, there were 236 of these vessels in port, with crews of one or two individuals each.[2]

The commercial fishing fleet can be divided not only by boat size, but also by the four major types of gear they use: mobile gear (draggers) and three categories of fixed gear (gill nets, longlines, and lobster pots). Other types of commercial fishing include jigging, harpooning, diving for sea urchins, and various types of trapping. Some supplement their income as recreational and sports fishing charters and seasonal whale-watching tours. However, groundfishing with mobile gear remains the predominant fishing strategy in Gloucester.

For the town of Gloucester, commercial fishing is still a primary industry (Gloucester was ranked second in 1995 in pounds landed on the eastern seaboard), but light industry and the service sector are gaining in importance, and foreign imports have taken the place of domestic landings for some local processors.[3] The community's largest fishery employer, Gorton's of Gloucester, processes and markets *only* imported fish; it has not purchased a pound of locally caught fish in thirty years. Foreign boats provide a more reliable supply of fish. The labor and harvesting costs are lower on foreign-flagged boats, and they operate under fewer restrictions. Most processors now rely on foreign suppliers to keep their businesses going, and their long-term interests are not as linked to the fate of the Gloucester-based fishing fleet as in the past.

Besides experiencing a reduction in its fishing fleet and supporting businesses over the past twenty years, the contemporary fishing industry of Gloucester has gone through many other changes caused by technological innovation, competition, and a recent scarcity of certain fishing stocks, along with increasing competition among a diversity of stakeholders. Reductions in allowable fishing days at sea, the closure of large areas, the loss of the Grand Banks in the Hague Line decision,[4] and a decline in fish stocks have reduced the viability of the groundfishing fleet. Nevertheless, local fishing and related businesses still employ an estimated 40 percent of Gloucester's population.

In 1996 there were 322 permitted vessels for groundfish in Gloucester. These vessels employed 826 fishermen. The families of the 826 fishermen included about 500 wives and 1,000 children. The average family size in the fishing industry is five.[5] This means that the total directly involved in fishing in 1996 was approximately 5,630. Those in the businesses indirectly dependent on fishing include approximately 5,200 workers and business owners and operators and their families, for a total fishery-dependent population of approximately 10,830.[6] In a more general sense, the rest of the residents of the Gloucester community also benefit from the waterfront and traditional character of a community steeped in fishing history. Tourists and artists, for example, are attracted to Gloucester because it represents a working fishing port, not just another seashore community.

Religion and World View

Fishing life is expressed and celebrated in symbols and social rituals. Rituals are repetitive seasonal actions that reveal the most deeply felt values of families and households. Rituals of saint worship, of the blessing of the fleet, and seafood festivals are integrated with other secular and religious symbols that are a part of Gloucester's cultural landscape. Symbols and associated rituals can also reflect persisting social arrangements, including working crews, family networks, social clubs, fisher-processor credit relationships, and fishing associations.

Gloucester's historical dependence on fishing is also revealed in the symbolic art and architecture of the community, both religious and secular. Dedicating places and monuments to fishing shows a deep community dependence on that occupation. Examples include Our Lady of Good Voyage Church, the Gloucester fisherman statue, and the entrance mural of Saint Ann's Church. A recent event of significance is the dedication of the plans for the statue of the fisherman's wife to complement the world-famous Gloucester fisherman statue.

The most celebrated annual ritual is the Saint Peter's festival, and 2000 marked the 73rd year of its celebration. This festival, sponsored by the Italian-American fishing colony of Gloucester, takes place on the weekend closest to the Feast Day of Saint Peter, June 29. Sicilian immigrants brought the tradition to Gloucester, which pays homage to Saint Peter, the patron saint of fishermen, and asks him to protect fishermen against the storms and other dangers encountered at sea. The procession of Saint Peter is accompanied by an outdoor Catholic mass, the blessing of the fishing fleet, carnival rides and ethnic food, and special competitive events, including seine boat races and the famous greased pole competition, held from a platform erected in the harbor. In this event, fishermen try to capture a flag at the end of a greased pole. Slipping off the pole sends contestants plummeting twenty feet into the water below. The event, watched by thousands of residents and visitors, is said to symbolize the fisherman's victory over the sea. The contestants are chosen to represent important families in the Sicilian fishing heritage of Gloucester, and the winners are celebrated as local heroes.

The rich cultural celebrations of Gloucester cannot, however, hide the trauma and stress of a community in decline. The Sicilian heritage has been undermined by the loss of the fishery resources that they depend on for survival. This crisis of community began almost two decades ago with the creation of the exclusive economic zone (200-mile territorial limit) in U.S. waters under the 1976 Magnuson Fisheries and Conservation Act.

THREATS TO SURVIVAL

Federal Intervention and Its Effects

The 1976 Magnuson Fisheries and Conservation Act, reauthorized in 1996 as the Magnuson-Stevens Act, was instituted to protect the marine resources of the United States. It established a 200-mile Exclusive Economic Zone (EEZ) to regulate fisheries in U.S. waters. To take advantage of the EEZ and revitalize community-based fisheries, the National Marine Fisheries Service (NMFS) was authorized to provide low-interest loans to build up a domestic fishing fleet. As a result, the New England groundfish fishery fleet experienced rapid expansion. At the time, virtually no social scientists were advising the NMFS on policy, and no assessment was made of the potential impact of increasing the number of boats and fishing gear on U.S. fishing communities. The consequences for Sicilian fishermen and their way of life were disastrous.

This loan program was based on a policy perspective that considered only economic opportunity in the EEZ without potential long-term impacts to communities such as the Sicilians of Gloucester. In New England, investors quickly took advantage of the loan program, and the fishing capacity of domestic fleets increased dramatically. Immediate results included a rapid increase in local economic capital, bolstered by gains in catch profits from increased landings. Under the Fishing Vessel Obligation Guarantee Program, just about every major East Coast port, including Gloucester, Boston, and New Bedford, Massachusetts; Portland and Rockland, Maine; and Newport, and Point Judith, Rhode Island, dramatically built up their fleets, including the number of powerful stern trawlers.

Key respondents in fishing communities claim that many of those taking advantage of the fishing vessel loan program were newcomers to the fishery. Moreover, they also claim that from 1977 to 1980 many new vessel owners were outsiders whose primary occupations (e.g., doctors and lawyers) marked them as fishery "investors," not fishermen. As fishery "investors," they had no prior social, cultural, or human capital invested in the local fishing communities, and were thus not bound by the responsibilities and reciprocal exchanges of local capital that supported traditional fishing families, households, and their community. Nor were investors attentive to the social networks, such as the Gloucester Fishermen's Wives Association and the Offshore Mariners Association of New Bedford, Massachusetts. In short, those now putting new boats to sea cast themselves only as individual entrepreneurs and ignored the long-standing social system. Since that same traditional social system had managed the fisheries with a long-term outlook, keeping harvesting in balance with the supply of fish, it is not a surprise that the waters off Gloucester rapidly became overfished.

Declining Fish Stocks

The buildup of the groundfish fleet resulted in intense pressure on stocks, both inshore and offshore. As competition for groundfish resources increased, the breakdown and loss of capital (human, social, cultural, biophysical) accelerated both within and among fishing-dependent communities. Competition and acrimony increased between the fleets of different ports and the fleets of different gear types in the same ports.

With the increase in fleet capacity and the pressure to provide return on investment, overfishing of stocks followed. In 1995 through 1997, the NMFS determined that the primary groundfish stocks in Gloucester's management area, called the New England Fishery Management Council, were seriously depleted. Their response to the growing crisis was to cut drastically the number of allowable days at sea for the groundfishing vessels from 260 to 88. The NMFS also eliminated significant exceptions from current effort control regulations and broadened area closures to protect juvenile and spawning fish. In 1997 a National Science Council review of the New England groundfish stock assessment confirmed that there was a significant overfishing capacity, directly traceable to the government loan program. The program led to a rapid rise in the number and capacity of boats, exceeding what the fishery could sustain.[7]

The overall impact of the groundfish declines and subsequent regulations was catastrophic, particularly in the harvesting and processing sectors. In 1980 there were 3,500 finfish harvesters (members of boat crews) and 5,700 workers in the onland processing sector in Massachusetts. By 1992 finfish harvesters in Massachusetts had decreased to 1,500 and processing workers to 2,700, a 58 percent and 53 percent decline, respectively, in twelve years.[8] The hardship fell not only on the new boats and investors, but also on the traditional Gloucester fishermen. There were declines in attendance and participation in local fishermen organizations, and some out-migration occurred when some older fishermen returned to Sicily and Portugal "in disgrace."

Rising Stress

Another impact is seen in the evidence of rising stress. Stress on social ties was expressed through fierce gear conflicts among draggers, gill netters, and longliners of groundfish. Conflict also comes from the decrease in catch share payments made to crewmen on draggers. As fuel costs and other operating expenses have risen, and allowable days at sea have been cut, captain/owners are beginning to lower the pay of deck hands. Stress levels were exacerbated by declines in catch profits and the ensuing tightening of terms for new credit and loans from local banks.

Reduced Crew

Another sign of distress is the drop in number of crew employed on the vessels. Some larger vessels are now operating inshore with skeleton crews of just two or four (e.g., a father-son operation with one or two hired crew). They cannot afford to work with a larger crew, nor can they afford to fish offshore for any extended periods. Deckhands are earning less and less as the captains they work for are forced to put more and more of the catch share into covering the operating expenses of the boat. One source estimated that a deckhand's earnings of $300 for a recent trip, considering his days at sea are twenty-four-hour, full-time activities, amounted to forty cents an hour.[9] Deckhands are the most vulnerable group in the Sicilian fishing community, since they are the most poorly educated and least occupationally flexible population in Gloucester.

Strain on Family Life

The economic strain has also jeopardized the traditional family life. Many women now work outside the home, and men who traditionally would spend most days outside the household at sea or on the docks find themselves spending more and more time at home. Because of traditional gender expectations, the stress between husbands and wives has increased. Limitations on days at sea and the increasing costs of operating, repairing, and insuring boats are underlying causes. Declines in health insurance coverage among fishing industry households are also an increasing source of stress. Relations that formerly made fishing families among the most stable and socially healthy organizations in the state are now strained.

Decline in Community Celebrations

The deepening crisis has led not only to increased domestic strife but also to avoidance of community ritual celebrations.

We used to go out to the club and go to church, but I don't do that anymore. What is the point? There is nothing good to talk about. We just go from the boat to the house. Sometimes we go to church, but it's usually now only on Easter or other holidays.[10]

The forces of change in the Sicilian community are also seen in the lack of participation in specific community cultural groups and the declining celebration of such key culturally associated rituals as the Saint Peter's festival. In Gloucester, participation in the local fishing association, the Societa Siciliana, decreased from 304 in 1991 to 89 in 1995 (a 70 percent decline). The Sons of Italy declined from 200 in 1991 to 79 members in 1995, a 60 percent drop. By comparison, in the same period, nonfishing associations were increasing in membership. For example, the Gloucester Elks, whose membership consisted mostly of newly arrived Boston suburbanites, increased from 76 (1991) to 185 (1995) members, a 143 percent increase.[11] One disturbing sign that Sicilian cultural values were no longer unquestioned was expressed by the actions of a newly appointed (non-Sicilian) religious leader in Gloucester. During this time of community crisis, he disparaged the celebration of local Sicilian saints days as "contrary to the wishes of the Catholic church."[12] Subsequent declines in parish attendance were in part attributed to such attacks of outsider ignorance against local cultural values.

Health Care Crisis

In the health care sector, increasing health care costs and the changing nature of eligibility for public programs led to a high proportion of the industry working without any health insurance. Lack of insurance caused even greater hardship in an already highly vulnerable population. A survey of 485 finfish fishing industry households in Massachusetts found that increased insurance costs and declines in income had forced many families to go without health insurance. In 1996, 47 percent of surveyed male adults, 37 percent of women, and 34 percent of children were uninsured at least one month during the year, representing an overall ten-year decrease of 35 percent in insured fishing family members for the region.[13]

In 1989 the total population at risk in Massachusetts fishing communities from lack of health insurance was 52 percent, including 43 percent uninsured and an additional 9 percent who were insured at the time of the survey but who had experienced an insurance gap during the last year. By comparison, the National Medical Expenditure Survey found that only 20 percent of the U.S. population was uninsured for all or part of the year 1989.[14] For the state of Massachusetts, at this time, the portion of uninsured adults was 13 percent. Thus, the 1996 uninsured rate in fishing communities in Massachusetts was at least three times higher than the statewide average.

Local Crisis

Most businesses supporting the local industry are themselves small, locally owned, and locally operated. Estimates suggest that the restrictions on groundfishing will eliminate more than 50 percent of these local businesses.[15] The press, too, paints a depressing picture of the fishery: "A Comeback Is No Sure Thing," "Plenty of Fish in the Sea? Not Anymore," "For Fishermen, a Legacy Lost," "Dilemma: Save Fish or Fishermen?" are some local headlines. Prophets of crisis further entrench the belief that the fishery is "dead-dying," but this perspective is one sided. It is driven by management, conservation, and development interests that ignore the historical record of ecologically sensitive self-management of the Sicilian fishing community, the rejuvenating powers of fish stocks, and the resilience of these New England fishing families. Families and communities must transform themselves to meet the demands of social and economic changes that are the legacy of poor management and a socially unconscious trend toward maximizing efficiency and profit regardless of the destructive effects on people and the environment. That legacy has brought a profound threat to Gloucester's fishing-dependent families while it enriches a pool of outside development interests and inside tourism promoters. Also in jeopardy are many occupational roles that continue to support the local fishing industry. These include processing plant workers, ice providers, truck drivers, electricians, boat operators and owners, deckhands, gear suppliers, lawyers, social service providers, welders, accountants, engineers, fuel suppliers, seafood processors, marine railway owners and operators, refrigeration service people, surveyors, and charter boat owners and operators.

Regulatory and Economic Responses

Government reaction to the crisis included a $25 million buyback program of groundfishing vessels and retraining programs for fishermen. According to a loan specialist for the NMFS Northeast Financial Services Office, the goal of the program "was to take out [eliminate] the most fishing capacity for the amount of money we had." Beginning with a $2 million pilot program, which bought out eleven vessels, the initiative progressed with another $23 million and a final buyout count of sixty-seven East Coast fishing vessels and their fishing permits. Bought-out vessels were scrapped or sunk at sea, or they were transferred to non-fishery use as research vessels for such organizations as the Maritime Discovery Center in Rochester, New York. Ironically, the buyback program represented an attempt to decrease the overcapacity in economic (fishing) capital originally created by the prior federal vessel loan program. As we have seen, the loan program kicked off a cascade of multiplier effects from the impact on fish stocks, reduced fish catches, dissolved credit relationships and social contracts, decreased cooperation and sharing on shore and at sea (e.g., sharing fishing information), and increased social problems as job satisfaction plummeted.

Vessels of all sizes have been affected, although the larger vessels are having the most difficulty. An informal survey of Massachusetts ports reveals that, between 1997 and 1999 more than thirty vessels (scallopers and draggers) have left the fishery altogether, have moved to a different region or country, are waiting to be scrapped, or are too expensive to be reoutfitted.[16] In New Bedford, the sister groundfishing port to Gloucester, eighty-three vessels have dropped out of the fleet over the last five years. This decline is accompanied by a severe economic decline in the shoreside sector where derelict vessels crowd the docks.

Retraining Programs

Retraining programs were initiated to redirect people into alternate occupational roles—roles for which many were ill suited after a lifetime spent in fishing. Furthermore, commercial fishermen—Sicilians and others—share many cultural values: independent natures, difficulty in relating to people with a different world view, linguistic barriers to retraining, unfamiliarity with set (clocked) schedules within a workplace, and the idea of fishermen forty to forty-five years of age that participating means giving up on fishing and a subsequent loss of face in front of one's peers. Indebtedness also constrains some who would try. A family (or families) with its homes mortgaged to a vessel cannot easily abandon that vessel to pursue another option. Nonetheless, despite these barriers and a lack of early successes, the retraining program, run by the Gloucester Fishermen and Family Assistance Center under the guidance of the Gloucester Fishermen's Wives Association, had by 1998 put some 200 fishermen and related industry workers through the program, a telling measure of the level of hardship in Gloucester.

RESPONSE: STRUGGLES TO SURVIVE CULTURALLY

In the case of the Gloucester fishing families, the threats they face have produced some active responses of resistance, but mostly the Gloucester Sicilians have responded with changes to themselves and their community, stemming from their reliance on an economic niche that is coming apart. Their responses include rising individual stress, declining health, more fractious relations with non-fishing neighbors, diminished community supports for families in trouble, and others. This section examines a number of the most visible of these responses.

Scarcity of fish, gentrification of the community, and recent regulations are resulting in significant changes in the social conditions for the fishing households and families in Gloucester. These changes are seen both on and off the water, in the household environment, and in the social and occupational networks of the community. On the water there is an increase in competition and a loss of economic viability. The larger vessels and their crew find themselves increasingly unprofitable. One symptom is the breakdown of shared information on the location of fishing grounds expressed as "chatter" (on the water conversation by marine radio). Chatter allows a fisher to share information with other boats on the location of good fishing strikes with the hope of benefiting by reciprocal exchange of information in the future.

The competition has also led to divisive squabbling between age cohorts. Older, established fishermen argue that they are more concerned with conservation issues, and they suspect that newcomers are going all out to catch as many fish as possible, including resorting to illegal net liners to increase the overall catch (by netting smaller fish species). Whether true or not, there has been conflict between the newer fishing families and the established families. This conflict was exacerbated by a belief that not all groups of fishers were fairly represented on the New England Fishery Management Council.

Health Effects

Social conflict within and between fishing families is also revealed through health effects, compounded with the high uninsured rate. These effects are, in their own way, a debilitating means of response from Gloucester's fisher families. A Gloucester doctor with twenty years of treating fishing families noted a rise in stress-related illnesses including hypertension, heart disease, and stroke owing to the fishing crisis. In other settings, heart disease and other illnesses, which impact a person's social relationships, have also been related to work dissatisfaction.

One fisherman came into the office and was all shook up because he had to throw away a lot of haddock. He went out fishing and caught 2,000 pounds of haddock in his first tow. He had to throw 1,500 pounds overboard. So he moved his bat and reset the net. He got 10,000 pounds, and all of it went overboard. So he moved his boat again, and this time he got 20,000 pounds. Well, for these fishermen, waste is a sin. So to throw all these fish overboard was really hard. This guy was so upset about it when he came in that he started having chest pains right in the office while he was talking about it. (President, Local Fishing Association)[17]

Community Relations

How outsiders perceive Gloucester fishermen reveals the cultural and economic changes facing the traditional fishing community. In response to the question, "Do you see a shift in the way people [in the community] think about fishermen and fishing in general," one community leader responded,

Gloucester is going through a gradual conversion from a self-sustaining community to a bedroom community . . . as a consequence of those people (fishers) who've been migrating out of the city, there's a tendency not to understand the way the fishing industry is run. I'll never forget the time I was standing on the wharf when I heard a man say to a fisherman on the deck of the boat, Can I have a haddock? And the guy said, I can't give it to you because I need it to make the box. And the person misunderstood what he said and he said, I didn't want it for nothing; I'd have paid for it. And the guy said, "No, no. I need it to make the box" [a box being a certain kilogram weight of fish in wooden boxes used as units of measure]. Well, he was speaking broken language, and the man didn't understand him. I did, and I heard the man turn around and say to the person he was with, "Jesus! Can you imagine that? And they get the [fish] for nothing."[18]

Despite efforts to manage under the present system, a significant decline in landings continues owing to restrictions on days at sea and area closures. There are just fewer fish. Causes for this decline are uncertain, but factors such as overfishing, near-shore climate change, and changes in migration patterns of stocks are certainly included. One consequence has been deteriorating community relations.

The Next Generation

Among the important questions regarding the future of Sicilian ground-fishing in Gloucester and throughout New England is the extent to which the fleet and its fishing community is reproducing itself. Are fishermen being replaced by their sons and nephews? Are they being displaced by new groups of immigrants based on alternative organizational structures? Is vertical integration within fisheries occurring, with the processing sector deploying its own fleets? These questions concern the future of the fleet and its ability to generate incomes that will continue to put fishing at the core of the Gloucester economy. Unfortunately, the youth of Gloucester are understandably reluctant to enter the fishery.

One informant, who taught high school in Gloucester for many years, noted that in 1974 a good 75 percent of those in biology classes had some ties to a fishing boat or the industry. Discussions of fishery biology and the industry were integrated into classroom lectures. In 1992–1993, when he retired from classroom duty, virtually no students had ties (or admitted having ties) to the industry.[19] Besides the decline in participation, there is now a certain shame factor associated with being in the fishery, which certainly influences youths' aspirations. This is strengthened by perceptions in the media and at the managerial level that fishermen have destroyed the

Three generations of Gloucester fishermen. Photo: Christopher L. Dyer.

resources (they are "fish killers"), and that it is no longer an economically (or socially) viable manner of making a living.

A local educator explains the loss of economic liability in the fishery:

When I first started to teach in 1974 on Cape Ann it was not uncommon for students to pick up side jobs on the wharf—literally putting themselves through college working on fish during the summer and after school. An awful lot also left school to work in the industry. It was an economic safety net. Now, those who did not return to school are hurting. Some of those kids really weren't going to get an education and would take deck hand jobs. But lots of people did get an education working in fish. The really good kids could go through UMASS [University of Massachusetts] working in fish—packing fish—working two shifts. This has been lost—is gone. Back in 1974, one of the most positive things I could say to a kid was you can get a job [in the fishery] anywhere in town. Now the entire economic network provided by fishing is missing.[20]

Thus, another aspect of the downturn in the fishery economy is the loss of dockside and processing work for students. Ten years ago, students could get double shifts at local processing plants, and many students financed their college education with money made by processing fish (e.g., the present mayor of Gloucester did this). Other students less skilled in the classroom might drop out and take jobs as deckhands. They could earn a lot of money this way, but at the expense of their education and future job mobility. Now, all students are encouraged to stay in school if they can because there are no jobs available for them in the local community other than at minimum wage. This has hurt families who, struggling economically, lack the resources to send academically capable sons and daughters to college. Meanwhile, those sons and daughters no longer have the opportunity to earn money for college themselves.

Repair shops and marine equipment, once readily available in Gloucester, must now be sought in New Bedford, Boston, or elsewhere. Yet, present trends in development have done nothing to revitalize any of the fishing facilities. Costs to operate and maintain vessels have soared while access to facilities dwindles: "Nowadays, you can't get anything fixed locally. We need a new propeller on our vessel, but we have to pay someone from Seattle $5,000 to come here to work on the part. And all this time our boat is just sitting costing us money."[21] Meanwhile, the Chamber of Commerce reports that, overall, the health of the business community in Gloucester, outside the fishing sector, is improving. This reflects the shift from an economy dependent primarily on fishing to a mixed economy of high technology, tourism, and light industry.[22]

Diversification

Government administrators often accuse fishermen of stubbornly rejecting change. The evidence suggests the contrary: fishermen take risks and try new approaches when there is a credible enough possibility of succeeding to warrant the risk. For example, some draggers converted their gear to herring fishing in the hope of succeeding in this new fishery. Herring stocks are abundant, but the market is undeveloped and current herring fishermen are uneasy about new entrants into a fishery they have long had to themselves. Nevertheless, various Gloucester fishermen converted their vessels for herring at a cost of $135,000. When they were unsuccessful at selling the catch they had to give up and absorb the loss. Fishermen are also investigating other species that are underutilized or have not been part of the traditional fisheries of Gloucester. For example, draggers are participating in a fishery for dogfish off of Cape May, and for squid off of Rhode Island. Others have gone after monkfish, whose livers are highly valued, or have invested in fish traps to harvest eels. Pessimism runs high, however, that seeking these new species will work. Overall, the ability to shift to other species and gear is limited by the capital investment in the fishing operation. The larger vessels in the Gloucester fleet are often saddled with debt, tied to home mortgages, and too specialized to rig with other gears without incurring further major debt.

Docking Pressures

The groundfishing fleet of Gloucester is concentrated inside a sheltered harbor, and affordable docking space is at a premium. After the introduction of ice plants in the late 1800s, iced fish could be marketed throughout the eastern seaboard, which established Gloucester as one of the primary seafood ports in the nation. Existing processing and cold-storage facilities have a combined capacity of nearly 95 million pounds.[23] If this infrastructure were to be replaced for other dockside uses, it would be prohibitively expensive to rebuild it if fish stocks ever recovered.

The modern state dock, built in 1982, was recently renovated with funds from the Economic Development Administration. There are deep draft berths for sixty-four commercial vessels at the state fish pier. However, the high docking fees and insurance requirements have kept most commercial vessels off this dock. Scattered among the working vessels are charter boat facilities and whale-watching firms which have been taking over spaces vacated by a dwindling groundfish fleet. Space limitations mean that most of the vessels must have some arrangement with a processing facility or a dealer in order to tie up their vessels. Drydocking (pulling a boat out of water for repair) with such facilities as the historic Gloucester Marine Railways have also changed over time with escalating industry costs. Some of the drydocking facilities have only a few spaces; others have upwards of twelve; and others may have more. Along the docks, space is also taken up by several corporate seafood-processing firms mixed with smaller seafood buyers, recreational boating facilities and processors, boat docks, and ice, fuel, and oil suppliers. Putting available docks to other uses as Gloucester shifts to a tourist economy will inhibit any future recovery and growth of the commercial fishing sector.

The Changing Market for Gloucester Fish

As we have seen, the support infrastructure is under severe pressure, and little of it could be lost without having a major impact on the ability of the present fleet to operate. Some hope is presented by the recent creation of a herring processing operation and the conversion of a local seafood processor into a large fish auction facility. The fish auction allows buyers to bid on specific catch of fish by species and boat, and it improves Gloucester fishermen's access to international sales. This may put an emphasis on product quality rather than volume, making it possible to catch fewer fish but get a higher price for them. Nevertheless, these encouraging signs belie the longer-term reality, the steady decline in local processing and marketing capacity. The fish dehydration plant that employed hundreds of workers for decades closed in 1984. There are currently a dozen local buyers, including five processors, but there were several times that number of buyers in Gloucester before the passage of the Magnuson Act. A great deal of ambivalence exists about the consequences of recent changes in the size of the fleet and seafood dealers' attempts to hang onto old markets or explore new marketing options.

The history of fish marketing has been characterized by an unbalanced economic relationship that usually favors the buyers. Recently the balance has shifted from dealers to fishermen, largely because of the increased competition for the dwindling fleet of suppliers. Thus, paradoxically, even though there are few markets, the fleet of large draggers in Gloucester is so reduced as to increase competition among *dealers* for the remaining fishermen. Too, as the number of markets decline, the options available to the remaining boats become more uncertain; there is a decrease in the flexibility of the market owing to reduced volume overall. Further, the effect on prices is limited. Today, higher fish prices mean that processor/marketers do not need to process as much fish through their facilities to remain viable. This does not help the suppliers (fishers), who are competing for a scarcer product and dealing with increasing costs. Thus there are both negative and positive consequences of a shrinking fleet, fewer overall pounds of fish, and increased fish prices at the dock.

Fish are generally sold whole frozen and shipped to secondary markets where they will be processed to their consumer form. It is ironic that Gorton's Seafood of Gloucester exclusively processes foreign quick frozen product (QFP) in lieu of local fish. Gorton's added strain with the locals when it upgraded its processing systems and eliminated laborers by automation and by raising the minimum educational requirement for hiring to the GED (high school graduation) level. Housewives and other ethnic workers with limited education and poor English skills, formerly able to find jobs in fish processing, have lost their jobs.

Credit

Another problem is the private ownership of facilities for off-loading boats, which effectively preclude the existence of spot markets with many buyers and sellers. These arrangements were traditionally mitigated by the establishment of implicit contractual arrangements. For example, in Gloucester, fishermen would be given credit for the purchase of fuel and ice with the implication that they would sell their catch through certain buyers, and that the debt accrued would be paid back with the catch. Debt relationships extended to the wider community to include bank loans for boats and second mortgages, food credit advanced at local grocery stores, and delayed payment on supplies and services from gear and repair shops servicing the industry.

In Gloucester, credit relations between banks and fishermen and between marine suppliers and fishermen have deteriorated. Traditionally, suppliers of marine services and trip supplies advanced boat captains oil, fuel, and ice. That practice is dying out. Captains could also postpone paying repair costs on their boats until they had brought in a good catch. That, too, is about gone. Five years ago, fishermen could also easily get loans and credit from banking institutions in town, and some linked their home mortgages to the boats when they purchased them, or when they made major repairs on the boats. A 1995 survey of seventy-five groundfishers in Gloucester reveals that 20 percent (15 out of 75) have committed their homes as collateral for a fishing vessel mortgage.[24] Today, it is virtually impossible to get a loan for fishing needs. Fishermen report that banking institutions are telling fishermen that they are "getting out of the fishing business" and cannot risk investing in fishing.

Social Impacts on the Fishing Community

Impacts of declining viability are reflected in loss of informal relationships of sharing in the fishing among Sicilian family, friends, and the social institutions. Losses in income for captains of dragger vessels have weakened the ties between crewmen and captains. Vessels formerly put out to sea with a crew of ten who shared in the catch profits enough for all to make a living, raise families, and own property. Many crews speak only Sicilian and have rarely worked outside the industry. Crew members also formed social and cultural units, spent time together onshore, took part in common rituals to honor saints and family, and drank and talked together in local fishermen's clubs and bars. The bounty of the catch was spread to the community through donations of money and fish. A traditional scene for a docking boat was the distribution of small amounts of fish to gathered locals using special "fish bags" supplied by the hardware store. Such distribution no longer occurs. Fishermen cannot afford the loss of even a small portion of the catch.

When captain owners, in order to cut costs, eliminate crew or decrease their pay, crew members feel bitter toward their former employers, and their long-standing social ties are weakened or destroyed as an outcome. Often middle-aged, and with no other work skills, they lose self-respect when forced to give up property and independence to rely on relatives and the community. Sicilian pride makes it difficult for many to seek public assistance, and they remain in denial in social isolation. Only when their plight is desperate, when they are losing their home and cannot pay bills, will they turn to others. Meanwhile, their resolute independence and history of informal (cash) salary arrangements makes them invisible to the social welfare system.

Onshore ties between dock owners and the fleet have also eroded. The Gloucester Marine Railways charges dock fees, which was not done in the past. The ability to pay fees has put pressure on the boat owner to collect on old or delinquent bills. Further, the Gloucester Marine Railways, once a thriving dry-dock facility for Sicilian fishing boats, can no longer extend traditional credit to the fishermen after it filed for Chapter 8 bankruptcy in 1996. The fuel, ice, and other products sold by processors are encountering shrinking demand. While there is competition among the processing sector for the business of an ever-declining population of fishers, they have an ever-shrinking capability to repay.

Obviously, fish marketing in Gloucester is in a difficult transition. Old systems of debt, loyalty, and uneven power relationships between fishermen and processors have been eroding under the economic difficulties and negative publicity facing the fleet yet new systems have not been fully developed to deal with new political and economic realities.

Summary

The Sicilian groundfish case study illustrates how a government policy to promote an expanded catch with low-interest federal loans for the purchase of new, larger fishing vessels and gear, combined with the loss of a historically utilized and significantly important fishing area through the 1984 Hague Line, contributed to drastic declines in available groundfish stocks. This situation destabilized the Sicilian fishing community and created stress and economic ruin for many families and households dependent upon the resources of the sea. These declines continue to have severe community impacts that are socially, culturally, and economically devastating to individuals, to fishing families, and to households in and around Gloucester. The most recent federal management actions being considered to turn around declines in fish stocks include rotating seasonal closure of large inshore areas in the Gulf of Maine. This would adversely impact hundreds of inshore fishers and their families in Massachusetts and Maine, and it is a direct and continuing consequence of the declines in groundfish stocks started with the overcapitalization of the 1970s groundfishing fleets. Had the Fishing Vessel Obligation Loan Program been more carefully monitored and reigned in when overfishing capacity loomed, the program could have favored community residents having a direct historical dependence on the fishery, such as Sicilian fishing families with long historical residence in Gloucester. With more careful management of both fish stocks and community needs, the profound consequences for Gloucester's fishing community could have been avoided.

With recent and proposed regulations on the fishery, degradation of their shore-based support industry, and an uphill battle against the public perception that the fishery is "dead," the Sicilian groundfishing families of Gloucester are again experiencing a great deal of stress and economic hardship. Increased competition and conflict, loss of days at sea, and increasing operating costs are all contributing to the crisis. Large-scale draggers are having the most difficult time, and deckhands on these draggers are the most vulnerable to the decreasing economic and social viability of the fishery. Gill netters and longliners are also suffering from new marine mammal regulations that curtail the areas they can fish.

Through organizations such as the Gloucester Fishermen's Wives, concerted efforts are being made to adapt constructively to the fishing crisis. Representatives of the fishing community are writing grants for federal assistance, promoting underutilized species (fish not usually marketed), and working with state and regional religious, service, and government organizations to diversify the options available to those in the fishing industry. To date, attempts to adapt to the new regulatory climate have been difficult but may improve with time if government management is intelligent and if resources are made available.

Switching to underutilized species, such as herring, carries high costs, and the difficulties of breaking into new markets also limits the success of such ventures. The introduction of the local fish auction is a positive development, and new initiatives to buy back vessels could somewhat alleviate the situation. However, many fisher households are at or near social and economic collapse. Efforts are being made and could be supported by management to diversify the fishery through retraining programs, comanagement of resources, and other initiatives to mitigate the crisis. Gloucester still retains its historical identity as an American fishing port, strong in tradition and commitment to the use of the marine environment, but what form this changing community will take in the future is as uncertain as the weather at sea. Gloucester's Sicilian families and their traditional support networks now face profound challenges to maintain a centuries-old way of life, fishing.

FOOD FOR THOUGHT

The destructive changes facing the Sicilians of Gloucester and other American fishing and farming communities in general are the result of a wider process in American society that is transforming all of us. Not more than a quarter century ago the American way of life still consisted mostly of people living close to nature—working on family farms or family fishing boats. Our lives depended on nature's harvest, and this harvest could be uncertain and cruel. This meant people and the communities they made up grew to depend on each other and worked together to decrease the uncertainty of a life close to nature. An appreciation of producing something together—a tangible product such as fish and crops—provides a sense of pride, awe, and humility which are mostly lost in our contemporary society where values and traditions of family and sharing are challenged by the myth that success in life is equated with money, no matter how we get it. Such an appreciation also gives us respect for our natural environment, where people are more a part of their natural surroundings than at odds with it.

The adaptive character of such "communities of nature" emphasize family values, helping one another, practicing religion, sharing what one has, and respect for each other. These characteristics are at the core of the traditional Sicilian fishing culture. Yet, these people are being overwhelmed by social changes and government ignorance which has put a premium on economic efficiency and profit regardless of the human consequences. There is much we can learn from the Sicilian fishing family about what we have lost—what we in many ways used to be. Instead of callously shrugging off their struggle to survive, we should learn what we can from "the finest kind"—the fishermen of Gloucester, and in that learning find culturally appropriate solutions to our own wider social dilemma of progress without humanity.

Questions

1. The Sicilian fishing community of Gloucester is, on the whole, losing its battle to survive as a community and retain its distinct way of life. Should our nation's ethnic richness be sacrificed to unrestrained economic forces? Explain.

2. Credit arrangements were key social links that underpinned Gloucester's Sicilian fishing community as well as its ties to non-Sicilian businesses and other infrastructure. Now those credit arrangements are unraveling. How might credit arrangements be reinstituted to reestablish those crucial ties?

3. How could the 1976 federal legislation, in another form, have accomplished the political goal of laying effective claim to the 200-mile limit without leading to (1) the overexploitation of the fisheries and (2) the destruction of the Sicilian fishing industry?

4. Gloucester's political leaders are encouraging the shift of the city's economic base to one emphasizing high-technology, tourism, and light industry. How can this shift occur without destroying the Sicilian fishing culture and community?

5. The government's reaction to the fishing crisis was to buy back vessels and institute a job retraining program for Sicilian fishing families. What social and cultural needs of the Sicilian community did these economic solutions not address, and what could be done to help fulfill these needs in the face of the fishing crisis?

NOTES

1. Christopher L. Dyer, and David Griffith, *Appraisal of the Social and Cultural Aspects of the Multispecies Groundfish Fishery* (Bethesda, Md.: Aguirre International and The National Oceanographic and Atmospheric Administration, 1996), 76.

2. National Marine Fisheries Service, *Data Base on Licensed Groundfish Vessels for the Northeast* (Bethesda, Md.: National Marine Fisheries Service and The National Oceanographic and Atmospheric Administration, 1995).

3. Department of Commerce/National Marine Fisheries Service, *Rankings of U.S. Ports by Ex-Vessel Landings*, (Bethesda, Md.: Author, 1996).

4. The Hague Line is a political division that splits the access to fishery re-

sources of the Grand Banks and associated waters between the United States and Canada. However, areas just north of the line, which American fishers argued was somewhat arbitrary, included some of the choicest fishing grounds, initially explored and fished by American vessels.

5. Christopher L. Dyer, *Field Notes, Multi-species Groundfish Study* (Gloucester, Mass., 1996).

6. Christopher L. Dyer and David Griffith, *An Appraisal of the Social and Cultural Aspects of the New England Multispecies Groundfish Fishery* (Bethesda, Md.: Aguirre International and the National Oceanographic and Atmospheric Administration, 1996), 18.

7. *Review of the New England Groundfish Stock Assessment* (Washington, D.C.: National Science Council, 1997), 28.

8. Ibid; Dyer and Griffith, *An Appraisal*, 57.

9. Ibid.

10. Ibid.

11. Dyer and Griffith, *An Appraisal*, 59.

12. Personal communication with David Bergeron, the coordinator of the Massachusetts Fishermen's Partnership, in Gloucester, 1998.

13. Christopher L. Dyer, and John J. Poggie. "The Natural Resource Region and Marine Policy: A Case Study from the New England Groundfish Fishery," *Marine Policy* 24 (2000): 252.

14. Ibid., 253.

15. Massachusetts Fishermen's Partnership, *Informal Survey of Groundfish Fleet Status*, (Massachusetts Fishermen's Partnership: Gloucester, Mass., 1998).

16. Ibid.

17. Personal communication with Angela Sanfelippo, the president of the Gloucester Fishermen's Wives Association, October 1995.

18. 1998 Oral History Project, Archives of the Gloucester Fishermen's Wives Association.

19. Dyer, Field Notes.

20. Personal communication, author's fieldnotes, 1996.

21. Ibid.

22. Interview with Gloucester Mayor Bruce Tobey, November 1995.

23. Department of Commerce, National Marine Fisheries Service, *Rankings of U.S. Ports*.

24. Caritas Christi Health Care System. *Heath Survey of the Fishing Population in Massachusetts* (Boston: Health Care for All, 1996), 52.

RESOURCE GUIDE

Published Literature

Barlett, K. *The Finest Kind: The Fishermen of Gloucester.* New York: W.W. Norton, 1977.

Clarke, Margaret Elwyn. "Managing Uncertainty: Family, Religion and Collective Action Among the Fishermen's Wives in Gloucester, Massachusetts," Social and Economic Papers no. 18. St. Johns, Newfoundland: Memorial University of Newfoundland, Institute of Social and Economic Research, 1988.

Doeringer, Peter, Philip Moss, and David Terkla. *The New England Fishing Economy: Jobs, Income and Kinship*. Amherst: University of Massachusetts Press, 1986.

Dyer, Christopher L., and David Griffith. *An Appraisal of the Social and Cultural Aspects of the Multispecies Groundfish Fishery*. Bethesda, Md.: Aguirre International and the National Oceanographic and Atmospheric Administration, 1996.

Prybot, Peter K. *White-Tipped Orange Masts: Gloucester's Fishing Draggers*. Gloucester, Mass.: Curious Traveler Press, 1998.

WWW Sites

Commonwealth Corporation Gloucester Fishermen and Family Assistance Center
http://www.commcorp.org/wss/Fisherman/default.htm

Gloucester Fishermen's Wives Association
http://www.gfwa.org

Massachusetts Fishermen's Partnership
http://www.shore.net/~mfp

Index

About the Editor and Contributors

BEN G. BLOUNT is a professor of anthropology and linguistics at the University of Georgia, where he teaches courses on coastal anthropology, human ecology, and cognitive anthropology. His current research focuses on the southern Atlantic Coast of the United States, the Bay Islands of Honduras, and the East African Coast. He serves on the Scientific and Statistical Committee of the South Atlantic Fishery Management Council.

ANGELA M. BUCK is a traditional food gatherer and cultural resource specialist with the Grant County Public Utility District. Angela is a Yakama and has lived at Priest Rapids since 1975.

ALLAN BURNS is a professor and chair of the Anthropology Department at the University of Florida. He works with Maya people in Yucatán and Chiapas, Mexico, Guatemala, and the United States on applied anthropology projects involving labor and employment, documentary film, and political asylum. He is author of *Mayan in Exile*.

CHRISTOPHER DYER is an applied anthropologist and serves as the coordinator of research and grant development for Meeting Street, East Providence, Rhode Island. He serves on the Social Science Advisory Committee of the New England Fisheries Management Council and is an advisor to the Massachusetts Fishermen's Partnership and the Gloucester Fishermen's Wives Association. Recent research on New England fishing communities is supported by the NOAA/Department of Commerce.

TOM GREAVES is an applied anthropologist and professor of anthropology at Bucknell University. A former president of the Society for Applied Anthropology, editor of the *American Anthropologist*, and recent chair of the Committee for Human Rights of the American Anthropological Association, Greaves has researched and written extensively about the contemporary struggle, human rights, and intellectual property rights of indigenous peoples, particularly those in North America.

JOHN A. GRIM is a professor of religion at Bucknell University whose special fields of interest are American Indian religions and religion and ecology. He undertakes field studies on the Crow Reservation, where he and his wife were adopted into the Birdinground family. *Aho kaashiilaa* (thanks) to co-author Magdalene and the Crow people for their efforts to educate American society about Crow history and life.

JO ANN KOLTYK is an independent scholar, writer, and educator. She has been a lecturer in the anthropology and folklore departments at the University of Wisconsin in Madison and at the Rock County campus in Janesville. Her book on the Hmong is entitled *New Pioneers in the Heartland: Hmong Life in Wisconsin*. Dr. Koltyk continues to research and write about the Hmong and issues concerning immigration and gender.

JULIA G. LONGENECKER is an anthropologist working in the Cultural Resource Protection Program, Confederated Tribes of the Umatila Indian Reservation, in northeastern Oregon State. Longenecker specializes in the handling of Native American human remains associated with inadvertent discoveries and works with law enforcement and the public to stop the looting of archaeological sites and Native American burial sites.

MAGDALENE MEDICINE HORSE-MOCCASIN TOP is the archivist at Little Big Horn College in Crow Agency, Montana, and serves as librarian at the college. She has undertaken archival research in the Library of Congress in Washington, D.C., and has been a consultant for the National Endowment for the Humanities.

ANTONIA MILLS teaches First Nations studies at the University of Northern British Columbia, Canada (http://quarles.unbc.ca/ideas/net/instructors/inst_fir.html; http://quarles.unbc/firstnationsstudies/index.html). She worked for the Gitxsan Witsuwit'en Tribal Council for their Delgamuukw land claims case and is continuing research on their reincarnation concepts and cases.

BROOKE OLSON teaches anthropology and American Indian studies at Ithaca College. Dr. Olson has worked on the development of culturally sensitive health programs for Native American diabetes, and currently she is doing research on land, identity, and empowerment among the Haudenosaunee (Iroquois).

ERNEST OLSON is an associate professor of anthropology at Wells College in Aurora, New York. He did his doctoral dissertation research in

Polynesia and has more recently worked on the issue of American Indians and sacred sites.

ROBERT B. PORTER, a member (Allegany heron clan) and former attorney general of the Seneca Nation, is a professor of law and the director of the Tribal Law and Government Center at the University of Kansas. He writes and teaches about decolonizing federal Indian control law and revitalizing indigenous governance and legal systems.

KURT RUSSO is the director of the International Indigenous Exchange Program at Northwest Indian College, coordinates the Arlecho Creek Forest Conservation Partnership for the Lummi Nation, is the executive director for the Florence R. Kluckhohn Center for the Study of Values, and serves on the board of the Native American Land Conservancy. He lives in Bellingham, Washington.

DARBY C. STAPP is an anthropologist working for Pacific Northwest National Laboratory at the U.S. Department of Energy's Hanford site in Washington State. His work involves protecting cultural resources at Hanford so that they will be available to future generations of Native Americans and others. Stapp also specializes in helping Native Americans develop cultural resource management skills to enable them to take an active role in managing the resources important to them.

CLIFFORD E. TRAFZER (Wyandot) is a professor of history and Native American studies at the University of California, Riverside, where he is also the director of the Native American Nations Research Center. The author of twenty books, Trafzer has spent the last three years working on cultural revitalization with the Chemehuevis of the Twenty-Nine Palms Band of Mission Indians.

MIGUEL VASQUEZ is an associate professor of anthropology at Northern Arizona University and a recent member of the executive committee of the Society for Applied Anthropology. Since 1991 he has worked closely in many collaborative projects with the Hopi Tribe and in rural development projects in Norway, Guatemala, California, and Arizona over the past thirty years.